𝕭attle of 𝕲ettysburg

The Official History by the Gettysburg National Military Park Commission

Compiled by

Lt. Col. George R. Large, U.S. Army (Ret.)

 Burd Street Press

Copyright © 1999 by Lt. Col. George R. Large, U.S. Army (Ret.)

ALL RIGHTS RESERVED—No part of this book may be reproduced in any form without permission in writing from the publisher, except by a reviewer who wishes to quote brief passages in connection with a review.

This Burd Street Press publication
was printed by
Beidel Printing House, Inc.
63 West Burd Street
Shippensburg, PA 17257-0152 USA

In respect for the scholarship contained herein, the acid-free paper used in this book meets the guidelines for permanence and durability of the Committee on Production Guidelines for Book Longevity of the Council on Library Resources.

For a complete list of available publications
please write
Burd Street Press
Division of White Mane Publishing Company, Inc.
P.O. Box 152
Shippensburg, PA 17257-0152 USA

Library of Congress Cataloging-in-Publication Data

Large, George R., 1935-
    Battle of Gettysburg : the official history by the Gettysburg
National Military Park Commission / compiled by George R. Large.
        p.   cm.
    Includes bibliographical references and index.
    ISBN 1-57249-171-X (acid-free paper)
    1. Gettysburg (Pa.), Battle of, 1863. I. Gettysburg National
Military Park Commission. II. Title.
    E475.53.L3   1999
    973.7'349--dc21   99-19685
                                                                CIP

PRINTED IN THE UNITED STATES OF AMERICA

CONTENTS

ILLUSTRATIONS

MAPS

PREFACE

The Battle of Gettysburg, fought during the first three days of July 1863, was the tragic culmination of Gen. Robert E. Lee's second and final invasion of the North. By the end of the three days of battle between Maj. Gen. George G. Meade's Army of the Potomac and General Lee's Army of Northern Virginia, close to 51,000 men in blue and gray would be killed, wounded, or missing. While no single day of the three days at Gettysburg matched the fury of the single-day Battle of Antietam, which ended Lee's first invasion of the North, no battle of the Civil War was bloodier or as important to the history of the United States.

Recognizing the importance of preserving the site where this great battle was fought, in 1893 the United States Congress passed legislation, which directed the appointment of a commission to establish the Gettysburg National Military Park. Congress further directed that the positions and activity of the various commands of both armies be carefully and impartially ascertained and suitably marked. The inscriptions on the markers that the Gettysburg National Military Park Commission erected in compliance with the congressional mandate provide a carefully researched, impartial history of the Battle of Gettysburg. This book provides that history.

INTRODUCTION

Among the many grand monuments erected on the Gettysburg battle-field to honor the men who fought there are 330 simple tablets of bronze on granite or cast-iron on iron pedestals. These tablets were placed there by the Gettysburg National Military Park Commission to mark the position and evolutions of the various commands of the Army of the Potomac and Army of Northern Virginia. The inscriptions on these tablets provide a carefully researched, authenticated account of the movement and other action of the men, both North and South, who fought the bloody battle there during the first three days of July 1863. Read separately as the visitor moves about the battlefield, the tablets present a sometimes-bewildering series of individual accounts of the battle. Assembled together in the order that the events occurred, the inscriptions on the tablets provide a concise, impartial historical account of the Battle of Gettysburg.

GETTYSBURG BATTLEFIELD PRESERVATION

Initial efforts to preserve the Gettysburg battlefield were under the guidance of the Gettysburg Battlefield Memorial Association (GBMA), a local organization formed soon after the battle with the goal of preserving the battlefield and memorializing the Union success at Gettysburg. Operating under an 1864 charter from the state of Pennsylvania, the GBMA became the official agency for establishing the landscape and controlling the placement of memorials, markers, and monuments on the battlefield. During its more than thirty years' existence, the GBMA performed a magnificent service in preserving major portions of the Union lines and supervising the placement of more than 400 monuments erected by the various Northern states that sent troops to the battle. In 1887 the United States Congress appropriated funds to be used by the GBMA for marking the positions of United States Regular commands. However, since the association's charter limited its expenditures to the Union lines, no effort could be made to establish the lines of the Army of Northern Virginia. In 1889, the association petitioned members of Congress to authorize the purchase of land along the Confederate lines of battle, and to mark the positions of every division, brigade, and regiment with tablets.

The petition by the GBMA to expand the battle site at Gettysburg coincided with efforts by various Civil War veterans groups, both North and South, to preserve the Civil War battlefields and to bring Federal oversight to the preservation of the principal battle sites. In 1890, Congress authorized the Chickamauga and Chattanooga National Military Park, and appropriated funds for preserving and marking the Antietam battlefield site. Legislation was also introduced in both houses of Congress to provide for marking the lines of battle and positions occupied by the Army of Northern Virginia on the Gettysburg battlefield, but this legislation did not pass.

There was no opposition to establishment of a national park at Gettysburg, but political wrangling over the composition of the proposed park's administrators delayed passage of implementing legislation for five years. It was not until February 11, 1895, that legislation establishing Gettysburg National Military Park became law. In the meantime, congressional proponents of the park concept inserted a clause into the Sundry Civil Appropriation Act of March 3, 1893, providing $25,000 for the battlefield. Provisions of the act provided: "For the purpose of preserving the lines of battle at Gettysburg, Pa., and for properly marking with tablets the positions occupied by various commands of the Armies of the Potomac and of Northern Virginia on the field, and for opening and improving avenues along the positions occupied by troops upon those lines, and for fencing the same, and for determining the leading tactical positions of the batteries, regiments, brigades, divisions, corps and other organizations, with references to the study and correct understanding of the battle and to mark the same with suitable tablets, each bearing a brief historical legend compiled without praise or censure, the sum of $25,000 to be expended under the direction of the Secretary of War".

Under the authority of the Sundry Civil Appropriation Act, Secretary of War Daniel Lamont appointed a three-man Gettysburg Battlefield Commission on May 25, 1893, and directed that it take immediate steps to preserve the lines of battle at Gettysburg. The original three men appointed to the commission were John P. Nicholson (Chairman), William H. Forney, and John B. Bachelder. Both Forney and Nicholson were veterans of the battle, Forney with the Confederate 10th Alabama Infantry and Nicholson with the Union 28th Pennsylvania Infantry. Bachelder was a highly respected, though controversial, historian of the battle and had served as superintendent of legends and tablets for the GBMA. Emmor B. Cope, an engineer officer who had been attached to the Army of the Potomac headquarters during the battle, was selected as the commission's engineer in July 1893. Both Bachelder and Forney died in 1894 and were replaced by two veterans of the battle, William M. Robbins, who had served with the 4th Alabama Infantry and Charles A. Richardson, with the 126th New York Infantry. The Battlefield Commission was retained as the Park Commission after the Gettysburg National Park was officially established in 1895. The law establishing the park also provided for transfer of property from the GBMA, giving the Park Commission complete control of the battlefield.

The composition of the commission remained unchanged until the death of Robbins in 1905. Another Confederate veteran, Lunsford L. Lomax, who had served with the 11th Virginia Cavalry at Gettysburg, replaced him. Lomax was the last appointment to the commission, even though it remained in existence for another 17 years. The Sundry Civil Appropriation Act of 1912 provided that vacancies on the commission would not be filled and that upon the departure of the last commissioner, the duties of the commission were to be performed as directed by the secretary of war. Lomax died in 1913 and Richardson in 1917, leaving Nicholson as the sole commissioner until his death in 1922. Upon Nicholson's death, E. B. Cope was appointed the first superintendent of the Gettysburg National Military Park, a position he held until his death in 1927.

The multi-talented team of Nicholson, Robbins, Richardson, and Cope operated remarkably well together during the commission's ten most active years. The accomplishments of the team placed an indelible stamp on the appearance and character of the Gettysburg National Military Park. It was during their tenure that most of the research and preparation of the history of the battle was done. Under the supervision of the GBMA, monuments erected by the different states that had provided them had already marked the positions of most of the Union troops. The focus of the Park Commission was on fixing and marking the positions and movements of the Confederate troops and United States Regulars—no small task more than 30 years after the battle. To obtain the information needed, the commission invited surviving Union and Confederate officers and soldiers to visit the field, and authorities of the Southern states were requested to send delegations representing Confederate commands to locate positions. The commission reported in their 1911 annual report to the secretary of war that 61,412 official letters had been written in connection with establishing the history of the battle. In that same report the commission reported that as the park approaches completion: "The commission have written in imperishable Bronze and Granite, 'without praise and without censure', the history of the Army of the Potomac and the Army of Northern Virginia on the Field of Gettysburg and with justifiable pride they refer to their work constructed upon the most scientific principles and minimum cost for work of such high character."

The Park Commission accomplished its work with amazingly little controversy. There were a few detractors, but the overwhelming opinion of the public was supportive. The thing that generated the most controversy was the commission's decision to continue the policy established by the GBMA for marking the position of the various commands. Under that policy the location of monuments, markers, and tablets was restricted to the respective positions occupied by the commands and bodies of troops in line of battle. Since the Army of the Potomac was on the defense during the battle, the result of the policy was that, for the most part, the positions of the Union troops are marked where the troops fought. However, the markers along the Confederate avenues only show from where the Confederate troops started their attacks. The park commissioners originally intended to mark Confederate advanced positions and in their 1905 annual report to the secretary of war "suggested that markers of little cost be placed to mark the farthest and most important advances of the Confederate forces (brigades) in the attack on the Union positions." However, the recommendation was never acted upon because of strong opposition from Northern veterans to placing Confederate markers behind Union monuments. Eleven Confederate brigade advanced position iron tablets were erected on the second day's battlefield, but they only show attack routes; none were placed at the farthest advance of the brigades. One positive result of the policy restricting the location of monuments is that much of the ground over which the Confederates advanced is uncluttered, appearing today much as it did at the time of the battle.

STATUS OF HISTORICAL TABLETS

The 330 bronze or cast iron historical tablets that were placed on the battlefield by the Park Commission are almost equally divided in number between those marking Union positions and those marking the positions of the Confederate commands. There are 166 tablets describing the actions of the commands of the Army of the Potomac during the battle. One hundred fifty-six of these are bronze tablets mounted on granite, erected on the positions of the corps, divisions, brigades, and United States Regular battalions and batteries. Ten of the Union tablets are cast iron, erected to mark positions of state artillery batteries that had not been marked with monuments by the states. There are 164 tablets on the battlefield marking the positions and describing the actions of commands of the Army of Northern Virginia. Ninety of these are bronze on granite, similar in character to those for the Army of the Potomac. The remaining 87 Confederate tablets are of cast iron. Thirteen of these are tablets showing additional brigade and division positions, and 74 mark the position of artillery batteries.

To complete the history of the battle, the Park Commission erected 19 cast iron itinerary tablets in the various Maryland and Pennsylvania towns, which the two armies passed through going to and leaving Gettysburg. Nine tablets describe the movements of the Army of the Potomac on June 29 through July 7, 1863. There are 10 tablets describing the movements of the Army of Northern Virginia on June 26 through July 5, 1863. Duplicates of these tablets were also erected on the battlefield, the Union ones on East Cemetery Hill and those for the Confederates on West Confederate Avenue near Hagerstown Road. These tablets were removed from the field in the early 1970s and placed in storage. Even though the tablets can not be found on the battlefield, the inscriptions on these tablets are included in this book because they are important to the Park Commission's history of the battle. Also, it is the intent of the Gettysburg National Military Park staff to return these tablets to the battlefield.

The inscriptions on 349 historical tablets erected on the Gettysburg battlefield by the Park Commission are presented in this book. Except for the 19 itinerary tablets, all still stand on the battlefield. The fact that they are still standing is a tribute to the stewardship of that hallowed ground by the Park Commission, the War Department, and the United States Park Service. Visitors to the battlefield may occasionally find that a cast iron tablet of interest has been removed from the field for restoration as part of the park maintenance program. Therefore, the number of tablets physically on the field may change from time to time.

PRESENTATION OF TABLET INSCRIPTIONS

The tablet inscriptions presented in the following pages were reproduced as they exist on the tablets standing on the battlefield, or in the case of the itinerary tablets, from Park Commission records in the Gettysburg National Military Park Archives. The inscriptions are assembled in the order that the five distinct phases of the second invasion of the North by the Army of Northern Virginia evolved. The first grouping describes the movement of the commands of the armies before and during the three days of the battle. The second, third, and fourth groupings describe the events of the first, second, and third days of the battle. While not a separate phase of the battle, the supporting artillery commands and other supporting units not directly engaged are presented separately in a fifth grouping. The final grouping describes the movement of the armies in the days immediately following the battle.

The tablet inscriptions within the groupings are further separated, first by listing those describing the activity of the various commands of the Army of the Potomac, followed by those describing the actions of the Army of Northern Virginia. The inscriptions are further ordered in the sequence that the events they describe evolved. The condensed history of the battle that the inscriptions provide is often too general to allow precise sequencing or ordering of the two armies together. Many of the commands in both armies fought on more than one day of the battle. The full inscription on the tablets for these commands is presented in the sequence that they were first engaged. That part of the narrative describing the engagement of the commands on subsequent days is again presented in the sequence that they were later engaged.

A short summary of the events that occurred during each phase, along with maps showing the location of the tablets, is provided to orient the reader and assist in identifying the location of the events described. The tablet inscriptions describing the events are then presented in the sequence that the commands described were engaged. This presentation allows the reader to use this book to obtain a quick overview of the entire campaign by reading the summary of events for the five phases, as a reference tool for study of the battle, and as a tour guide to the battlefield. It should be noted that the tablet number shown at the bottom of the tablet inscriptions appears on the maps at the tablet's location on the field. These numbers were assigned by the author for tablet location purposes and are not on the actual tablets. The itinerary tablets were not assigned numbers because they are not physically standing on the battlefield.

The history of the Battle of Gettysburg presented in the following pages is the history of that great battle prepared by the Gettysburg National Military Park Commission. The battle summary presented is also based on the commission's history of the battle. The reader may encounter differences between the history by the Park Commission and the "popular" history of the battle. No attempt was made to either identify all of the differences or dwell on those that are apparent. These differences are the source of other research and other books.

PART
I

Before the Battle
June 1863

SECOND INVASION OF THE NORTH

Less than 10 months after the end of his Maryland Campaign of 1862, Gen. Robert E. Lee again turned his Army of Northern Virginia northward. The Battle of Antietam, or Sharpsburg as it was known in the South, that forced Lee to end the first invasion of the North was the bloodiest single day's battle in American history. The battle that ended the second invasion would prove to be the single most pivotal event leading to the end of the war and return of the seceded states to the Union nearly two years later.

The Battle of Antietam was a strategic defeat for the South because it forced Lee to return to Virginia and ended any hope of recognition and active support by the European powers. On the other hand, the Army of Northern Virginia scored an impressive tactical victory by fighting the vastly superior Army of the Potomac to a draw. Back in Virginia, Lee's army continued to defeat the Union forces that were sent after it, scoring impressive victories in the battles of Fredericksburg and Chancellorsville. Despite these victories, the Army of Northern Virginia was a battered army. The dwindling resources of the South could not provide the provisions of war that the Army of Northern Virginia desperately needed. Perhaps the most debilitating of all was the loss of irreplaceable men and leaders such as Lt. Gen. Thomas "Stonewall" Jackson, who was accidentally killed by his own men at Chancellorsville.

The decision to invade the North again was born out of the desperation that the Confederacy faced in the summer of 1863. The western theater was near collapse, with only Vicksburg still holding. General Lee prevailed over those that wanted to send part of his army to prevent the fall of Vicksburg. Lee's position was that there was little that his army could do to save the West; but scoring a major victory in Union territory would sufficiently strengthen the active peace movement in the North to force the Federal government to sue for peace. Another reason for an invasion of the North was to resupply the army. All of the supplies that the Army of Northern Virginia so

3

desperately needed could be found in the rich towns and lush fields of western Maryland and eastern Pennsylvania.

THE MARCH TO PENNSYLVANIA

The Army of Northern Virginia that General Lee started moving toward Pennsylvania on June 3, 1863, was not the same army that had only days before won such an impressive victory at Chancellorsville. Without Stonewall Jackson's strong presence, the winning organization of two large infantry corps under Jackson and Lt. Gen. James Longstreet was no longer practical. Lee reorganized the army into three corps with three divisions each. Longstreet retained First Corps with the divisions of Maj. Gens. John Hood, Lafayette McLaws, and George Pickett. Jackson's old Second Corps was given to Lt. Gen. Richard Ewell with the divisions of Maj. Gens. Jubal Early, Edward Johnson, and Robert Rodes. A new Third Corps was formed with the divisions of Maj. Gens. Richard Anderson, Henry Heth, and William Pender, commanded by Lt. Gen. A. P. Hill. All of the commanders were seasoned combat leaders, but many were now in higher level command positions that they had not previously experienced. Ewell and Hill were new to corps command and Heth, Pender, and Rodes were new division commanders.

Lee's plan was to move his three infantry corps northwestward through the Shenandoah and Cumberland Valleys into Pennsylvania. Maj. Gen. J. E. B. Stuart's Cavalry Division, which had also been beefed up with three additional brigades, was to screen the right flank of the army and delay the Army of the Potomac when it started north. Stuart also led three of his brigades on a foray east of the Union army, a move that may have doomed the invasion before it started. Ewell's Second Corps led the march north through the valleys, followed by Longstreet's First Corps. Hill's Third Corps waited at Fredericksburg until the Union army, in position across the river, also moved north, then followed the First and Second Corps north into Pennsylvania.

The Union army that moved north to position itself between Lee's advance and Washington was commanded by Maj. Gen. Joseph Hooker. Even with heavy losses at Chancellorsville that had not been replaced, the Army of the Potomac was still larger and better equipped than the one it was now pursuing northward. The army's defeat at Chancellorsville was the last in a pattern of defeats and subsequent change of army commanders. It had fought four major battles in the past ten months under four different commanders and would soon have the fifth for the biggest battle of all.

The Army of the Potomac was organized into seven infantry corps with nineteen divisions and a cavalry corps with three divisions. To facilitate a rapid move northward, Hooker divided his army into two wings.

One wing was led by Maj. Gen. John Reynolds, consisting of his own corps and those under Maj. Gens. Oliver Howard and Daniel Sickles. Hooker led the other wing of four corps under Maj. Gens. Winfield Hancock, George

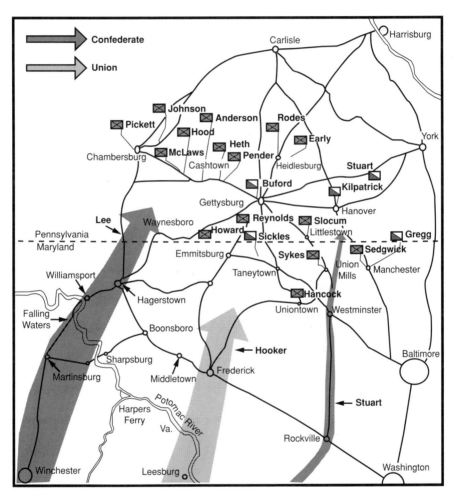

March to Gettysburg
Locations are night of June 30, 1863

Meade, John Sedgwick, and Henry Slocum. Hooker moved the army into Maryland with skill and speed. By June 26, the army had crossed the Potomac River without Lee's knowledge and was assembled in the vicinity of Frederick. Two days later Hooker was relieved of command of the Army of the Potomac. He was replaced by one of his corps commanders, Maj. Gen. George Meade. Maj. Gen. George Sykes was given command of Meade's Fifth Corps. Hooker had intended to move the army west to intercept Lee's supply line in the lower Cumberland Valley, and had already moved two corps in that direction. After assessing information that the Confederates were now approaching the Susquehanna River and the Pennsylvania state capitol, and in keeping with his orders to protect Washington and Baltimore, General Meade changed the direction of the army. He issued orders for the army to move toward York, Pennsylvania on June 29. General Reynolds, retaining command of the three corps wing of the army, was to lead the move north.

MEETING AT GETTYSBURG

Perhaps for the first time, J. E. B. Stuart had allowed his army commander to be "blind-sided." The Army of the Potomac had been across the Potomac two days before General Lee learned—not from his chief of cavalry—of its close presence. The Army of Northern Virginia had moved rapidly into Union territory. Upon crossing the Potomac the army fanned out to scour the countryside. When Lee learned of the close presence of the Union army, his own army was spread over some thirty miles of the Pennsylvania countryside. Ewell's Corps was arrayed near the Susquehanna River between York and the state capitol at Harrisburg. Longstreet's Corps was at or near Chambersburg and Hill's Corps was in the vicinity of Cashtown. Lee sent urgent orders for a concentration of his army in the vicinity of Cashtown. His orders included the admonishment that there was to be no decisive engagement before the army was together.

The town of Gettysburg was not the objective of either army, but a meeting at Gettysburg was inevitable because 10 roads converged there. Brig. Gen. John Gordon's Brigade of Maj. Gen. Jubal Early's Division, Ewell's Corps was the first of the two armies to enter the town on June 26. The brigade paused there for a short period of time, but then in a hurry, moved on. The brigade did report that there was a source of badly needed shoes there. On the morning of June 30, after learning about the supply of shoes, Henry Heth sent Brig. Gen. James J. Pettigrew's Brigade from its camp at Cashtown to investigate.

Mindful of Lee's order not to become seriously engaged, Pettigrew cautiously moved his brigade along the Chambersburg Pike toward the town of Gettysburg. It was late afternoon when his forward line of skirmishers encountered cavalry outposts along a creek, known as Willoughby Run, west of town. Advancing to a position near the Lutheran Seminary, Pettigrew saw that Gettysburg was not occupied, but he observed a large body of Union cavalry approaching the town on Emmitsburg Road. With little exchange of fire, Pettigrew withdrew and put his brigade in bivouac about midway between Cashtown and Gettysburg. Pettigrew rode on to Cashtown to report his encounter with Union troops to Heth and A. P. Hill. Having heard nothing about the location of the Union army from Stuart's cavalry, Hill immediately notified General Lee of Pettigrew's encounter, informing him that he would move on Gettysburg in force the next morning.

The Union troops that Pettigrew encountered were from the advance guard of Reynolds' wing of the Army of the Potomac. Led by Brig. Gen. John Buford, the advance guard consisted of two brigades from his First Cavalry Division and one battery of artillery. Buford also did not want a major engagement and was content to let Pettigrew withdraw and let the situation develop. He deployed his troopers along Willoughby Run, north and south of Chambersburg Pike and sent out pickets to the north and west. He was certain that the Confederates would return in the morning.

* * *

The itinerary tablet inscriptions that describe the movement of the Union and Confederate armies before and during the Battle of Gettysburg are presented here. These tablets were removed from the battlefield, but the Gettysburg National Military Park staff plans to return them to the field as funding permits.

ITINERARY TABLET INSCRIPTIONS
ARMY OF THE POTOMAC

ARMY OF THE POTOMAC

June 29 1863

Headquarters Army of the Potomac moved from Frederick to Middleburg First and Eleventh Corps marched from Frederick to Emmitsburg Second Corps from Monocacy Junction via Liberty and Johnsville to Uniontown Third Corps from near Woodsborough to Taneytown Fifth Corps from Ballinger's Creek via Frederick and Mount Pleasant to Liberty Sixth Corps from Hyattstown via New Market and Ridgeville to New Windsor Twelfth Corps from Frederick to Taneytown and Bruceville.

First and Second Brigades First Cavalry Division from Middletown via Boonsborough Cavetown and Monterey Springs to near Fairfield Reserve Cavalry Brigade of the First Division from Middletown to Mechanicstown Second Cavalry Division from New Market and Ridgeville to New Windsor Third Cavalry Division from Frederick to Littletown and the Artillery Reserve from Frederick to Bruceville.

Skirmishes at Muddy Branch and Westminster Md. and at McConnellsburg and near Oyster Point Pa.

ARMY OF THE POTOMAC

June 30 1863

Headquarters Army of the Potomac moved from Middleburg to Taneytown First Corps marched from Emmitsburg to Marsh Run Third Corps from Taneytown to Bridgeport Fifth Corps from Liberty via Johnsville Union Bridge and Union to Union Mills Sixth Corps from New Windsor to Manchester Twelfth Corps from Taneytown and Bruceville to Littlestown First and Second Brigades of First Cavalry Division from near Fairfield via Emmitsburg to Gettysburg Second Cavalry Division from New Windsor to Westminster and thence to Manchester Third Cavalry Division from Littlestown to Hanover and the Artillery Reserve from Bruceville to Taneytown.

8

Fight at Hanover Pa. and skirmishes at Westminster Md. and at Fairfield and Sporting Hill near Harrisburg Pa.

ARMY OF THE POTOMAC

July 1 1863

First Corps marched from Marsh Run Eleventh Corps from Emmitsburg to Gettysburg Second Corps from Uniontown via Taneytown to near Gettysburg Third Corps from Bridgeport via Emmitsburg to the field of Gettysburg Fifth Corps from Union Mills via Hanover and McSherrystown to Bonaughtown Sixth Corps from Manchester en route to Gettysburg Twelfth Corps from Littlestown via Two Taverns to the Field of Gettysburg Second Cavalry Division marched from Manchester to Hanover Junction from whence the First and Third Brigades proceeded to Hanover while the Second Brigade returned to Manchester Third Cavalry Division moved from Hanover via Abbotsville to Berlin and the Artillery Reserve First Regular and Fourth Volunteer Brigades from Taneytown to near Gettysburg The Vermont Brigade from the defense of Washington joined the First Corps on the Field of Gettysburg.

Battle of Gettysburg (first day) and skirmish at Carlisle Pa.

ARMY OF THE POTOMAC

July 2 1863

Second Fifth and Sixth Corps Lockwood's Brigade from the Middle Department First and Third Brigades Second Cavalry Division Third Cavalry Division and Artillery Reserve reached the Field of Gettysburg First and Second Brigades First Cavalry Division marched from Gettysburg to Taneytown and Merritt's the Reserve Brigade of First Division from Mechanicstown to Emmitsburg.

Battle of Gettysburg (second day) and skirmishes at Hunterstown and near Chambersburg Pa.

ARMY OF THE POTOMAC

July 3 1863

First and Second Brigades First Cavalry Division marched from Taneytown to Westminster the Reserve Brigade of First Cavalry Division from Emmitsburg to the Field of Gettysburg and the Second Brigade Second Cavalry Division from Manchester to Westminster.

Battle of Gettysburg (third day) and fight at Fairfield.

ITINERARY TABLET INSCRIPTIONS
ARMY OF NORTHERN VIRGINIA

───────────

ARMY OF NORTHERN VIRGINIA

June 26 1863

Headquarters of the Army with Hood's Division Longstreet's Corps crossed the Potomac at Williamsport Md. and marched to Greencastle Pa. McLaws's Division Longstreet's Corps crossed the river and encamped near Williamsport Pickett's Division Longstreet's Corps with the Reserve Artillery marched through Hagerstown to Greencastle.

Rodes's and Johnson's Divisions Ewell's Corps with Jenkins's Cavalry Brigade were on the road from Chambersburg to Carlisle Pa. Early's Division Ewell's Corps with French's 17th Virginia Cavalry had a skirmish with the 26th Penna. Militia Infantry Gordon's Brigade Early's Division marched through Gettysburg halting a short time in the town Anderson's Division Hill's Corps marched from Hagerstown and encamped two miles north of Greencastle Hampton's Chambliss's and Fitz Lee's Brigades Stuart's Cavalry Division marched from Buckland via Brentville to near Wolf Run Shoals on the Occoquan River Va.

Robertson's and Jones's Brigades of Stuart's Cavalry Division guarding gaps in lower Blue Ridge.

───────────

ARMY OF NORTHERN VIRGINIA

June 27 1863

Headquarters of the Army moved from Greencastle to Chambersburg Pa. Rodes's and Johnson's Divisions Ewell's Corps arrived at Carlisle Early's Division marched from Mummasburg via Hunterstown New Chester and Hampton to Berlin Gordon's Brigade Early's Division reached York McLaws's Division Longstreet's Corps marched from Williamsport via Hagerstown Middleburg and Greencastle to five miles south of Chambersburg Hood's Division reached Chambersburg and Pickett's Division marched three miles further north Anderson's Division Hill's Corps marched via

10

Chambersburg to Fayetteville Pa. Heth's and Pender's Divisions Hill's Corps to the same place by other routes Hampton's Chambliss's and Fitz Lee's Brigades Stuart's Cavalry Division marched from Wolf Run Shoals on Occoquan River via Fairfax Station Annandale and Dranesville Va. And crossed the Potomac into Maryland below Seneca Creek Robertson's and Jones's Brigades Stuart's Cavalry Division remained in Virginia to guard the passes of the Blue Ridge.

―――――――

ARMY OF NORTHERN VIRGINIA

June 28 1863

Rodes's and Johnson's Divisions Ewell's Corps were at Carlisle Jenkins's Cavalry Brigade was sent to reconnoiter the defenses of Harrisburg Early's Division Ewell's Corps marched from Berlin by way of Weiglestown to York Gordon's Brigade Early's Division marching on through York to Wrightsville on the Susquehanna River.

Hill's Corps in camp at Fayetteville Longstreet's Corps at or near Chambersburg.

Hampton's Chambliss's and Fitz Lee's Brigades Stuart's Cavalry Division marched via Darnestown and Rockville Md.

―――――――

ARMY OF NORTHERN VIRGINIA

June 29 1863

Heth's Division Hill's Corps marched from Fayetteville to Cashtown Pender's and Anderson's Divisions remaining at Fayetteville.

Johnson's Division Ewell's Corps countermarched from Carlisle to Greenville Pa. Rodes's Division Ewell's Corps remained at Carlisle and Early's Division at York and Wrightsville.

Longstreet's Corps remained in position near Chambersburg.

Three Brigades of Stuart's Cavalry Division marched through Cooksville Sykesville and Westminster Md. to Union Mills Pa.

―――――――

ARMY OF NORTHERN VIRGINIA

June 30 1863

Heth's Division Hill's Corps at Cashtown Pettigrew's Brigade Heth's Division marched nearly to Gettysburg but was recalled Pender's Division

Hill's Corps marched from Fayetteville to Cashtown   Anderson's Division Hill's Corps remained at Fayetteville.

Rodes's Division Ewell's Corps marched from Carlisle via Petersburg to Heidlersburg   Johnson's Division Ewell's Corps marched from Greenville to Scotland Pa.   Early's Division Ewell's Corps returned from York via Weiglestown and East Berlin and encamped three miles from Heidlersburg.

Pickett's Division Longstreet's Corps remained at Chambersburg guarding wagon trains   McLaws's and Hood's Divisions Longstreet's Corps marched from there to Fayetteville except Law's Brigade which was sent to New Guilford.

Stuart's Cavalry Division marched from Union Mills Md. via Hanover to Jefferson and had a fight at Hanover Pa. with Kilpatrick's 3d Cavalry Division.

———

ARMY OF NORTHERN VIRGINIA

July 1 1863

Heth's and Pender's Divisions Hill's Corps marched from Cashtown to Gettysburg   Anderson's Division Hill's Corps marched from Fayetteville via Cashtown to near Gettysburg.

Rodes's Division Ewell's Corps marched from Heidlersburg via Middletown to Gettysburg   Early's Division Ewell's Corps to Heidlersburg and thence by the direct road to Gettysburg   Johnson's Division Ewell's Corps from Scotland via Cashtown to Gettysburg.

Pickett's Division Longstreet's Corps remained with the wagon trains at Chambersburg   McLaws's and Hood's Divisions Longstreet's Corps except Law's Brigade on outpost duty at New Guilford marched from Fayetteville to Marsh Creek within four miles of Gettysburg.

Stuart's Cavalry Division marched from Jefferson via Dover and Dillsburg to Carlisle   Robertson's and Jones's Brigades of Cavalry crossed the Potomac at Williamsport and marched to Greencastle Pa.

———

ARMY OF NORTHERN VIRGINIA

July 2 1863

McLaws's and Hood's Divisions Longstreet's Corps marched from Marsh Creek to the Field at Gettysburg   Law's Brigade Hood's Division marched from New Guilford to Gettysburg arriving about noon   Pickett's

Division Longstreet's Corps marched from Chambersburg and arrived in the vicinity of Gettysburg soon after sunset.

Stuart's Cavalry Division marched from Carlisle via Hunterstown to near Gettysburg Hampton's Cavalry Brigade being in front had an engagement with Union Cavalry in the evening at Hunterstown Pa.

Robertson's and Jones's Brigades Stuart's Cavalry Division marched from Greencastle to Chambersburg.

———————

ARMY OF NORTHERN VIRGINIA

July 3 1863

Pickett's Division Longstreet's Corps arrived on the field early in the morning.

Robertson's and Jones's Brigades Stuart's Cavalry Division marched from Chambersburg via Cashtown and Fairfield to a position on the right flank of the Confederate Army Jones's Brigade had a severe fight with the 6th United States Cavalry near Fairfield Pa.

Imboden's Brigade of mounted Infantry reached the field at noon.

PART II

The First Day
July 1, 1863

FIRST DAY BATTLE SUMMARY

After his encounter with Pettigrew's Brigade the previous day and with knowledge that General Lee appeared to be concentrating his army in the vicinity of Gettysburg, Brigadier General Buford was well aware that the Confederates would likely arrive in force early. He would not be disappointed in his assessment. Confederate Maj. Gen. Henry Heth's four-brigade Division departed Cashtown for Gettysburg at about five o'clock in the morning. The column was led by Brig. Gen. James Archer's Alabama Brigade, followed by Brig. Gen. Joseph Davis', Col. J. M. Brockenbrough's, and Brig. Gen. J. J. Pettigrew's Brigades. Third Corps commander, Lt. Gen. A. P. Hill, also ordered Maj. Gen. Dorsey Pender's Division to follow Heth's.

Expecting little opposition, Archer moved his brigade rapidly along the Chambersburg Pike toward Gettysburg. About five miles from town, Archer's advance skirmishers ran into Buford's pickets posted at the Marsh Creek crossing. Pushing the Union pickets back, Archer's Alabamians continued to advance until they came onto Herr's Ridge at about eight o'clock. There they came under fire from Lt. John Calef's Battery A Second U.S. Artillery and halted to bring their own artillery forward. Alerted by the scattered exchange of fire between the advancing Rebels and his withdrawing patrols, Buford had already sent word to Maj. Gen. John Reynolds, First Corps Commander, that the Confederate infantry was advancing in force toward Gettysburg and asked for relief as soon as possible.

MORNING BATTLE

Arriving on Herr's Ridge, Heth called Davis' Brigade forward to establish a battleline with Archer's Brigade south of Chambersburg Pike, Davis' Brigade north of the Pike. Skirmishers were ordered forward against Buford's line of two dismounted cavalry brigades on McPherson's Ridge; Col. William Gamble south of the Pike, Col. Thomas Devin to the north. Even with one

17

fourth of their number acting as horse holders in the rear, the dismounted troopers with their breechloading carbines and support by Calef's Battery, laid down a heavy volume of fire. General Heth, thinking that he had encountered infantry, paused to await the arrival of reinforcements before committing the main body of his brigades. After nine o'clock, with his artillery up and skirmishers probing the Union line, Heth determined that only a light cavalry force was between him and Gettysburg. He ordered the main bodies of Archer's and Davis' Brigades to sweep them aside.

Observing the battle from the cupola of the Lutheran Seminary, it soon became obvious to Buford that his line of dismounted troopers could not hold for long. Heth was pushing forward with a much larger force, soon to be joined by Pender's Division that could be seen approaching from the west. Buford's outposts, which he had posted to the north, had also reported that a large force of Confederates was approaching from that direction. Without reinforcement, he would be forced to withdraw or be overrun. As he was making preparations to withdraw to Cemetery Hill, Buford saw in the distance a Union infantry column approaching from the south on Emmitsburg Road.

General Reynolds was leading his First Corps toward Gettysburg when he got the message about the Confederate advance from Buford. Upon hearing the sound of battle, he directed his lead division under Brig. Gen. James Wadsworth to move cross-country, straight to the fighting, and galloped forward for a personal reconnaissance. Reynolds was briefed on the situation by Buford and after quickly studying the situation, concurred with Buford that the terrain was indeed excellent for defensive battle and that the Confederates must not be allowed to occupy the high ground south of the town. Deciding to hold the position, Reynolds rather than the commanders of the Army of the Potomac or Army of Northern Virginia selected the location of the battle that would end the second Confederate invasion of the North. With the decision made, he sent a message to Maj. Gen. Oliver Howard urging him to bring his Eleventh Corps to Gettysburg as quickly as possible. He also sent a message to General Meade that the enemy was advancing on Gettysburg in strong force and that he would delay them as long as possible. With that, he rode back to personally direct Wadsworth's Division into position.

Buford's Cavalry had been fighting two full hours when the First Corps infantry started relieving them at about ten o'clock. Gamble moved his troopers to the left of the arriving infantry, and Devin's Brigade was sent to picket the approaches from the north. The cavalry's success in delaying the Confederate advance could be credited to their tenacity and to Heth's lack of knowledge of the enemy situation.

General Reynolds directed Brig. Gen. Solomon Meredith's famous Iron Brigade and two regiments of Brig. Gen. Lysander Cutler's Brigade to take

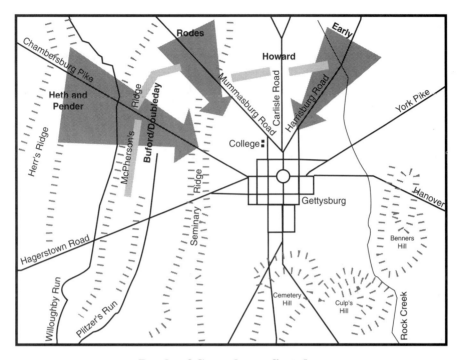

Battle of Gettysburg, first day

position on McPherson's Ridge, south of the Chambersburg Pike. Cutler's three remaining regiments were sent north of the railway cut on the other side of the Pike. These were Reynolds' final commands. He was killed instantly by a rifle bullet to the head while directing the deployment of the Iron Brigade on the edge of a wooded area now known as Reynolds Woods. Command passed to Maj. Gen. Abner Doubleday.

Heth was soon aware that he had more to contend with than dismounted cavalry, but he was committed. As the Union infantry was taking up position, Archer's and Davis' Brigades were crossing Willoughby Run and moving up to sweep McPherson Ridge. The Iron Brigade went on the attack as soon as they were deployed. Moving through Reynolds Woods, the brigade fell upon Archer's flank and rear with devastating results. The Confederates attempted to pull back, but many were captured, including Archer, the first Confederate general to be captured under General Lee's command. The Iron Brigade pushed the Confederates back across Willoughby Run and took position on the east slope of Herr's Ridge.

To the north of the Pike the results were similar but reversed. Davis' Brigade outflanked Cutler's three regiments north of the railway cut and forced them back to Seminary Ridge. As the elated Confederates pursued the retreating Federals over the crest of McPherson Ridge and into the quarter-mile-wide valley between McPherson and Seminary ridges, they funneled into a deep cut on the unfinished railroad bed. What appeared to be a covered approach proved to be a trap. Major General Doubleday quickly took advantage of the situation by rushing Cutler's two regiments that were south of the Pike to the cut. The hapless Rebels saw the muzzles of rifles pointed down at them from the sides of the cut so high and steep that they could not return fire. Many heeded the ordered surrender; those that didn't suffered heavily as they ran the gauntlet back through the cut. With as many as half its number killed, wounded or captured, Davis pulled his brigade back across Willoughby Run. After the repulse of Davis' Brigade, Doubleday ordered the Iron Brigade to pull back to McPherson Ridge, re-establishing the line held about four hours earlier by Buford's cavalry.

General Heth had not had a good morning. He had advanced skirmishers to meet what was supposed to be militia but encountered Buford's Army of the Potomac cavalry. The infantry brigades from the vanguard of the Union First Corps met the two brigades that he sent to push the cavalry aside. Archer's and Davis' Brigades were pushed back to Herr's Ridge with heavy loss. Seeing more Union troops arriving but not knowing their strength, Heth decided to continue the engagement with artillery and wait before sending his infantry back across Willoughby Run.

AFTERNOON BATTLE

The remaining two First Union Corps divisions arrived on the field and were taking up position by noon. Brig. Gen. Thomas Rowley, arriving with two of his Third Division brigades, was sent to reinforce the Iron Brigade on McPherson's Ridge; Col. Roy Stone's Brigade to the right and Col. Chapman Biddle's to the left. Brig. Gen. John Robinson's Second Division went into position on Seminary Ridge. Maj. Gen. Oliver Howard's Eleventh Union Army Corps had also arrived on the field. Taking command of the battlefield by virtue of his seniority, Howard directed Maj. Gen. Carl Schurz's Third Division to connect with the First Corps' right and extend the line to Oak Hill, a dominant height where McPherson and Seminary Ridges converge. Brig. Gen. Francis Barlow's First Division was ordered to take position on Schurz's right. The corps' Second Division under Brig. Gen. Adolph Von Steinwehr occupied Cemetery Hill as the corps reserve.

Surprises were in store for both sides that day as the Army of the Potomac and the Army of Northern Virginia converged on Gettysburg. As the two Eleventh Corps divisions moved across the open fields north of the town, Maj. Gen. Robert Rodes' Division of the Confederate Second Corps appeared on the field from the north. The corps commander, Lt. Gen. Richard Ewell, riding forward with the corps vanguard, immediately saw the strategic advantage of Oak Hill and ordered Rodes to occupy it. To counter this threat to the right flank of the Union line, Howard bent the north end of the Union line back to the east. He ordered Schurz's Division to form a line facing north with its left flank on the Mummasburg Road. Barlow was ordered to extend the line from the Third Division's right flank, northeast to Rock Creek. In so doing, a gap of about a quarter of a mile was formed between the two Union corps. Observing the danger that the Confederates on Oak Hill presented to the right flank of his corps, Doubleday quickly ordered Brig. Gen. Henry Baxter's and Brig. Gen. Gabriel Paul's Second Division Brigades to extend the right flank of the First Corps to Mummasburg Road. He also ordered Brig. Gen. Lysander Cutler's First Division Brigade to change front and take position on the Second Division's left.

Wanting to hit the Union flank before the Federals could establish an east-west line, Rodes decided to launch a hasty attack with three of his five brigades. Posting Brigadier General George Doles' Brigade on the left to hold off the arriving Union reinforcements and holding Brigadier General S. D. Ramseur's Brigade in reserve, Rodes ordered his three attack brigades forward. The attack was made without preliminary reconnaissance or the advancement of a skirmish line. The result was a miserable failure. Brigadier General Alfred Iverson's Brigade and three regiments of Colonel E.A. O'Neal's Brigade were to advance against the right flank of the Union First Corps. Iverson was to attack the flank of Baxter's Brigade as O'Neal conducted a frontal assault. O'Neal's badly led brigade was hurled back in disorder before Iverson could get his brigade moving. Brig. Gen. Junius Daniel's Brigade, which was supposed to cover Iverson's right flank, became too disoriented and scattered to assist in the attack. Iverson's Brigade, with both flanks now exposed, advanced against the Union line posted behind a low stone wall east of Forney Field. The Confederate line was ripped apart in front of the stone wall. Pinned down by Paul and Baxter's Brigades, Iverson's right flank was assaulted by Cutler's Brigade. Three of Iverson's four North Carolina Regiments were almost annihilated.

It was now about three o'clock in the afternoon of a very long day for both sides. General Lee was now on Herr's Ridge, assessing the situation that his army had stumbled into. What first appeared to be a disaster in the making for the Confederates was taking a turn for the better. Rodes was starting to recover from his ill-fated hasty attack. Daniel's Brigade, which had drifted wide in its effort to support Iverson, was now engaging Stone's Brigade at the angle where the First Union Corps' line bent to the east. Ramseur's Brigade was moving from its position in reserve to assail First Corps' right wing, and Dole's Brigade was showing progress in the gap between the two Union Corps, preventing them from linking up. Maj. Gen. Jubal Early's Confederate Division, with almost perfect timing, had also arrived from York, Pennsylvania to threaten the right flank of the Union Eleventh Corps. Observing the pieces fall together as if planned, Lee decided to discard the caution that he came onto the field with and press the attack. He ordered A. P. Hill to send both Heth's and Pender's Divisions to sweep McPherson Ridge.

The First and Third Divisions of the Eleventh Corps had been on the field north of the town about two hours. Under intense artillery fire from Oak Hill and pressure from Dole's Brigade, Schurz's Third Division had made little progress in linking up with First Corps. Barlow's First Division, with Col. Leopold Von Gilsa's First Brigade in the lead, had moved about a mile north of town to a position between Harrisburg Road and Rock Creek. Brig. Gen. Adelbert Ames' Second Brigade, arriving to reinforce the First Brigade, sent four companies across Rock Creek as skirmishers and deployed the remainder of the brigade on a hill, now known as Barlow Knoll, overlooking Rock Creek. With Ames' Brigade securing the flank, Barlow ordered Von Gilsa to attack Dole's flank to the left front. Von Gilsa's Brigade advanced over the hill and into the woods beyond where it encountered Brig. Gen. John Gordon's Brigade from Early's Division coming to Dole's support. The fight was intense but short. Supported by Dole's Brigade and effective enfilading fire from Col. H. P. Jones' Artillery Battalion east of Rock Creek, Gordon's six regiments of Georgia Infantry quickly cleared the hill. Falling back to the Almshouse, the Federals were attempting to form a line with the division reserve when Brig. Gen. Harry Hays' Brigade and Hoke's Brigade under Col. Isaac Avery struck them on the flank. Flanked and under intense pressure from superior forces, the Eleventh Corps line collapsed into a complete rout at about four o'clock.

The collapse of the Union right flank also forced the First Corps to give up the ground it had fought so hard for all day. Paul's Brigade, which had repulsed repeated attacks on its position behind the stone wall, was forced to withdraw under heavy fire. Baxter's Brigade had already pulled back to the rail-cut on Seminary Ridge. Pender's fresh division, along with Heth's bloodied brigades, was successfully forcing the line on McPherson Ridge. Meredith's Iron Brigade, suffering heavy losses, repulsed its attackers and held on until the Confederates carried Biddle's exposed position. Meredith and Stone were then compelled to fall back to Seminary Ridge. The remnants of First Corps that attempted to establish a line around the Seminary were soon assaulted by Pender's Division following from McPherson Ridge and by Rodes' Division pushing south along Seminary Ridge. Greatly outnumbered and with only the support of Gamble's spent cavalry brigade, the Federals were forced to retreat to Cemetery Hill.

As the First Union Corps' infantry and artillery funneled through the town toward Cemetery Hill, they encountered streets already clogged with troops from the Eleventh Corps. The result was near chaos. Had the Confederates pursued in force, it would have been much worse. Fortunately for the hapless Federals the Confederates did not, allowing many units to reach Cemetery Hill. Some stayed there with Von Steinwehr's Division but many continued on southward.

By four-thirty the first day's battle was essentially over. Early's Division was in the streets of Gettysburg, rounding up large numbers of prisoners, but the fight was over. The casualties were extremely high for both sides. Nearly one-fourth of the attacking Confederates had fallen or had been captured as compared to more than half of the Union troops deployed on the field that day. Lee's natural inclination was to pursue his beaten opponent up Cemetery Hill to complete the victory. However, not knowing the location of the remainder of the Army of the Potomac, he was hesitant to commit to a general engagement until his other divisions arrived. A. P. Hill's Corps was in no condition for further battle that day, nor was Rodes' Division of Ewell's Corps. Hoping that Early's Division was still fresh enough, but not knowing the condition of his Second Corps troops or the difficulty of the terrain, Lee sent a verbal order for Ewell to carry Cemetery Hill, if he thought it practicable. When nightfall came, no follow-up attack on Cemetery Hill had been made.

Baltimore Street, Gettysburg, circa 1885

Courtesy USAMHI-MOLLUS

Baltimore Sreet, Gettysburg, 1998

Photograph by Author

View of Chambersburg Pike, circa 1885

Looking from McPherson's Ridge to Herr's Ridge. Heth's Division formed for attack in open field on left.

Courtesy USAMHI-MOLLUS

View of Chambersburg Pike, 1998

Note tree growth on Herr's Ridge.

Photograph by Author

The Railroad Cut, circa 1885. Looking east.

Courtesy USAMHI-MOLLUS

The Railroad Cut, 1998

Photograph by Author

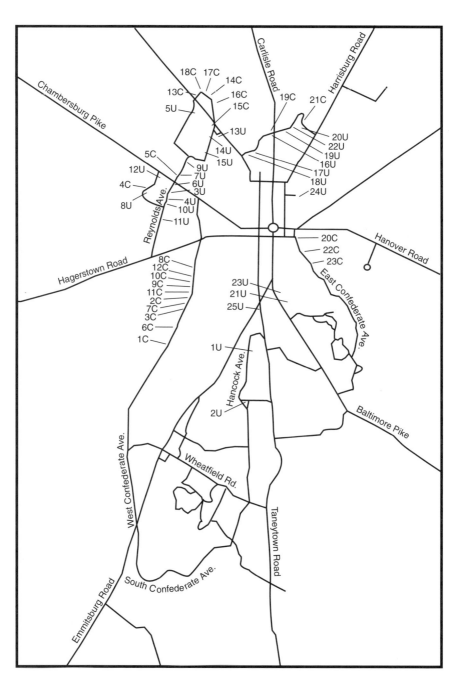

First day tablet locations

FIRST DAY TABLET INSCRIPTIONS
ARMY OF THE POTOMAC

ARMY OF THE POTOMAC
Major General George G. Meade
Commanding

The Army consisted of Eight Corps

First Corps	Major General John F. Reynolds
	Major General Abner Doubleday
	Major General John Newton
Second Corps	Major Winfield S. Hancock
	Brigadier General John Gibbion
Third Corps	Major Daniel E. Sickles
	Major General David B. Birney
Fifth Corps	Major General George Sykes
Sixth Corps	Major General John Sedgwick
Eleventh Corps	Major General Oliver C. Howard
	Major General Henry W. Slocum
Twelfth Corps	Brigadier General Alpheus S. Williams
Cavalry Corps	Major General Alfred Pleasonton
Reserve Artillery	Brigadier General Robert O. Tyler

July 1. The First and Eleventh Corps arrived and were engaged north and west of Gettysburg and fell back to Cemetery Hill in rear of the town. The Twelfth Corps and a large part of the Third Corps arrived at the close of the day.

July 2. The remainder of the Third Corps and the Fifth and Second Corps arrived in the morning. The Sixth Corps in the Afternoon. The Third Corps having advanced was attacked by Longstreet's Confederate Corps and Anderson's Division of Hill's Corps. The Fifth Corps and the First Division of the Second Corps going to the support of the Third Corps an engagement ensued until nightfall when the Union forces had been driven back from their advanced position and the Confederates repulsed.

28

July 3. The Twelfth Corps having by order vacated a large part of its line on Culps Hill on the night of the 2D and Johnson's Division of Ewell's Corps having occupied the works. The Twelfth Corps in the morning attacked and regained the lines it had previously vacated. Hill's Corps and Pickett's Division of Longstreet's Corps in the afternoon attacked the line of the Second Corps and were repulsed with great Loss. Stuart's Confederate Cavalry in the afternoon attacked the Second Cavalry Division and the Second Brigade Third Cavalry Division and was repulsed.

No. 1U   Tablet on Granite Marker located—Hancock Avenue

ARMY OF THE POTOMAC
CAVALRY CORPS
Major General Alfred Pleasonton

First Division   Brigadier General John Buford

Second Division   Brigadier General David McM. Gregg

Third Division   Brigadier General Judson Kilpatrick

Headquarters Guard
   Co. C 1st Ohio   Capt . Samuel N. Stanford

Horse Artillery
   First Brigade   Capt. James M. Robertson
   Second Brigade   Capt. John C. Tidball

June 29. Buford's Division advanced and extended its lines to left as far as Hagerstown to discover Confederate forces if any on left of the Army. Gregg's Division moved to right of the Army to Westminster covering the country toward York and Carlisle by reconnoissances and patrols. Kilpatrick's Division advanced to Hanover.

June 30. Gamble's and Devin's Brigades Buford's Division advanced to Gettysburg. Kilpatrick's Division encountered Stuart's Cavalry at Hanover. Two brigades of Gregg's Division were ordered to Gettysburg. Huey's Third Brigade was left at Westminster.

July 1. Gamble's and Devin's Brigades encountered Heth's Division Hill's Corps on second ridge west of Gettysburg. When 1st and 11th Corps retreated to Cemetery Hill the Cavalry took position first on the left connecting with the town and later further to the left in front of Little Round Top.

July 2. On the arrival of the 3D Corps Buford's command was ordered to Westminster. Kilpatrick's Division marched toward Gettysburg and was ordered to the right and was attacked at Hunterstown by a detachment of Stuart's command which was repulsed.

July 3. Merritt's Brigade arrived and skirmished with the Confederate right while the 6th U. S. advanced to Fairfield and became engaged. Kilpatrick with Farnsworth's Brigade took position on left of battle line and made a charge in the afternoon on the Confederate right but was repulsed with loss including General Farnsworth killed. Gregg's Division on the right was attacked by Stuart's Cavalry in the afternoon but with the aid of Custer's Brigade Kilpatrick's Division the attack was repulsed.

Casualties   Killed 5 Officers 86 Men   Wounded 39 Officers 315 Men Captured or Missing 8 Officers 399 Men   Total 852

No 2U   Tablet on Granite Marker located—Pleasonton Avenue

ARMY OF THE POTOMAC
CAVALRY CORPS
FIRST DIVISION
Brig. Gen. John Buford

First Brigade   Col. Wm. Gamble
Second Brigade   Col. Thos. C. Devin
Reserve Brigade   Brig. Gen. Wesley Merritt

June 29. Engaged in picketing scouting and patrolling westerly and northerly to Hagerstown. Finding no Confederate force Gen. Buford with the First and Second Brigades re-crossed the mountains and encamped near Fairfield.

June 30. Arrived at Gettysburg at 11 A. M. as a detachment of Heth's Confederate Division was about to enter but withdrew on the approach of the two Brigades of the Division. Gen. Buford deployed his Cavalry along the ridge east of Willoughby Run between the Mummasburg and Fairfield Roads with pickets well advanced.

July 1. Was attacked between 8 and 9 A. M. by Heth's Division and Pegram's Artillery Battalion which were held in check until the arrival of First Corps. The Second Brigade picketed the approaches from the north and retarded the advance of Ewell's Corps until Eleventh Corps arrived. About 4 P. M. retreated to Cemetery Hill and formed on left of town and bivouacked for the night in front of Little Round Top.

July 3. Started in the morning for Westminster to guard Army trains. The Reserve Brigade Cavalry Corps arrived about noon on the Emmitsburg Road and engaged for four hours the Confederate right.

Casualties   Killed 1 Officer 27 Men   Wounded 12 Officers 104 Men Captured or Missing 6 Officers 268 Men   Total 418

No. 3U   Tablet on Granite Marker located—South Reynolds Avenue

---

ARMY OF THE POTOMAC
CAVALRY CORPS   FIRST DIVISION
FIRST BRIGADE
Col. William Gamble
8th, 12th Illinois   (4 Cos.) 3rd Indiana
(6 Cos.) 8th New York Cavalry

June 30. Started early for Gettysburg and encountered two Mississippi regiments and a section of artillery and after a short skirmish proceeded to Gettysburg when a detachment of Major Gen. Heth's Division about to enter the town withdrew towards Cashtown leaving pickets four and a half miles from Gettysburg.

July 1. Between 8 and 9 A. M. Confederates advanced in force from Cashtown. The Brigade dismounted and with Battery A 2D U. S. Artillery held its position for more than two hours against infantry and artillery in superior numbers and until Major Gen. J. F. Reynolds arrived with First Corps after which the Brigade was engaged on the left of the infantry. On retiring to the Cemetery Hill the Brigade took position left of the town with Second Brigade and later in front of Little Round Top.

July 2. Relieved by Third Corps and marched to Taneytown en route to Westminster.

Casualties   Killed 1 Officer 12 Men   Wounded 6 Officers 52 Men   Captured or Missing 28 Men   Total 99

No. 4U   Tablet on Granite Pedestal located—South Reynolds Avenue

---

ARMY OF THE POTOMAC
CAVALRY CORPS   FIRST DIVISION
SECOND BRIGADE
Col. Thomas C. Devin
6th   9th New York   17th Pennsylvania
3D (2 Cos.) West Virginia Cavalry

June 30. Started early for Gettysburg and encountered two Mississippi Regiments and a section of artillery and after a short skirmish proceeded to Gettysburg arriving there as a detachment of Major Gen. Heth's Division was about to enter the town but withdrew towards Cashtown leaving pickets four and a half miles from Gettysburg.

July 1. Between 8 and 9 A. M. the Confederates advanced in force from Cashtown. The Brigade Dismounted and with Battery A 2D U. S. held its position for more than two hours against infantry and artillery in superior numbers until arrival of Eleventh Corps and then held the approach by the York Pike. Later ordered to the Emmitsburg Road and formed line with right flank resting on the town. Bivouacked for the night in front of Little Round Top.

July 2. Relieved by Third Corps and marched to Taneytown en route to Westminster.

Casualties   Killed 2 Men   Wounded 3 Men   Captured or Missing 23 Men   Total 28

No. 5U   Tablet on Granite Pedestal located—Buford Avenue

——————

ARMY OF THE POTOMAC
FIRST CORPS
Major General John F. Reynolds
Major General Abner Doubleday
Major General John Newton

First Division   Brigadier General James S. Wadsworth
Second Division   Brigadier General John C. Robinson
Third Division   Brigadier General Thomas A. Rowley
                        Major General Abner Doubleday
Artillery Brigade   Colonel Charles S. Wainright

July 1. Arrived at Gettysburg between 10 A. M. and noon. Relieved Buford's Cavalry and became engaged with Archer's and Davis's Brigades Heth's Division Hill's Corps. General Reynolds fell mortally wounded about 10.15 A. M. The Confederates having been reinforced from Hill's and Ewell's Corps made a vigorous attack at 2 P. M. with superior numbers along the entire line. At 4 P. M. the Corps retired and took positions on Culps Hill and Cemetery ridge.

July 2 & 3. Wadsworth's Division occupied the north point of Culps Hill connecting with 12th Corps on right and Robinson's and Rowley's Divisions on Cemetery Ridge with detachments elsewhere.

Casualties including Corps and Division Staff: Killed 42 Officers 624 Men   Wounded 262 Officers 2969 Men   Captured or Missing 80 Officers 2079 Men   Total 6056

No. 6U   Tablet on Granite Marker located—South Reynolds Avenue

——————

ARMY OF THE POTOMAC
FIRST CORPS
FIRST DIVISION
Brig. General James S. Wadsworth

First Brigade   Brig. Gen. Solomon Meredith
                              Col. Wm. W. Robinson

Second Brigade   Brig. General Lysander Cutler

July 1. Arrived at 10 A. M. the first Union Infantry on the field. Formed across Chambersburg Pike relieving First Division Cavalry Corps and was immediately attacked by Archer's and Davis's Brigades Heth's Confederate Division which was repulsed with heavy losses. At 2 P. M. both sides having been heavily reinforced the fighting was renewed with great energy. The two brigades fighting separately where most needed. At 4 P. M. the Confederates having advanced in superior numbers and enveloping both flanks the Division retired by order of the general commanding to Cemetery Hill and went into position on north side of Culps Hill.

July 2 & 3. Entrenched on Culp's Hill and repulsed attacks made in the evening of second and morning of third.

Casualties   Killed 19 Officers 280 Men   Wounded 98 Officers 1131 Men Captured or Missing 15 Officers 612 Men   Total 2155

No. 7U   Tablet on Granite Marker located—North Reynolds Avenue

━━━━━━━━━━━

ARMY OF THE POTOMAC
FIRST CORPS   FIRST DIVISION
FIRST BRIGADE
Brig. Gen. Solomon Meredith
Col. William W. Robinson
19th Indiana   24th Michigan
2D   6th   7th Wisconsin Infantry

July 1. Arrived at 10 A. M. went into position and charged Brig. Gen. Archer's Brigade in Reynolds's Woods forced the Confederate line across Willoughby Run capturing Brig. Gen. Archer and many prisoners. The 19th Indiana 24th Michigan and the 2D and 7th Wisconsin retired and formed line in Reynolds Woods the 6th Wisconsin having come to the support of Second Brigade against Brig. Gen. Davis's Brigade Major Gen. Heth's Division. At 4 P. M. being outflanked and hard pressed the Brigade retired under a heavy fire of infantry and artillery to Seminary

Ridge and thence to Cemetery Hill and to the north slope of Culps Hill and entrenched.

July 2. Repulsed without loss a sharp attack at right. About sunset the 6th Wisconsin went to the support of Third Brigade Second Division Twelfth Corps and assisted in repelling attacks during the night.

July 3. Repulsed a sharp attack in the morning without loss.

Casualties   Killed 13 Officers 158 Men   Wounded 54 Officers 666 Men Captured or Missing 13 Officers 249 Men   Total 1153

No. 8U   Tablet on Granite Pedestal located—Meredith Avenue

ARMY OF THE POTOMAC
FIRST CORPS   FIRST DIVISION
SECOND BRIGADE
Brig. Gen. Lysander Cutler
7th Indiana   76th   84th   95th   147th New York
56th   (9 Cos.) Pennsylvania Infantry

July 1. Arrived at 9.45 A. M. and took position in the right of Reynolds's Woods. The 76th and 147th New York and 56th Penna. north of the railroad cut were fiercely attacked by Brig. Gen. Davis's Brigade Major Gen. Heth's Division but the 84th and 95th New York assisted by 6th Wisconsin made a charge on the cut through which Brig. Gen. Davis's Brigade attempted to retreat and captured many prisoners and two stands of colors. The Brigade held its first position until 2 P. M. when it was relieved by Second Brigade Third Division and went into position on Oak Ridge on the left of Second Division and assisted in the capture of a large part of Brig. Gen. Iverson's Brigade. Remained under a heavy fire until 4 P. M. when it retired to Cemetery Hill and took position on Culps Hill. The 7th Indiana here joined the Brigade.

July 2. At night the 84th and 147th New York went to the support of the Third Brigade Second Division Twelfth Corps and was actively engaged remaining through the night.

July 3. Repulsed an attack in the morning and remained in position until the close of the battle.

Casualties   Killed 6 Officers 122 Men   Wounded 44 Officers 465 Men Captured or Missing 2 Officers 363 Men   Total 1002

No. 9U   Tablet on Granite Pedestal located—North Reynolds Avenue

---

ARMY OF THE POTOMAC
FIRST CORPS
THIRD DIVISION
Brig. Gen. Thos. A. Rowley   Major Gen. Abner Doubleday

First Brigade   Col. Chapman Biddle
                         Brig. Gen. T. A. Rowley
Second Brigade   Col. Roy Stone
                         Col. Langhorne Wister
                         Col. E. L. Dana
Third Brigade   Brig. Gen. Geo. J. Stannard
                         Col. Francis V. Randall

July 1. Arrived about 11 A. M. The First Brigade took position in field on the left of Reynolds Woods. Second Brigade on Chambersburg Pike relieving Second Brigade First Division. These brigades were actively engaged from 2 to 4 P. M. and retired with the Corps and took position south of the cemetery fronting Emmitsburg Road. The Third Brigade joined at dusk.

July 2. At sunset sent to support of Third Corps on its right at Emmitsburg Road and captured 80 prisoners and recaptured 4 guns.

July 3. In position on left of Second Division Second Corps. Assisted in repulsing Longstreet's assault capturing many prisoners and three stand of colors.

Casualties   Killed 13 Officers 252 Men   Wounded 89 Officers 1208 Men
Captured or Missing 16 Officers 525 Men   Total 2103

No. 10U   Tablet on Granite Marker located—South Reynolds Avenue

---

ARMY OF THE POTOMAC
FIRST CORPS   THIRD DIVISION
FIRST BRIGADE
Col. Chapman Biddle
Brig. Gen. Thomas A. Rowley
80th New York   121st   142D   151st Penna. Infantry

July 1. Arrived and went into position about 11. 30 A. M. left of Reynolds's Woods. The 151st Penna. having been sent to reinforce Second Brigade on right of Reynolds's Woods. The remaining regiments with Battery B 1st Penna. formed line facing west and held this position until near 4 P. M. when being pressed with superior numbers in front and outflanked on the left the Brigade retired to Seminary Ridge. On the withdrawal of the Corps the Brigade retired to Cemetery Hill and formed on the left along Taneytown Road and remained there until noon the next day.

July 2. Between 5 and 6 P. M. the Brigade was moved to the left centre from which First Division Second Corps had been taken to support Third Corps.

July 3. Remained in the same position and assisted in repelling Longstreet's assault in the afternoon taking many prisoners. At 6 P. M. withdrew to former position on Taneytown Road.

Casualties   Killed 8 Officers 103 Men   Wounded 41 Officers 516 Men Captured or Missing 8 Officers 222 Men   Total 898

No. 11U   Tablet on Granite Pedestal located—South Reynolds Avenue

------

ARMY OF THE POTOMAC
FIRST CORPS   THIRD DIVISION
SECOND BRIGADE
Col. Roy Stone   Col. Langhorne Wister
Col. Edmund L. Dana
143D   149th   150th Pennsylvania Infantry

July 1. Arrived and went into position at McPherson buildings between Reynolds Woods and the Railroad Cut and was subjected to a heavy front and enfilading artillery fire from the right. Repulsed repeated attacks of Brig. Daniel's Brigade Major Gen. Rodes's Division from the right as well as front attacks until pressed on both flanks and in front by superior numbers. It retired to Seminary Ridge and held temporary breast works there until the Corps retired before overwhelming numbers to Cemetery Hill when the Brigade with the Division took position at the left of the cemetery on and near the Taneytown Road.

July 2. Late in the afternoon moved to left and took position previously occupied by First Division Second Corps.

July 3. Remained in the same position under the heavy artillery fire in the afternoon.

The strength of the Brigade July 1st   1315

Casualties   Killed 4 Officers 105 Men   Wounded 35 Officers 430 Men Captured or Missing 8 Officers 271 Men   Total 853

No. 12U   Tablet on Granite Pedestal located—Stone Avenue, McPherson Ridge

------

ARMY OF THE POTOMAC
FIRST CORPS
SECOND DIVISION
Brig. General John C. Robinson

First Brigade   Brig. Gen. Gabriel Paul
                         Col. S. H. Leonard
                         Col. Adrian R. Root
                         Col. Peter Lyle
                         Col. R. Coulter
Second Brigade   Brig. General H. Baxter

July 1. Arrived at the Seminary about noon hotly engaged on the right and right centre from about 2 P. M. until 4 P. M. when on the advance of Rodes's Confederate Division against the front and flanks the Division by order the Commanding General retired with the Corps through Gettysburg to Cemetery Hill on the left of the cemetery parallel to Emmitsburg Road.

July 2. Relieved about noon by Third Division Second Corps and placed in reserve and thereafter sent to support of the Third Eleventh and Second Corps at different times and places.

July 3. At daylight moved to the support of batteries on Cemetery Hill. At 9 A. M. sent to the support of Twelfth Corps and at 3 P. M. took position on the right of Second Corps and remained until the close of the battle.

Casualties   Killed 9 Officers 82 Men   Wounded 68 Officers 548 Men
Captured or Missing 52 Officers 931 Men   Total 1690

No. 13U   Tablet on Granite Marker located—Robinson Avenue

ARMY OF THE POTOMAC
FIRST CORPS   SECOND DIVISION
SECOND BRIGADE
Brig. Gen. Henry Baxter
12th Mass   83D   97th New York
11th   88th   90th Pennsylvania Infantry

July 1. Arrived about noon took position on right of Corps on Mummasburg Road with Second Brigade First Division on left. Repulsed an attack of Col. O'Neal's Brigade then changed front and with the assistance of Second Brigade First Division captured 1000 prisoners and three stand of colors of Brig. Gen. Iverson's Brigade. Afterwards relieved by First Brigade and retired to the Railroad Cut to support Battery B 4th U. S. At

4 P. M. retired to Cemetery Hill and constructed breastworks. The 11th Penna. was transferred to the First Brigade.

July 2. About 10 A. M. relieved by Second Brigade Second Division Second Corps and placed in reserve. At 4 P. M. supported a battery of Eleventh Corps. At sunset moved to the support of Third Corps then returned to support of Eleventh Corps.

July 3. Moved to the rear of the cemetery early in the morning in support of Twelfth Corps. At 2 P. M. formed on right and rear of Third Division Second Corps and there remained until the close of the battle. The Brigade went into action with less than 1200 men.

Casualties   Killed 7 Officers 3 Men   Wounded 31 Officers 227 Men Captured or Missing 12 Officers 338 Men   Total 648

No. 14U   Tablet on Granite Pedestal located—Doubleday Avenue, north end

Note: Numbers inscribed for killed, wounded and captured or missing total 618, not 648.

━━━━━━━━━━

ARMY OF THE POTOMAC
FIRST CORPS   SECOND DIVISION
FIRST BRIGADE
Brig. Gen. Gabriel R. Paul
Col. Samuel H. Leonard   Col. Adrian R. Root
Col. Richard Coulter   Col. Peter Lyle
16th Maine   13th Massachusetts
94th   104th   New York   107th Penna. Infantry

July 1. Arrived about noon and went into position on the ridge near the Seminary and threw up Breastworks. About half past 2 P. M. moved to the right of Corps in support of Second Brigade. Repulsed repeated attacks and was engaged until 4 P. M. then retired to Seminary Ridge and constructed Breastworks. The 11th Penna. was transferred from the Second Brigade.

July 2. About noon relieved by Third Division Second Corps and went to rear in support of batteries on Cemetery Hill. At sunset moved to the left to support the Third Corps and returned to Cemetery Hill.

July 3. At 9 A. M. went to support of Twelfth Corps and at 3 P. M. to the left and took position on right of Second Corps in support of a battery and there remained until the close of the battle.

Casualties   Killed 2 Officers 49 Men   Wounded 36 Officers 321 Men Captured or Missing 40 Officers 593 Men   Total 1041

No. 15U   Tablet on Granite Pedestal located—Doubleday Avenue, south end

---

ARMY OF THE POTOMAC
ELEVENTH CORPS
Major General Oliver O. Howard

First Division   Brigadier General Francis C. Barlow
                         Brigadier General Adelbert Ames
Second Division   Brigadier General Adolph Von Steinwehr
Third Division   Major General Carl Schurz
Artillery Brigade   Major Thomas W. Osborn

July 1. Schurz's Division in advance arrived at 10.30 A. M. was formed in line northwest of the town. Barlow's Division formed on Schurz's right. Steinwehr's Division was placed on Cemetery Hill. The line in front was attacked by brigades of Rodes's and Early's Divisions. About 4 P. M. the Corps was forced back and retired through the town to Cemetery Hill and formed on each side of the Baltimore Pike.

July 2. The Corps remained in the same position until about 4 P. M. when the Confederate artillery opened fire from Benner's Hill and Cemetery Ridge but was silenced by artillery under Colonel Wainright and Major Osborn. At 8 P. M. Hays's Louisiana and Hoke's North Carolina Brigades attacked the position on East Cemetery Hill but were repulsed.

July 3. At 1 P. M. all the Confederate artillery within direct range opened fire on this position which was followed by an unsuccessful charge on the 2d. Corps position.

Casualties   Killed 33 Officers 336 Men   Wounded 120 Officers 1802 Men   Captured or Missing 62 Officers 1448 Men   Total 3801

No. 16U   Tablet on Granite Marker located—West Howard Avenue

---

ARMY OF THE POTOMAC
ELEVENTH CORPS
THIRD DIVISION
Major General Carl Schurz

First Brigade   Brig. Gen. Alex Schimmelfennig
                         Col. George Von Amsberg
Second Brigade   Col. W. Krzyzanowski

July 1. Arrived about noon and advanced to connect with the right of First Corps. The First Division on the right but was repulsed by a strong artillery and infantry fire from Rodes's Division Ewell's Corps. Engaged until past 4 P. M. and then retreated through the town to Cemetery Hill bringing up the rear of the Corps and took position behind stone walls with the First Division on right and Second on left. Skirmishers in houses 300 to 500 yards front.

July 2. In position in two lines behind stone walls of the cemetery. At 7 P. M. the First Brigade was sent to support the First Division on right. One regiment remained there four regiments went further to the right and assisted in repelling at 9 P. M. an attack made through woods on First Corps. Between 8 and 9 P. M. an attack on East Cemetery Hill was made by Hays's Louisiana Brigade and a detachment from Second Brigade was hastened to the point of attack and after a short and vigorous hand to hand conflict the attack was repulsed..

July 3. Not engaged except skirmishing.

July 4. Detachment from Division entered town and captured over 300 Confederates left on the retreat of their forces.

Casualties   Killed 20 Officers 113 Men   Wounded 56 Officers 628 Men Captured or Missing 33 Officers 626 Men   Total 1476

No. 17U   Tablet on Granite Marker located—West Howard Avenue

———————

ARMY OF THE POTOMAC
ELEVENTH CORPS   THIRD DIVISION
FIRST BRIGADE
Brig. Gen. Alex Schimmelfennig
Col. George Von Amsberg
82D Illinois   45th   157th New York
61st Ohio   74th Pennsylvania Infantry

July 1. Arrived 1 P. M. and advanced to connect with the right of First Corps on Oak Hill but was met by heavy artillery and musketry fire and after being engaged between two and three hours and pressed closely upon the front and flank by superior numbers the Brigade was compelled to retire with the Corps at 4 P. M. through the town to Cemetery Hill. The streets and alleys of the town became congested with the mass of infantry and artillery and many were captured. The Brigade formed and took position on Cemetery Hill between the First and Second Divisions of the corps.

July 2. At 4 P. M. the Brigade was subjected to a heavy artillery fire converging on Cemetery Hill. At dark a sudden attack was made on the right and the Brigade was sent to the support of Brig. Gen. A. Ames and returned after midnight except the 74th Penna. which remained under the command of Brig. Gen. Ames.

July 3. Skirmishing not engaged.

Casualties   Killed 8 Officers 50 Men   Wounded 20 Officers 276 Men
Captured or Missing 28 Officers 425 Men   Total 807

No. 18U   Tablet on Granite Pedestal located—West Howard Avenue

---

ARMY OF THE POTOMAC
ELEVENTH CORPS   THIRD DIVISION
SECOND BRIGADE
Col. W. Krzyzanowski
58th   119th New York   82d Ohio
75th Pennsylvania   26th Wisconsin Infantry

July 1. Arrived about 1 P. M. marched through the town to the front and took position on the line of the Corps on right of First Brigade and was engaged with Brig. Gen. Doles's Brigade Major General Rodes's Division and other forces for more than two hours. About 4 P. M. the Corps having been flanked and forced back by superior numbers it retired through the town to Cemetery Hill and took position behind stone walls. Skirmishers were actively engaged in houses from three to five hundred yards in front.

July 2. In same position until between 8 and 9 P. M. when a fierce attack on East Cemetery Hill was made by Brig. Gen. Hays's Brigade and Battery I 1st New York was momentarily captured but the 58th and 119th New York were hastened to its support and assisted in its recapture and in repelling the attack.

July 3. Not engaged beyond skirmishing but subjected to a heavy artillery fire.

July 4. The 119th New York and the 26th Wisconsin made a reconnaissance going about two miles to the east of the town and captured many stragglers.

Casualties   Killed 12 Officers 63 Men   Wounded 36 Officers 352 Men
Captured or Missing 5 Officers 201 Men   Total 669

No. 19U   Tablet on Granite Pedestal located—East Howard Avenue

---

ARMY OF THE POTOMAC
ELEVENTH CORPS
FIRST DIVISION
Brig. Gen. Francis C. Barlow   Brig. Gen. Adelbert Ames

First Brigade   Col. Leopold Von Gilsa
Second Brigade   Brig. Gen. Adelbert Ames
                         Col. Andrew L. Harris

July 1. Arrived about 10.00 A. M. and went into position on a hill about a
    mile north from the town the left extending southwesterly connecting the
    Third Division. Attacked by Dole's and Gordon's Georgia Brigades un-
    der enfilading fire from Jones's Artillery Battalion. Hoke's and Hays's
    Brigades of Early's Division moved across Rock Creek upon the right
    and rear and compelled a retreat through the town to Cemetery Hill and
    the Division took position on East Cemetery Hill and at its base, the First
    Corps on the right, Third Division on the left.

July 2. About 8 P. M. was attacked by Hoke's and Hays's Brigades which
    swept up among the batteries at the top. The attack was repulsed about
    9.00 P. M. with the aid of First Brigade Third Division Second Corps.

July 3. At 1 P. M. heavy cannonade opened and continued with consider-
    able effect for an hour and a half followed by a charge on the Second
    Corps on the left which was repulsed with great loss.

Casualties   Killed 9 Officers 113 Men   Wounded 46 Officers 631 Men
Captured or Missing 15 Officers 492 Men   Total 1306

No 20U   Tablet on Granite Marker located—East Howard Avenue

ARMY OF THE POTOMAC
ELEVENTH CORPS   FIRST DIVISION
FIRST BRIGADE
Col. Leopold Von Gilsa
41st   (9 Cos.) 54th   68th New York
153D Pennsylvania Infantry

July 1. The Brigade except the 41st New York having been temporarily left
    at Emmitsburg arrived about noon and took position a mile northerly
    from town on left of Harrisburg Road and right of Rock Creek Second
    Brigade on right and Third Division on left. Advanced over a knoll into
    woods in front and encountered Brig. Gen. Gordon's Brigade and was
    attacked by Brig. Gen. Doles's Brigade Major Gen. Rodes's Division
    and subjected to a severe enfilading artillery fire from Lieut. Col. Jones's
    Battalion on a knoll east of Rock Creek and forced back to the Almshouse
    where being outflanked the Brigade fell back with the Corps to Cem-
    etery Hill and took position behind a stone wall on the right of Corps. The
    41st New York rejoined the Brigade in the night.

July 2. Remained in position all day engaged as skirmishers. An attack in the evening on Cemetery Hill on the left was repulsed with the aid of First Brigade Third Division Second Corps.

July 3. Under artillery fire for an hour and a half but not engaged.

Casualties   Killed 4 Officers 50 Men   Wounded 21 Officers 289 Men Captured or Missing 6 Officers 157 Men   Total 527

No. 21U   Tablet on Granite Pedestal located—East Cemetery Hill

---

ARMY OF THE POTOMAC
ELEVENTH CORPS   FIRST DIVISION
SECOND BRIGADE
Brig. Gen. Adelbert Ames
Col. Andrew L. Harris
17th Conn. 25th   75th   107th Ohio Infantry

July 1. Arrived about noon and advanced along the Harrisburg road. Four companies of the 17th Conn. advanced as skirmishers across Rock Creek to the Bender House. The rest of the Brigade taking position on Barlow Knoll at left of First Brigade. Was hotly engaged until 4 P. M. when being enfiladed by artillery and flanked by superior numbers the Brigade with the Division was forced to retire and retreated through the town to Cemetery Hill to a position along a stone wall at right angles to the Baltimore Pike facing town.

July 2. Remained under a hot sharpshooter fire from houses in town until sunset when Brig. Gen. Hays's Brigade charged penetrating the line left open by the removal of 17th Conn. to the right shortly before and reached the batteries on the hill where after a hand to hand conflict the attack was repulsed with heavy loss including the colors of the 8th Louisiana captured by 107th Ohio.

July 3. No other engagement than sharp skirmishing.

Casualties   Killed 5 Officers 63 Men   Wounded 24 Officers 342 Men Captured or Missing 9 Officers 335 Men   Total 778

No. 22U   Tablet on Granite Pedestal located—East Howard Avenue

---

ARMY OF THE POTOMAC
ELEVENTH CORPS
SECOND DIVISION
Brig. General Adolph Von Steinwehr

First Brigade   Col. Charles R. Coster
Second Brigade   Col. Orland Smith

July 1. Arrived about 2 P. M. and went into position on Cemetery Hill supporting Battery I First New York Artillery and covered the commanding position there skirmishers taking possession of a church and near by house to prevent occupancy by Confederate sharpshooters. The First and Third Divisions having advanced in a line extending from Rock Creek to Mummasburg Road to connect with right of First Corps became hotly engaged with Hoke's and Hays's Brigades. Early's Division moved toward town in rear of the Union right and the First Brigade was sent to hold them. The Brigade retreated through town and joined the Second Brigade about 4.30 P. M.

July 2. Heavy artillery firing from 4 to 6 P. M. Between 8 and 9 P. M. the Division was attacked by Hays's Louisiana Brigade which penetrated to Battery I First New York Light Artillery and was repulsed with great loss.

July 3. Not engaged but subject to the fire of sharpshooters and artillery.

Casualties   Killed 3 Officers 104 Men   Wounded 14 Officers 493 Men
Captured or Missing 14 Officers 318 Men   Total 946

No. 23U   Tablet on Granite Marker located—Baltimore Pike, opposite National Cemetery

---

ARMY OF THE POTOMAC
ELEVENTH CORPS   SECOND DIVISION
FIRST BRIGADE
Col. Charles R. Coster
134th   154th New York
27th   73D Pennsylvania Infantry

July 1. Arrived about 2 P. M. and went into position on Cemetery Hill supporting Battery I 1st New York. Skirmishers occupying a church and near by house. Advanced about 3.30 P. M. through the town and faced to the right and intercepted the advance of Brig. Gen. Hays's and Brig. Gen. Hoke's Brigades Major Gen. Early's Division they moving toward town in rear of First Division Eleventh Corps and held them from the line of retreat of that Division to Cemetery Hill. Retired to East Cemetery Hill about 4.30 P. M. and resumed former position on the right of Second Brigade with Third Division on the right.

July 2. In same position during the day under fire of artillery and sharpshooters. At 8 P. M. Brig. Gen. Hays's Brigade charged the position and was repulsed with heavy loss. The 27th Penna. bore a conspicuous part in repelling this attack. Battery I 1st New York was temporarily captured but was immediately recovered.

July 3. Not actively engaged.

Casualties   Killed 3 Officers 53 Men   Wounded 8 Officers 220 Men Captured or Missing 12 Officers 301 Men   Total 597

No. 24U   Tablet on Granite Pedestal located—Coster Avenue, Gettysburg

---

ARMY OF THE POTOMAC
ELEVENTH CORPS   SECOND DIVISION
SECOND BRIGADE
Col. Orland Smith
33D Massachusetts   136th New York
55th   73D Ohio Infantry

July 1. Arrived at 2 P. M. and went into position on Cemetery Hill in line behind stone walls along Emmitsburg and Taneytown Roads facing northwest and supporting Battery I 1st New York. The 33D Mass. was detached during the battle and placed on the right of the Corps under the command of Brig. Gen. A. Ames. The 136th New York was on the extreme left of the Corps connecting on its right with the 55th and 73D Ohio.

July 2. Sharpshooting was kept up all day by the Union troops from stone walls and by the Confederates from houses in the town with considerable loss.

July 3. Sharp skirmishing continued with artillery firing from Confederate batteries east of the town.

Casualties   Killed 51 Men   Wounded 5 Officers 273 Men   Captured or Missing 2 Officers 17 Men   Total 348

No. 25U   Tablet on Granite Pedestal located—Taneytown Road, across from National Cemetery

FIRST DAY TABLET INSCRIPTIONS
ARMY OF NORTHERN VIRGINIA

ARMY OF NORTHERN VIRGINIA
General Robert E. Lee
Commanding

The Army Consisted of Three Army Corps

First Army Corps	Lieutenant General James Longstreet
Second Army Corps	Lieutenant General Richard S. Ewell
Third Army Corps	Lieutenant General Ambrose P. Hill
Cavalry Division	Major General J. E. B. Stuart

July 1. Heth's and Pender's Divisions Hill's Corps reached the field about 1 P. M. and were soon engaged on the north and west of town with the First and Eleventh Corps of the Army of the Potomac. Johnson's Division Ewell's Corps and Anderson's Division Hill's Corps reaching the field about dark were not engaged Longstreet's Corps on the march. Stuart's Cavalry Division marching from Dover to Carlisle.

July 2. McLaw's and Hood's Divisions Longstreet's Corps arrived on the field about 3 P. M. and formed facing the Union left. An assault was made by the two divisions assisted by Anderson's Division Hill's Corps. The Union troops were dislodged from Emmitsburg Road and Peach Orchard engagement lasting until night losses heavy. Pickett's Division Longstreet's Corps on the march. Johnson's Division Ewell's Corps about dusk advanced to the assault of Culp's Hill in connection with Early's Division Ewell's Corps. Rodes's Division Ewell's Corps held position west of town not engaged. Heth's and Pender's Divisions Hill's Corps occupied Seminary Ridge facing Union line not engaged. Stuart's Cavalry on left flank of Confederate Army.

July 3. Pickett's Division Longstreet's Corps reached the field in the morning. Assaulted the Union line on Cemetery Ridge about 3 P. M. assisted by Hill's Corps. The assault failed with great loss. An attack made on the left by Johnson's Division Ewell's Corps reinforced by three brigades of the Corps failed. Stuart's Cavalry Division engaged with 2d Union Cavalry

46

Division and 2d Brigade 3d Cavalry Division on the Confederate left about 1 P. M.

July 4. The Army took up the line of march during the night.

No. 1C   Tablet on Granite Marker located—West Confederate Avenue

———————

ARMY OF NORTHERN VIRGINIA
THIRD ARMY CORPS
Lieutenant General Ambrose P. Hill

Anderson's Division	Major General R. H. Anderson
Heth's Division	Major General Henry Heth
	Brigadier General J. J. Pettigrew
Pender's Division	Major General William D. Pender
	Brigadier General James H. Lane,
	Major General I. R. Trimble
Artillery Reserve	
Nine Batteries	Colonel R. Lindsay Walker

July 1. The Corps was near Cashtown. Heth's Division at 5 A. M. moved towards Gettysburg. Two brigades with artillery advancing across Willoughby Run were soon engaged. Archer's Brigade was driven across the run. After resting an hour Heth's Division formed line west of Willoughby Run and advanced with Pender's Division in reserve. 2.30 P. M. the right of Ewell's Corps appeared on the left. Pender's Division was ordered forward. After a severe contest the Union forces were driven back and through the town. The two divisions bivouacked on the ground gained. Anderson's Division bivouacked two miles in rear.

July 2. Anderson's Division extended to the right along the crest of hills facing Cemetery Ridge Pender's Division occupying the crest from the Seminary and joining Anderson's Division with Heth's Division in reserve the artillery in position on Seminary Ridge. The First Corps ordered to attack the left of Union forces the Third Corps to co-operate. General Anderson moved forward three brigades connecting with the left of McLaws's Division and drove the Union forces from their position. Anderson's right becoming separated from Mclaws's left and no support coming to these brigades they returned to their former line.

July 3. The Corps occupied the same position. Reserve batteries were placed facing the Union lines. The Confederate line held by Anderson's Division half of Pender's and half of Heth's the remainder of Corps ordered to report to General Longstreet as a support in the assault to be made on the Union position on Cemetery Ridge. About 1 P. M. the artillery along the line opened fire. 3 P. M. the assault was made and failed. Anderson's Division was held in reserve. The troops fell back to former positions.

July 4. The Corps took up the line of march during the night.

Casualties   Killed 837   Wounded 4407   Missing 1491   Total 6735

No. 2C   Tablet on Granite Marker located—West Confederate Avenue

———

C. S. A.
ARMY OF NORTHERN VIRGINIA
THIRD ARMY CORPS
HETH'S DIVISION
Major Gen. Henry Heth   Brig. Gen. J. J. Pettigrew

First Brigade	Brig. Gen. J. J. Pettigrew
	Col. J. K. Marshall
Second Brigade	Col. J. M. Brockenbrough
Third Brigade	Brig. Gen. James A. Archer
	Col. B. D. Fry
	Col. S. G. Shepard
Fourth Brigade	Brig. Gen. Joseph R. Davis
Artillery Brigade	
Four Batteries	Lieut. Col. John J. Garnett

July 1. The Division moved at 5 A. M. from Cashtown toward Gettysburg. About 3 miles from town the advance met the Union Forces. Archer's and Davis's Brigades moved forward on the right and left of the turnpike were soon engaged. The Brigades were forced to retire with heavy loss. After resting for an hour the Division was advanced in line of battle to the right of the pike and met with stubborn resistance. Rodes's Division Second Corps appeared on the left and formed a line at right angles. The Union troops retired to a wooded hill in the rear and finally gave way. The Division bivouacked on the ground won.

July 2. The Division in the morning was relieved by Anderson and held in reserve.

July 3. The Division occupied the position of the day before and was ordered to report to Lieut. Gen. Longstreet to unite in the attack on the Union centre. The assault was made and failed. The Division returned to its former position.

July 4. At night the Division took up line of march.

Casualties   Killed 411   Wounded 1905   Missing 534   Total 2850

No. 3C   Tablet on Granite Marker located—West Confederate Avenue

---

C. S. A.
ARMY OF NORTHERN VIRGINIA
HILL'S CORPS   HETH'S DIVISION
ARCHER'S BRIGADE
5th Battalion and 13th Alabama 1st 7th 14th Tennessee Infantry

July 1. The Brigade moved from Cashtown early in the morning towards Gettysburg. After a march of six miles came in view of the Union forces. The Brigade was deployed on the west side of Willoughby Run and about 10 A. M. advanced encountered 1st Brigade First Division beyond the run. The firing continued for a short time when a large force appearing on the right flank and opening a cross fire the position became untenable the Brigade was forced back across the run but advanced with the Division later in the day. The advance in the morning reached this position.

July 2. Not engaged.

July 3. Formed part of the column of Longstreet's assault.

July 4. The Brigade took up the line of march during the night to Hagerstown.

No. 4C   Tablet on Granite Pedestal located—Meredith Avenue

Note: Another tablet for Archer's Brigade—No. 66C, located on West Confederate Avenue—is included with the activity of July 3.

C. S. A.
ARMY OF NORTHERN VIRGINIA
HILL'S CORPS   HETH'S DIVISION
DAVIS'S BRIGADE
2nd, 11th, 42nd Mississippi 55th North Carolina Infantry

July 1. Formed west of Herr's Tavern crossed Willoughby Run about 10 A. M. Advanced in line and soon encountered artillery supported by 2nd Brigade 1st Division First Corps. The engagement was stubborn. The advance was made to the railroad cut after a short interval the attack was renewed at the cut and the Brigade was forced back losing many killed and wounded. A large force advancing on the right and rear opening a heavy flank fire the order was given to retire. About 3 P. M. the Brigade again moved forward with the Division and reached the suburbs of the town. The Brigade in the advance in the morning reached the railroad cut.

July 2. Not engaged.

July 3. Formed part of the column of Longstreet's assault.

July 4. The Brigade took up the line of march during the night to Hagerstown.

No. 5C   Tablet on Granite Pedestal located—Reynolds Avenue, railroad cut

Note: Another tablet for Davis' Brigade—No. 67C, located on West Confederate Avenue—is included with the activity of July 3.

C. S. A.
ARMY OF NORTHERN VIRGINIA
HILL'S CORPS   HETH'S DIVISION
PETTIGREW'S BRIGADE
11th 26th 47th 52nd North Carolina Infantry

July 1. Crossing Willoughby Run at 2 P. M. met the 1st Brigade 1st Division First Corps in Reynolds Woods and drove it back after a bloody struggle. Advancing to the summit of the ridge encountered and broke a second Union line and was then relieved by troops of Pender's Division.

July 2. Lay in woods west of the Run. In evening took position near here.

July 3. In Longstreet's assault the Brigade occupied the right center of the Division and the course of the charge brought it in front of the high stone wall north of the Angle and 80 yards farther east, it advanced very nearly to that wall. A few reached it but were captured. The skeleton regiments retired led by Lieutenants and the Brigade by a Major the only field officer left.

July 4. After night withdrew and began the march to Hagerstown.

Present on the first day about 2000 Killed 190 Wounded 915 Missing about 300   Total 1405

No. 6C   Tablet on Granite Pedestal located—West Confederate Avenue

---

C. S. A.
ARMY OF NORTHERN VIRGINIA
HILL'S CORPS   HETH'S DIVISION
BROCKENBROUGH'S BRIGADE
40th 47th 55th Regiments and 22nd Battalion Virginia Infantry

July 1. Crossed the Run at 2 P. M. between Chambersburg Pike and Reynolds Woods. Engaged Union forces on McPherson ridge and with other troops on left drove them back to next ridge capturing two flags and many prisoners with some sharpshooters in the barn. Soon afterwards the Brigade was relieved by Pender's Division.

July 2. Lay in the woods west of the Run. In the evening took position near here.

July 3. In Longstreet's assault this Brigade was on the left flank of the column and as it approached the Union position was exposed to a severe fire of musketry on the left flank and artillery and musketry in front. It pushed beyond the Emmitsburg Road but was met by a heavy front and flank fire from the Union lines north of the Bryan Barn and compelled to fall back.

July 4. After night withdrew and began the march to Hagerstown.

Present on the first day about 2000   Killed 180   Wounded 717   Missing about 500   Total 1397

No. 7C   Tablet on Granite Pedestal located—West Confederate Avenue

———————

C. S. A.
ARMY OF NORTHERN VIRGINIA
THIRD ARMY CORPS
PENDER'S DIVISION
Major Gen. William D. Pender   Brig. Gen. James H. Lane
Major Gen. I. R. Trimble

First Brigade	Col. Abner Perrin
Second Brigade	Brig. James H. Lane
Third Brigade	Brig. Gen. Edward L. Thomas
Fourth Brigade	Brig. Gen. A. M. Scales
	Lieut. Col. G. T. Gordon
	Col. W. Lee J. Lowrance
Artillery Battalion Four Batteries	Major William T. Poague

July 1. The Division moved about 8 A. M. in the direction of Gettysburg following Heth's division. A line of battle was formed on the right and left of the Pike 3 miles from the town. About 3 P. M. a part of Ewell's Corps appeared on the left and the Union forces making a strong demonstration an advance was ordered. Heth became vigorously engaged. The Division moved to the support passing through the lines forced the Union troops to Seminary Ridge. The Division reformed on the Ridge the left resting on Fairfield Road.

July 2. In position on the ridge not engaged except heavy skirmishing along the line.

July 3. During the morning two Brigades ordered to report to Lieut. Gen. Longstreet as a support to Gen. Pettigrew and were placed in rear of right of Heth's Division which formed a portion of the column of assault. The line moved forward one mile in view of the fortified position on Cemetery Ridge, exposed to severe fire. The extreme right reached the works but was compelled to fall back. The Division reformed where it rested before making the attack.

July 4. The Division during the night took up the line of march.

Casualties   Killed 262   Wounded 1312   Missing 116   Total 1690

No. 8C   Tablet on Granite Marker located—West Confederate Avenue

———————————

C. S. A.
ARMY OF NORTHERN VIRGINIA
HILL'S CORPS   PENDER'S DIVISION
LANE'S BRIGADE
7th   18th   28th   33rd   37th North Carolina Infantry

July 1. Crossed Willoughby Run about 3.30 P. M. and advanced on the right of the Division in the final and successful movement against the Union forces on Seminary Ridge held back Union Cavalry which threatened the flank and had a sharp conflict at the stone wall on Seminary Ridge just south of Fairfield Road.

July 2. Lay with its right in McMillan's Woods with skirmish line advanced.

July 3. In Longstreet's assault the Brigade supported the centre of Pettigrew's Division advancing in good order under the storm of shot and shell and when near the Union works north of the Angle pushed forward to aid the fragments of the front line in the final struggle and was among the last to retire.

July 4. After night withdrew and began the march to Hagerstown.

Present 1355   Killed 41   Wounded 348   Missing 271   Total 660

No. 9C   Tablet on Granite Pedestal located—West Confederate Avenue

———————————

C. S. A.
ARMY OF NORTHERN VIRGINIA
HILL'S CORPS   PENDER'S DIVISION
PERRIN'S BRIGADE
1st Rifles   12th   13th   14th Regiments and 1st Provisional South Carolina Infantry

July 1. Crossed Willoughby Run about 3.30 P. M. with its left in Reynolds Woods and advancing relieved Heth's line. Took a prominent part in the struggle by which the Union forces were dislodged from Seminary Ridge and pursuing them into town captured many prisoners. The Rifle Regiment was on duty as train guard and not in the battle of this day.

July 2. Supported artillery south of Fairfield Road. At 6 P. M. advanced a battalion of Sharpshooters which skirmished with Union outposts until dark. At 10 P. M. took position on Ramseur's right in the Long Lane leading from the town to the Bliss House and Barn.

July 3. In the same position and constantly engaged in skirmishing.

July 4. After night withdrew and began the march to Hagerstown.

Present about 1600   Killed 100   wounded 477   Total 577

No. 10C   Tablet on Granite Pedestal located—West Confederate Avenue

———

C. S. A.
ARMY OF NORTHERN VIRGINIA
HILL'S CORPS   PENDER'S DIVISION
SCALES'S BRIGADE
13th   16th   22nd   38th North Carolina Infantry

July 1. Crossed Willoughby Run about 3.30 P. M. relieving Heth's line and advancing with left flank on Chambersburg Pike took part in the struggle until it ended. When the Union forces made their final stand on Seminary Ridge the Brigade charged and aided in dislodging them but suffered heavy losses. Gen. A. M. Scales was wounded and all the field officers but one were killed or wounded.

July 2. In position near here with skirmishers out in front and on flank.

July 3. In Longstreet's assault the Brigade supported the right wing of Pettigrew's Division. With few officers to lead them the men advanced in good order through a storm of shot and shell and when the front line neared the Union works they pushed forward to aid it in the final struggle and were among the last to retire.

July 4. After night withdrew and began the march to Hagerstown.

Present about 1250   Killed 102   Wounded 381   Missing 116   Total 599

No. 11C   Tablet on Granite Pedestal located—West Confederate Avenue

C. S. A.
ARMY OF NORTHERN VIRGINIA
HILL'S CORPS   PENDER'S DIVISION
THOMAS'S BRIGADE
14th   35th   45th   49th Georgia Infantry

July 1. In reserve north of Chambersburg Pike on left of the Division. At sunset moved to position in McMillan's Woods.

July 2. On duty in support of artillery. At 10 P. M. advancing took position in Long Lane with left flank in touch with McGowan's Brigade and the right near the Bliss House and Barn.

July 3. Engaged most of the day in severe skirmishing and exposed to a heavy fire of artillery. After dark retired to this Ridge.

Present about 1200   Killed 34   Wounded 179   Missing 57   Total 270

No. 12C   Tablet on Granite Pedestal located—West Confederate Avenue

———————

ARMY OF NORTHERN VIRGINIA
SECOND ARMY CORPS
Lieutenant General Richard S. Ewell

Early's Division	Major General Jubal A. Early
Johnson's Division	Major General Edward Johnson
Rodes's Division	Major General R. E. Rodes
Artillery Reserve	Eight Batteries
	Colonel J. Thompson

July 1. The Corps occupied the left of the Confederate line and reached the field in the following order Rodes's Division by Newville Road about noon and deploying along Oak Ridge soon became engaged Early's Division on the Harrisburg Road about 1 P. M. and united with Rodes's left in an attack on the First and Eleventh Corps Union troops and drove them through the town to Cemetery Ridge. Johnson's Division reached the field about night and not engaged late in the night moved along the railroad and took position on the left of Corps and northeast of town.

July 2. In the early morning Johnson's Division was ordered to take possession of a wooded hill on the left. Skirmishers were advanced and a desultory fire kept up until 4 P. M. when the artillery from Benner's Hill opened the firing continued for two hours. The batteries were withdrawn much crippled. The Division about dusk was advanced to the assault in connection with Early's Division on the right the battle continuing until after dark. A partial success was made by a portion of each division but not being supported on the right was withdrawn to the former positions.

July 3. Early in the morning an attack was made by Johnson's Division having been reinforced by three brigades from the Corps two other assaults were made but failed. Early's Division was withdrawn and occupied its former position in the town and not engaged. At night the Corps fell back to the range of hills west of the town.

July 4. The Corps took up line of march during the night.

Casualties   Killed 809   Wounded 3823   Missing 1305   Total 5937

No. 13C   Tablet on Granite Marker located—Buford Avenue

C. S. A.
ARMY OF NORTHERN VIRGINIA
SECOND ARMY CORPS
RODES'S DIVISION
Maj. Gen. R. E. Rodes

Daniel's Brigade	Brig. Gen. Junius Daniel
Doles's Brigade	Brig. Gen. George Doles
Iverson's Brigade	Brig. Gen. Alfred Iverson
Ramseur's Brigade	Brig. Gen. S. D. Ramseur
O'Neal's Brigade	Col. E. A. O'Neal
Artillery Battalion Four Batteries	Lieut. Col. Thomas H. Carter

July 1. Rodes's Division advancing by the Newville Road occupied Oak Ridge about noon. The line formed and advanced in the following order. Dole's Brigade deployed in the valley north of town and left of Division and was opposed by troops of the Eleventh Corps. O'Neal's and Iverson's Brigades advanced on ridge and meeting a portion of First Union Corps were driven back with heavy loss. Daniel's Brigade was ordered to the support of Iverson but became separated by a change of direction moved to the railroad on the right where Heth's Division was engaged. Ramseur held in reserve. After a severe conflict the Union troops retired.

July 2. The Division occupied ground near and west of town and was not engaged.

July 3. The Brigades of Daniel and O'Neal were ordered to report to Gen. E. Johnson on the left early in the morning and joined in the attack on Culp's Hill. The remainder of the Division held the position of day before and at night retired to Seminary Ridge.

July 4. The Division took up the line of march during the night.

Casualties   Killed 421   Wounded 1728   Missing 704   Total 2853

No. 14C   Tablet on Granite Marker located—Rear of Peace Memorial, Oak Hill

———

C. S. A.
ARMY OF NORTHERN VIRGINIA
EWELL'S CORPS   RODES'S DIVISION
O'NEAL'S BRIGADE
3rd   5th   6th   12th   26th Alabama Infantry

July 1. Soon after arriving at this position three regiments attacked the Union flank, the 5th Regiment being ordered to guard the wide interval between the Brigade and Doles's Brigade in the valley on the left and the 3rd Regiment joining Daniel's and afterwards Ramseur's Brigade. The three regiments were repulsed with heavy loss but the entire Brigade took part in the general attack soon made by the Confederates which finally dislodged the Union forces from Seminary Ridge.

July 2. The Brigade in position all day in or near the town but not engaged.

July 3. The 5th Regiment lay in the southern borders of the town firing upon the Union artillery with their long range rifles. The other regiments moved to Culp's Hill to reinforce Johnson's Division.

July 4. Moved to Seminary Ridge. At night began the march to Hagerstown.

Present 1794   Killed 73   Wounded 430   Missing 193   Total 696

No. 15C   Tablet on Granite Marker located—Doubleday Avenue, southeast of Peace Memorial

———

C. S. A.
ARMY OF NORTHERN VIRGINIA
EWELL'S CORPS   RODES'S DIVISION
IVERSON'S BRIGADE
5th   12th   20th   23rd North Carolina Infantry

July 1. The Brigade was one of the first of the Division in the battle. It advanced against the Union line posted behind stone fence east of Forney Field. Its right being assailed by 2nd Brigade First Corps and its left exposed by the repulse of O'Neal a vigorous assault by Union forces in front and on left flank almost annihilated three regiments. The 12th Regiment on the right being sheltered by the knoll suffered slight loss and the remnants of the others joined Ramseur's Brigade and served with it throughout the battle.

July 2. Lay all day in the town. At dusk moved to aid in an attack on Cemetery Hill but two of Early's Brigades having been repulsed the Brigade withdrew.

July 3. With other brigades in the sunken road southwest of town. At night withdrew to Seminary Ridge.

July 4. Marched at 2 P. M. as wagon train guard on road to Hagerstown.

Present 1470   Killed 130   Wounded 382   Missing 308   Total 820

No. 16C   Tablet on Granite Pedestal located—Doubleday Avenue, southeast of Peace Memorial

---

C. S. A.
ARMY OF NORTHERN VIRGINIA
EWELL'S CORPS   RODES'S DIVISION
DANIEL'S BRIGADE
32nd   43rd   45th   53rd Regiments and 2nd Battalion North Carolina Infantry

July 1. The Brigade formed the right of Division and its line extended from Forney Field to the railroad near the McPherson Barn. The regiments did not at first move together nor attack the same troops. The 43rd and 53rd Regiments aided by O'Neal's 3rd Alabama and Iverson's 12th North Carolina attacked the Union line in the Sheads and Forney Field. The 45th Regiment and 2nd Battalion fought the 2nd Brigade 3rd Division First Corps near the railroad cuts and being joined by the 32nd Regiment and other troops compelled retreat. The regiments fought under a heavy artillery fire. The Brigade was reunited and lost heavily in the struggle which dislodged the Union forces from Seminary Ridge.

July 2. On Seminary Ridge all day. After night moved into town.

July 3. Marched before daylight to Culp's Hill to aid Johnson's Division.

July 4. Occupied Seminary Ridge. At night began the march to Hagerstown.

Present 2100   Killed 165   Wounded 635   Missing 116   Total 916

No. 17C   Tablet on Granite Pedestal located—Doubleday Avenue, west of Peace Memorial

C. S. A.
ARMY OF NORTHERN VIRGINIA
EWELL'S CORPS   RODES'S DIVISION
RAMSEUR'S BRIGADE
2nd   4th   14th   30th North Carolina Infantry

July 1. Soon after Iverson's and O'Neal's Brigades had each suffered the repulse of three regiments with heavy losses Ramseur's Brigade moved from its position here and vigorously assailed the right wing of the Union forces. The 14th and 30th Regiments with O'Neal's 3rd Alabama turned the flank of the Union troops while the 2nd and 4th Regiments together with Doles's Brigade and part of O'Neal's struck them in the rear. A struggle ensued in which both sides suffered severely and the conflict here only ended with the retreat of the Union Corps from Seminary Ridge. In that retreat the Brigade made active pursuit and captured many prisoners.

July 2. Skirmishing on the southern borders of the town.

July 3. In sunken lane southwest of town.

July 4. In line on Seminary Ridge. At night began the march to Hagerstown.

Present 1909   Killed 23   Wounded 129   Missing 44

No. 18C   Tablet on Granite Pedestal located—Buford Avenue, southwest of Peace Memorial

---

C. S. A.
ARMY OF NORTHERN VIRGINIA
EWELL'S CORPS   RODES'S DIVISION
DOLES'S BRIGADE
4th   12th   21st   44th Georgia Infantry

July 1. About 1 P. M. the Brigade formed line in the fields east of Oak Hill and skirmished with Union 2nd Brigade First Cavalry Division and aided Gordon's Brigade in dislodging the Union forces from Barlow Knoll and their line from thence to the Heidlersburg Road. Then joined Ramseur and others in their attack upon the rear of First Corps which after a long struggle was compelled to retire from Seminary Ridge. The Brigade took many prisoners from the First and Eleventh Corps which it pursued to the southern borders of the town.

July 2. Lay all day in the town on West Middle Street. After dark moved out to aid in a contemplated attack on Cemetery Hill.

July 3. In line with other brigades in the sunken road southwest of town.

July 4. On Seminary Ridge all day. At night began the march to Hagerstown.

Present 1369   Killed 86   Wounded 124   Missing 31   Total 241

No. 19C   Tablet on Granite Pedestal located—Howard Avenue, west of Carlisle Road

---

C. S. A.
ARMY OF NORTHERN VIRGINIA
SECOND ARMY CORPS
EARLY'S DIVISION
Maj. Gen. Jubal A. Early

Hays's Brigade   Brig. Gen. Harry T. Hays
Smith's Brigade   Brig. Gen. William Smith
Hoke's Brigade   Col. Isaac E. Avery
                          Col. A. C. Godwin
Gordon's Brigade   Brig. John B. Gordon
Artillery Battalion
  Four Batteries   Col. H. P. Jones

July 1. The Division arrived about noon within two miles of Gettysburg by Harrisburg Road. Formed line across road north of Rock Creek. Gordon's Brigade ordered to support of a brigade of Rodes's Division engaged with a division of the Eleventh Corps which had advanced to a wooded hill in front of town. The remainder of the Division was ordered forward as Gordon's Brigade was engaged. After a short and severe contest the Union troops were forced through the town losing many prisoners. Later in the day Gordon's Brigade ordered to the York Road in support of Smith's Brigade. Hays's and Hoke's Brigades occupied the town.

July 2. In the early morning Hays's and Hoke's Brigades took position to front and left of town. Gordon's Brigade in reserve moved to the rear of the brigades. Smith's Brigade remained in this position until nearly dusk when Hays's and Hoke's Brigades advanced on Cemetery Hill. The brigades reached the crest of hill but not being supported on the right were forced to retire. Gordon's Brigade advanced to support the attack.

July 3. At daylight Smith's Brigade was ordered to support of Johnson's Division on the left. Hays's and Hoke's Brigades formed line in town holding the position of previous day. Gordon's Brigade held the line of the day before. The Division not further engaged.

July 4. In the morning the Division was withdrawn to Cashtown Road to west of town.

Casualties   Killed 156   Wounded 806   Missing 226   Total 1188

No. 20C   Tablet on Granite Marker located—East Confederate Avenue

---

ARMY OF NORTHERN VIRGINIA
EWELL'S CORPS   EARLY'S DIVISION
GORDON'S BRIGADE
13th   26th   31st   38th   60th   61st Georgia Infantry

July 1. Arrived on the field from Harrisburg road in early afternoon and formed line on North side of Rock Creek. About 3 P. M. moved across the creek to support of Rodes's left which was attacked from Barlow Knoll. Charged the Union forces upon this hill and after a most obstinate resistance succeeded in breaking the line. The Brigade was afterwards moved to the support of Smith's Brigade on the York Road. The Brigade captured a large number of prisoners during the day.

July 2. Moved to the railroad in support of Hays's and Avery's Brigades in their attack on Cemetery Hill.

July 3. Occupied the position at foot of Cemetery Ridge and not engaged.

July 4. At 2 A. M. the Brigade was withdrawn and moved to Cashtown Road.

Casualties   Killed 71   Wounded 270   Missing 39   Total 380

No. 21C   Cast Iron Tablet located—East Howard Avenue

C. S. A.
ARMY OF NORTHERN VIRGINIA
EWELL'S CORPS   EARLY'S DIVISION
HAYS'S BRIGADE
5th   6th   7th   8th   9th Louisiana Infantry

July 1. Advancing at 3 P. M. with Hoke's Brigade flanked Eleventh Corps aided in taking two guns pursued retreating Union troops into town capturing many and late in evening halting on East High St.

July 2. Moved forward early into the low ground here with its right flank resting on Baltimore St. and skirmished all day. Enfiladed by artillery and exposed to musketry fire in front it pushed forward over all obstacles scaled the hill and planted its colors on the lunettes capturing several guns. Assailed by fresh troops and with no supports it was forced to retire but brought off 75 prisoners and 4 stands of colors.

July 3. Occupied a position on High St. in town.

July 4. At 2 A. M. moved to Seminary Ridge. After midnight began the march to Hagerstown.

Present about 1200   Killed 36   Wounded 201   Missing 95   Total 332

No. 22C   Tablet on Granite Pedestal located—East Confederate Avenue

---

C. S. A.
ARMY OF NORTHERN VIRGINIA
EWELL'S CORPS   EARLY'S DIVISION
HOKE'S BRIGADE
6th   21st   57th North Carolina Infantry

July 1. Advanced at 3 P. M. with Hays's Brigade flanked Eleventh Corps aided in taking two guns repulsed First Brigade Second Division and captured many prisoners. Late in evening took position here.

July 2. Skirmished all day at 8 P. M. with Hays's Brigade charged East Cemetery Hill. Severely enfiladed on the left by artillery and musketry it pushed on over infantry line in front scaled the hill planted its colors on the lunettes and captured several guns. But assailed by fresh forces and having no supports it was soon compelled to relinquish what it had gained and withdraw. Its commander Col. Isaac E. Avery was mortally wounded leading the charge.

July 3. Ordered to railroad cut in rear and later to High Street in town.

July 4. At 2 A. M. moved to Seminary Ridge. After midnight began the march to Hagerstown.

Present about 900   Killed 35   Wounded 216   Missing 94   Total 345

No. 23C   Tablet on Granite Pedestal located—East Confederate Avenue

PART III

The Second Day
July 2, 1863

SECOND DAY BATTLE SUMMARY

As dawn was breaking on July 2, 1863, the commanders of the Army of the Potomac and Army of Northern Virginia were on the field, and their armies were rapidly converging on Gettysburg. All of the Union army was close at hand except for the Sixth Corps, more than 30 miles away, which could not arrive until late in the day. The Twelfth Corps had arrived via the Baltimore Pike late the previous afternoon. Brig. Gen. Alpheus Williams' Division went into position east of Rock Creek and Brig. Gen. John Geary's Division formed a thin line along Cemetery Ridge to the vicinity of Little Round Top. The Second Corps started arriving at about 6 A.M. on the north end of Cemetery Ridge, relieving the depleted First Corps elements to the left of the cemetery. The Third Corps had also arrived early in the morning and occupied the south end of Cemetery Ridge, on the low ground between Cemetery Hill and Little Round Top to the left of Second Corps. To the great discomfort of the corps commander, Maj. Gen. Daniel Sickles, his position was lower than the high ground along Emmitsburg Road, less than a mile to his front.

Fearing an early attack on the army's right flank, General Meade ordered reinforcement of the battered First and Eleventh Corps. The entire Twelfth Corps was sent to Culp's Hill and the arriving Fifth Corps was held nearby in reserve on Baltimore Pike. The removal of Geary's Division from the area of Little Round Top forced the Third Corps to extend its line further to the vicinity of Little Round Top, but the summit was not occupied. Buford's Cavalry Division was now guarding the Union army's left flank.

The Army of Northern Virginia was concentrating even faster. All Second and Third Corps divisions were on the field. Maj. Gen. Edward Johnson's Second Corps Division had moved during the night to a position northeast of Culp's Hill. Maj. Gen. R. H. Anderson's Third Corps Division had also arrived during the night and was positioned further to the Confederate right along Seminary Ridge. With the exception of Maj. Gen. George Pickett's Division and Brig. Gen. E. M. Law's Brigade of Maj. Gen. John Hood's Division, Lt. Gen. James Longstreet's First Corps was also on the field. Maj. Gen. Lafayette

McLaws's and Hood's Divisions had bivouacked nearby during the night and were on the field in stand-by positions early. Law's Brigade, on picket duty at New Guilford, departed at 3 A.M. on a twenty-five-mile march to join Hood at Gettysburg. Pickett's Division, guarding trains at Chambersburg, would not arrive until sunset.

General Lee's intention was to attack as early as possible. Based on a report from an early-morning reconnaissance, which revealed that the Round Tops were unoccupied and the southern end of Cemetery Ridge only sparsely so, Lee developed his plan of attack. Longstreet's Corps, supported by Anderson's Division from Hill's Corps, would conduct an oblique attack up Emmitsburg Road into the rear of the Union position on Cemetery Hill. Ewell's Corps would launch a simultaneous attack on the Union right to prevent movement of Union reinforcements to the area of Longstreet's attack. Ewell was to launch his attack on the sound of Longstreet's guns.

ATTACK ON THE UNION LEFT

Longstreet did not start the movement of Hood and McLaws's Divisions from their stand-by positions until the arrival of Law's Brigade about noon. A series of marches and countermarches were made in order to conceal their flanking movement from the Union signal station on Little Round Top. These time consuming marches further delayed an already late start. Upon reaching their jump-off positions on Warfield Ridge, the Confederates found that more delay was needed to adjust to a clearly changed enemy situation. Spotting Union troops on Emmitsburg Road at the Peach Orchard, Hood's Division moved further to the right to a position which partially enveloped the Union left. Longstreet's guns opened on the Union line to start the long delayed attack at about 4 P.M.

The Union troops that the Confederates observed in the Peach Orchard were there as a result of General Sickles' repositioning of his Third Corps. Sickles' distress over his position on Cemetery Ridge increased upon learning that the Confederates were moving to the Union army left. A strong reconnaissance force, which was sent across the Emmitsburg Road, encountered Brig. Gen. Cadmus Wilcox's Brigade of Anderson's Division in the woods beyond. With the presence of Confederates to his front confirmed, Sickles also learned that Buford's cavalry had been withdrawn, exposing his corps to attack from the left. Having failed to obtain approval from Meade's staff to move his corps forward to the high ground, Sickles decided to do it on his own. At about 2 P.M., he ordered Maj. Gen. David Birney's Division to advance to the high ground to the southwest and Brig. Gen. Andrew Humphreys' Division to move west to Emmitsburg Road.

Birney placed Brig. Gen. Hobart Ward's Second Brigade on the high ground above Devil's Den on the left of the division. Brig. Gen. Charles Graham's First Brigade was positioned in the Peach Orchard along Emmitsburg Road, bending back to the east on the south side of the orchard. The Third

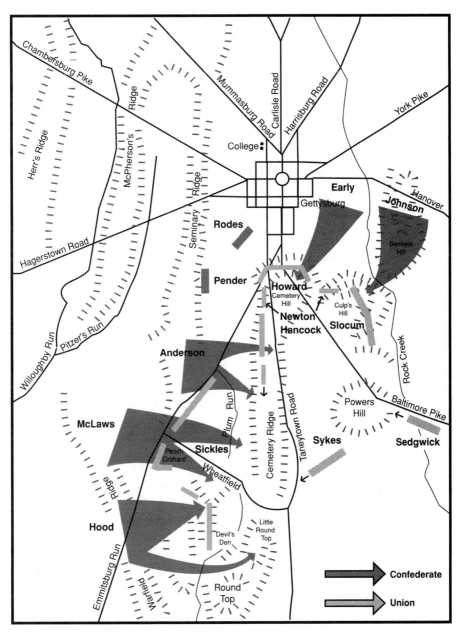

Battle of Gettysburg, second day
Union positions are as of 4 p.m.

Brigade under Col. Regis De Trobriand remained in column in the area of the Wheatfield between the First and Second Brigades in order to support either. Two brigades of Humphreys' Division extended the line from Graham's Brigade in the Peach Orchard to the northeast along Emmitsburg Road. Brig. Gen. Joseph Carr's First Brigade held the front line along the road with Col. William Brewster's Second Brigade behind in reserve. Col. George Burling's Third Brigade advanced in rear of Second Brigade but was soon sent to support Birney's Division.

Redeployment of the Union Third Corps was complete by about 3 P.M. The result was a long, isolated, two-sided defensive line which the corps did not have sufficient forces to cover. The dominant terrain, Little Round Top, was left unoccupied, and a large gap remained between the corps' right and the left of Second Corps. Both sides of the line faced thick woods from which the enemy could spring an attack, crushing the corps in a vice. The precarious position of the corps was immediately apparent to General Meade when he arrived to inspect Sickles' unauthorized deployment; but it was too late to order a withdrawal because the Confederates were already attacking the line. Meade ordered the dispatch of a Second Corps division and all of the Fifth Corps to reinforce the Third. The reinforcements had not started to arrive when the Confederates struck the southern side of Sickles' line.

Lee's plan of attack on the Union left called for rolling divisional assaults from right to left—Hood first, followed by McLaws, then Anderson. Brigades were also in echelon to obtain maximum strength. Hood attacked from two lines of two brigades each; Law's Brigade to the right of Brig. Gen. J. B. Robertson's Brigade made up the first line. Brig. Gen. Henry Benning's Brigade formed behind Law's Brigade on the second line, Brig. Gen. George Anderson's Brigade to the left behind Robertson's. The original attack order would have taken the division to the northeast, parallel to Emmitsburg Road, but the enemy situation dictated otherwise. Law's Brigade moved to sweep around Sickles' left flank onto the then unoccupied Little Round Top. Robertson's Brigade, conforming to Law's movement, hit Ward's Brigade deployed along the hill running north from Devil's Den. Robertson carried the position but with two of his regiments caught up in Law's sweep around Devil's Den, and finding the remaining two flanked by the 17th Maine of De Trobriand's Brigade, was forced to fall back. Ward's men rushed back into their former positions.

Robertson's message to General Hood for reinforcement would not soon be acted upon because Hood had been carried from the field, severely wounded in the arm by a shell fragment. General Law, the senior brigade commander, was not present to take immediate command. However, Generals Benning and Anderson had moved their brigades without orders to the sound of the battle. Benning moved to Robertson's right and Anderson came in with four of his five regiments on the left. The 7th Georgia Infantry of Anderson's Brigade had been sent south to screen against Union cavalry. The Confederate force was now more than Ward and De Trobriand could handle. Benning, with two of Robertson's regiments, swept Devil's Den and the hill above of Union forces, capturing three guns. Anderson's Brigade charged through the woods into De Trobriand's line at the south edge of the Wheatfield. Even with Cols. Jacob Sweitzer's and William Tilton's Brigades of Brig. Gen. James Barnes' First Fifth Corps Division already positioned in the woods on the west side of the Wheatfield, Anderson's Brigade charged past them, pushing De Trobriand across the field to the northern end. There it encountered Brig. Gen. John Caldwell's First Division of the Second Union Corps. Pressured to the front and flanked on the left, Anderson retired to the crest of Rose Hill.

General Barnes' First Division led the Fifth Corps march to reinforce the Third Corps. Prior to reaching the Wheatfield, Col. Strong Vincent's Brigade, which was leading the division, was detached and rushed to Little Round Top. The move was made at the urging of the Union army's chief engineer, Brig. Gen. Gouverneur Warren, who had found the strategic position empty and took the initiative to find forces to defend it. Barnes cooperated, allowing Vincent's Brigade to reach the summit just before Law's Confederates did.

Law's reinforced brigade had little difficulty from Union forces in its sweep past Devil's Den into Plum Run Valley at the base of Little Round Top. Quickly pushing three Union regiments from the valley, Law dispatched two Alabama regiments under Colonel Oates to clear the remaining Union opposition from the wooded northwest slope of Big Round Top. After an initial sharp engagement with a detachment of sharpshooters, Oates' men had only the steep, boulder-strewn slope to oppose their advance to the top. Looking across the valley between the two hills while they paused to catch their breath, the Confederates could see that the summit of Little Round Top was still empty, except for a few Union signalmen.

Moving through the wooded valley and onto the steep slope beyond, the Confederates were stopped by a heavy volley of musketry from the 20th Maine of Vincent's Brigade. Arriving only minutes before, Vincent deployed his brigade behind a natural defensive line below the summit of the hill. A third Alabama regiment, along with the two Texas regiments from Robertson's Brigade, moving on line to Oates' left, made contact, and the battle for Little Round Top was under way. The valley between the Round Tops quickly became a slaughterhouse. Even though outnumbered, the 20th Maine would not yield, but the right of Vincent's line was having less success against the charging Texas regiments. Again, the determined efforts of General Warren prevented the loss of Little Round Top and perhaps the battle. Brig. Gen. Stephen Weed's Third Brigade of Brig. Gen. Romeyn Ayres' Second Fifth Corps Division halted at Little Round Top and rushed onto the summit just in time to repel the charging Texas regiments. The first of Weed's regiments to arrive, the 140th New York commanded by Col. P. H. O'Rorke, charged over the crest without pausing to deploy, throwing the Texans back down the hill.

The battle for Little Round Top raged for over two hours; hand-to-hand, charge and counter charge. Union losses were severe, including Weed, Vincent, and O'Rorke killed. Confederate losses were equally heavy, but they would not give up their determined assault against equally determined Federals. Finally after dark, with their momentum lost and no reinforcement in sight, the spent Confederates withdrew to the base of the hill, linking up with the survivors of the fight for Devil's Den.

General Longstreet held McLaws' Division back from the fight for about an hour, hoping that movement to counter Hood's attack would weaken opposition to its attack. The division's four brigades were formed in two lines as Hood's Division had been. Brig. Gen. J. B. Kershaw's Brigade on the right of the first line with Brig. Gen. William Barksdale's on the left. Brig. Gen. P. J. Semmes' Brigade was on line behind Kershaw and Brig. Gen. W. T. Wofford's behind Barksdale. It was past 5 P.M. when Kershaw, soon followed by Semmes, attacked. Kershaw's regiments advanced to the Rose Farm where they divided; two regiments and a battalion moved north to the Peach Orchard while the remainder moved to attack Union positions on Rose Hill and in the area of the loop.

Advancing on Tilton's and Sweitzer's position in the woods west of the Wheatfield, Kershaw encountered Caldwell's Union Division advancing on his right. Being hit by severe artillery fire from the left, Kershaw's regiments fell back to join Semmes. Pursuing the retreating Confederates, Brig. Gen. Samuel Zook's Third Brigade of Caldwell's Division advanced through the woods to an open field to the west. Thinking that they were being relieved, Tilton and Sweitzer withdrew their brigades before Caldwell's Division arrived, leaving Zook's Brigade exposed. Semmes and Kershaw resumed the attack and with Anderson's Brigade pushed the Federals back through the Wheatfield. Caldwell's First Brigade under Col. Edward Cross, which had gone to Weed's support above Devil's Den, was now threatened on the flank and rear. Seeing the urgency of the situation, Caldwell sent his reserve brigade under Col. John Brooke, along with Sweitzer's, back into the Wheatfield. Colonels Hannibal Day and Sidney Burbank's Brigades of Army Regulars from Ayres' Division also advanced across Plum Run Valley to the high ground to relieve Cross and the battered remnants of the Third Corps elements there. The Regulars took up position facing the Wheatfield as Brooke and Sweitzer were pushing the Confederates back into the woods south of the field. Once again, the Wheatfield was in Union hands, but the fight for it was not over.

Longstreet had finally allowed McLaws to release Barksdale and Wofford's Brigades to charge into the Peach Orchard. In their exposed position, Graham's reinforced brigade could do little to stop them. Wofford continued eastward along Wheatfield Road, flanking Brooke and Sweitzer's attacking brigades. Nearly surrounded, the brigades turned to fight their way back through the Wheatfield. It was a most desperate hand-to-hand fight. Day and Burbank's Regulars, caught in a killing crossfire, were also retreating.

Anderson, Semmes, and Kershaw's Confederates joined Wofford's in sweeping the Union line across Plum Run Valley to the base of Little Round Top. The loss in men and hard to replace leaders was onerous for both sides. Anderson was wounded and Semmes mortally so. Sickles was carried from the field with a severe leg wound, and Caldwell lost three of his four brigade commanders, two of them killed.

Barksdale's Brigade was in hot pursuit of the Union forces fleeing from the Peach Orchard. With Barksdale in front, urging his men on to Cemetery Ridge, the brigade pushed past the Trostle House, where Sickles' headquarters had been. The 21st Mississippi Infantry, on the right of the assault line, captured two batteries of artillery north of Wheatfield Road. The other three regiments inclined to the left and headed for the large gap between the left of Second Corps' line and Little Round Top.

General Meade was moving the Twelfth Corps from Culp's Hill to reinforce the line on Cemetery Ridge and his chief of artillery, Brig. Gen. Henry Hunt, was moving to cover the gap in the line with artillery until it arrived. Hunt had massed a strong line of artillery on the crest and down the slope in front of Plum Run. Seeing the urgency of the situation, Maj. Gen. Winfield Hancock ordered reinforcements from Brig. Gen. John Gibbon and Brig. Gen. Alexander Hays' Second Corps Divisions to move southward to plug the gap. The first to arrive, Col. George Willard's Brigade from Hays' Third Division, was sent to check Barksdale's advance.

Charging across Plum Run through a hail of canister, Barksdale's Mississippians were hit in the flank by Willard's countercharging New York regiments. Both Barksdale and Willard fell mortally wounded. Without their dynamic leader and unsupported on both flanks, the Mississippians withdrew. The first reinforcements to arrive from the Twelfth Corps, Brig. Gen. Henry Lockwood's Independent Brigade, assisted in pushing the Confederates to a line near Emmitsburg Road, recovering the artillery captured by the 21st Mississippi.

General Humphreys' thin line along Emmitsburg Road was now all that remained of Sickles' salient, and that had become a very dangerous position. Having been flanked by McLaws' Division on the left and confronted by Maj. Gen. R. H. Anderson's Division advancing in front, there was no choice but to withdraw. First changing front to the left in order to connect with Union troops in the Wheatfield, the division gradually withdrew to the left of Hancock's position on Cemetery Ridge.

Following instructions to maintain contact with Longstreet's left, three of Anderson's five brigades started their advance when Barksdale's Brigade charged into the Peach Orchard. Brigadier General Wilcox's Brigade on the right, Perry's Brigade commanded by Col. David Lang in the center, and Brig. Gen. A. R. Wright's on the left. Because of a mix-up in orders, Brig. Gen. Carnot Posey ordered his four regiments out at different times as skirmishers, and his brigade did not participate in the attack on Cemetery Ridge. Brig. Gen. William Mahone's Brigade remained in reserve, supporting the artillery.

Wilcox's and Perry's Brigades, pursuing Humphreys' Division, were rapidly closing on the gap in the Union line on Cemetery Ridge. The 19th Massachusetts and 42nd New York, arriving as reinforcements from Gibbon's Division, were immediately sent by Hancock down the slope to support Humphreys. Charging into the Confederate line, already in disorder from Humphreys' resistance and the artillery that had devastated Barksdale's charge, the fresh Union troops halted Wilcox's advance at the foot of the hill. Perry's Brigade, advancing on Wilcox's left, was also stopped at the foot of the ridge. After reaching Cemetery Ridge on the left of Gibbon, Humphreys turned on his pursuers. Colonel Brewster's Brigade of New Yorkers charged back down the slope into Perry's three Florida regiments, capturing the 8th Florida colors and recovering abandoned guns. With severe losses and none of the requested support in sight, Wilcox and Perry fell back.

A little farther to the north, Wright's Georgia Brigade was having more success. It had been the first to make contact, striking two regiments from Brig. Gen. William Harrow's First Brigade of Gibbon's Division that Hancock had sent out to Emmitsburg road north of the Codori House. Capturing many prisoners and guns, Wright's men continued on in hot pursuit of the fleeing Federals. They broke through the Union line at the stone wall south of the Angle and charged onto the crest beyond, capturing more guns. But the momentary victory soon turned into a desperate struggle for survival. Blue columns from the Twelfth and First Corps were converging on the position. With Wilcox's and Perry's Brigades withdrawing from the right and no support on the left, assailed on both flanks and columns converging on the rear, Wright turned his men to fight their way back across Emmitsburg Road with heavy losses.

At Little Round Top, the Union build-up was also forcing the Confederates back. Col. William McCandless' First Brigade of the Fifth Corps' Third Division, supported by Col. David Nevin's Third Brigade, Third Division, Sixth Corps, charged into the Confederates that had gained the northwest slope of Little Round Top, forcing them back into the Wheatfield. The Union brigades stopped at a stone wall in rear of the field. Now dark, the organized fight was over. Caldwell's battered division returned to the Second Corps line, and the remains of the Third Corps were placed in reserve along Taneytown Road. The Fifth Corps extended the line up Big Round Top. Brigades from Sixth Corps were used to fill gaps in the line and establish a line to the east from the Round Tops to protect the rear.

With the repulse of Anderson's advance on the left, McLaws thought it prudent to order his brigades back to the Peach Orchard and the woods west of the Wheatfield. Longstreet and Anderson's Confederates had little ground gained to show for their efforts. The loss of about a third of their numbers was a high price to pay for Devil's Den and the woods around to the Peach Orchard.

Perhaps their greatest success was in pulling the bulk of the Union force away from Ewell's front where the fight was still raging.

ATTACK ON THE UNION RIGHT

It was Lee's intent that Ewell's Corps would make a strong demonstration at the time of Longstreet's attack to keep Meade from pulling forces from his weighted right to reinforce the area of Longstreet's attack. The only demonstration conducted during most of the time of the battle to the south came from Maj. J. W. Latimer's Artillery Battalion. Taking position at about 4 P.M. on Benner's Hill, which offered neither cover nor concealment, the battalion opened a two-hour exchange with the well-positioned Union artillery on the heights across the valley. It was very much a one-sided exchange. Latimer's cannoneers suffered severe losses and did little to hold the Federals in position.

By the time Maj. Gen. Edward Johnson's Division started its assault on Culp's Hill at dusk, most of the Twelfth Corps, which had been building breastworks there since morning, had moved to reinforce the left and center of the Union line. Brig. Gen. George Greene's Third Brigade of Brig. Gen. John Geary's Second Division, supported by Wadsworth's depleted First Corps Division, were all that was left to stop Johnson's attack. Greene's five regiments of New Yorkers had taken position at the summit of Culp's Hill on the right of Wadsworth's thin line, connecting with the now vacated Second Brigade line on the right. The empty breastworks of the corps' First Division extended those of the Second Brigade southeast to the hill's lesser summit. Unable to cover the corps line, Greene sent the 137th New York to the Second Brigade's position. The 137th was taking up its new position when the brigade's line was attacked.

General Johnson attacked on a three-brigade front: Jones' Brigade, commanded by Lt. Col. R. H. Duncan on the right; Nicholl's Brigade, under Col. J. M. Williams in the center; and Brig. Gen. George Steuart's Brigade on the right. Duncan and Williams led their brigades against Greene's line on the main summit, making repeated assaults on the line, but could not break it. Steuart's Brigade moved onto the lesser of the summits, occupied the empty breastworks they found, and attacked Greene's right. The 137th New York changed front and supported by three depleted regiments from Wadsworth's Division, repulsed the attack. Now well after dark, the struggle slowed to individual firing from lines no more than 100 yards apart. Johnson's Fourth Brigade, commanded by Brig. Gen. James Walker, was held across Rock Creek in reserve. It crossed the creek after dark and joined Steuart's Brigade in occupying the Union breastworks. The Twelfth Corps units returning from the army left to find their breastworks occupied, formed line along Baltimore Pike in front of them. The stage was set for the battle to resume at first light.

With Johnson's belated attack under way, General Ewell moved to implement the planned attack on Cemetery Hill. Under the plan, Jubal Early's Division was to attack the north side of Cemetery Hill, and R. E. Rodes' Division would attack the western side. Given the depleted and demoralized state of the First and Eleventh Union Corps units that occupied Cemetery Hill, the chances for success were better there than at any other place on the field that day. But the hour was late and the disorganization that plagued Ewell's Corps during the Battle of Gettysburg continued.

General Early could only put two of his four brigades on the assault line. Smith's Brigade was still out on York Pike, where it had been for two days guarding against a reported approach of Union cavalry. Holding Gordon's Brigade in reserve, Early sent a line of two brigades, Hays on the right of Avery, toward the steep northeast face of East Cemetery Hill. It was about 8 P.M. and getting darker by the minute when the line struck the first of the Eleventh Corps lines at the bottom of the hill. The men of the Eleventh, still reeling from their rout the previous day, put up little resistance. Colonel Avery fell mortally wounded early in the charge, but his men swept on up the hill with Hays' Brigade. The brigades planted their colors in the abandoned gun positions on the crest of the hill; determined to hold until the support they expected arrived.

No other Confederates were advancing up the slopes of Cemetery Hill to support the two gallant brigades on the crest. Gordon advanced his brigade to the base of the hill, but Early stopped the advance when he saw that there was no advance from Rodes' Division. There was probably no single reason for Rodes not sending his brigades up the slope alongside Early's Brigades. Perhaps still shaken from his near disaster the previous day, Rodes did not show the same aggression that he displayed upon his arrival on the field. With no advance from Mahone's Brigade, Anderson's Division, and Pender's Division in the assault on his right, and Ewell's hesitancy that delayed the advance on the left, Rodes did not prepare his brigades for an attack until it was too late. Well past dark and the situation on the crest uncertain, Rodes did not advance.

Reinforcements were arriving on the crest but they were from the Union side. Hancock's Second Corps again responded to shore up the Union line. Col. Samuel Carroll's First Brigade of Hays' Division, followed by several regiments of the First Corps, went to the relief of the Eleventh Corps. Expecting Rodes' brigades to advance through the darkness, the Confederates on the crest held their fire, even though receiving fire from the advancing columns. Carroll's advance had closed with the Confederates before they returned fire. Still, the Confederates repulsed several attacks before they conducted an orderly withdrawal, bringing with them many prisoners and four stands of colors. Unsupported, the most successful penetration of the Union line of the day had ended.

The withdrawal of Hays' and Avery's Brigades ended the second day of the battle. Advances had been made against the entire Union line, except for the western side of Cemetery Hill. Lodgments had been established on the Union right and left, but nowhere were the Confederate gains decisive. But with the arrival of Pickett's fresh division and the belated appearance of Stuart's Cavalry, the fight would continue the next day.

View of Round Tops from Valley of Death, circa 1885

Courtesy USAMHI-MOLLUS

View of Round Tops from Valley of Death, 1998

Photograph by Author

Entrance to Devil's Den, 1885

Courtesy USAMHI-MOLLUS

Entrance to Devil's Den, 1998

Photograph by Author

View from Little Round Top showing Wheatfield, circa 1885

Courtesy USAMHI-MOLLUS

View from Little Round Top, 1998

Photograph by Author

View of Peach Orchard, circa 1885
Looking toward Round Tops.

Courtesy USAMHI-MOLLUS

View of Peach Orchard, 1998

Photograph by Author

View from East Cemetery Hill, circa 1885
Culp's Hill is to the right front, Benner's Hill center distance.

Courtesy USAMHI-MOLLUS

View from East Cemetery Hill, 1998

Photograph by Author

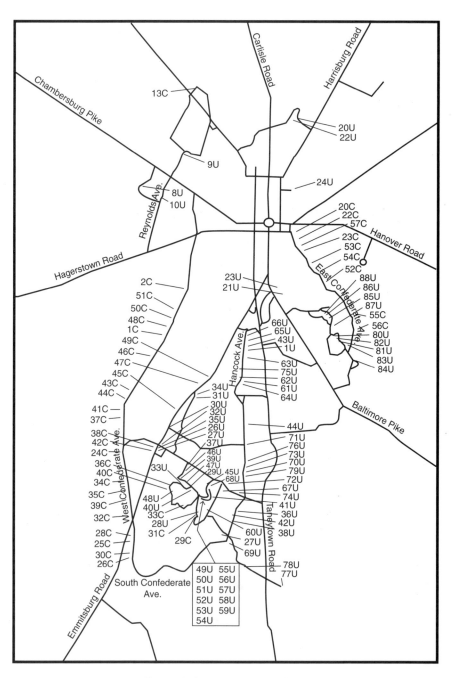

Second day tablet locations

SECOND DAY TABLET INSCRIPTIONS
ARMY OF THE POTOMAC

ARMY OF THE POTOMAC
Major General George G. Meade
Commanding

July 2. The remainder of the Third Corps and the Fifth and Second Corps arrived in the morning. The Sixth Corps in the afternoon. The Third Corps having advanced was attacked by Longstreet's Confederate Corps and Anderson's Division of Hill's Corps. The Fifth Corps and the First Division of the Second Corps going to the support of the Third Corps an engagement ensued until nightfall when the Union forces had been driven back from their advanced position and the Confederates repulsed.

No. 1U   Tablet on Granite Marker located—Hancock Avenue

Note: The complete inscription on this tablet is presented in Part II—Day One— Page 28.

ARMY OF THE POTOMAC
THIRD CORPS
Major General Daniel E. Sickles
Major General David B. Birney

July 1. This Corps was at Emmitsburg. Complying with General Howard's urgent request received at 3:10 P. M. General Sickles marched his Corps except two brigades and two batteries to Gettysburg.

July 2. At daybreak these troops rejoined the Corps massed on the left of Cemetery Ridge. During the forenoon the Confederates advanced towards the Union left. A reconnaissance disclosed their formation in three columns. Buford's Cavalry on the left flank had been withdrawn. About 2 P. M. this Corps, then the extreme left of the Union line, changed front to check the enemy until the 5th Corps could march from the Union right and occupy the Round Tops. The 3rd Corps, about 9800 men, formed line of battle from Plum Run to the Peach Orchard, thence along the Emmitsburg road 300 yards past the Rocer House. Birney's Division on left and Humphreys' Division along Emmitsburg road against three divisions, about 17000 strong under Longstreet. The Confederate batteries opened about 3 o'clock. The Infantry advancing soon after against the 3rd Corps left. Following an oblique order of battle, at 5:30 P. M. the enemy attacked the 3rd Corps left centre. Reinforcements repulsed this attack and occupied the Round Tops, relieving Birney's Division except at the Peach Orchard. About 6:30 P. M. the 3rd Corps centre at the Peach Orchard was broken after a stubborn resistance uncovering the left of Humphreys' Division which changed front and slowly retired following Birney to Cemetery Ridge and again advancing to Emmitsburg Road. Held that line until morning, the battle continuing until 7:30 P. M. General Sickles was severely wounded about 6 o'clock, General Birney taking command.

July 3. In support of the left centre on Cemetery Ridge.

Casualties   593 Killed   3029 Wounded and 589 Missing   Total 4211

No. 26U   Tablet on Granite Marker located—Emmitsburg Road, Peach Orchard

———

ARMY OF THE POTOMAC
THIRD CORPS
FIRST DIVISION
Major General David B. Birney
Brigadier General J. H. Hobart Ward

July 1. This Division was at Emmitsburg covering roads from Fairfield and Gettysburg. Shortly after 3 P. M. marched to Gettysburg leaving De Trobriand's Brigade.

July 2. This Brigade rejoined. At about 7 A. M. Birney relieved Geary's 2D Division 12th Corps, his left resting near Little Round Top, his right joining Humphreys on Cemetery Ridge. Picket line holding Emmitsburg road. Shortly after 2 P. M. Division wheeled to the left occupying high ground from Plum Run to Peach Orchard and thence along Emmitsburg Road to the Sherfy House, Wards Brigade on the left, De Trobriand's in the centre, and Graham's on the right. Burling's Brigade Humphreys' Division in reserve near Birney's centre. Confederate artillery opened at 3 o'clock. Soon after, three brigades of Hood's Division attacked Ward on Birney's left, extending later to De Trobriand. These attacks were successfully resisted. At 5:30 P. M. two brigades of McLaw's Division attacked Birney's right and centre. Two brigades of 5th Corps advanced to the rocky knoll at De Trobriand's right but withdrew after a brief contest.

Here occurred the first break in Birney's line. Movement against south face of the Peach Orchard checked by batteries in Birney's right centre. The Confederates renewed their attack on Birney's centre. Caldwell's Division 2D Corps now arrived, and, with troops from the 5th Corps, relieved Birney except at the Peach Orchard. About 6:30 P. M. Birney's right at the Peach Orchard was attacked on both fronts and broken opposite Sherfy House after stubborn resistance. Through this gap the Confederates swept forward crushing Birney's right which rejoined its Division.

July 3. The Division was held in reserve and detachments moved to threatened points.

Casualties   Killed 22 Officers 249 Men   Wounded 106 Officers 1278 Men   Captured or Missing 12 Officers 344 Men   Total 2011

No. 27U   Tablet on Granite Marker located—Emmitsburg Road, Peach Orchard

---

ARMY OF THE POTOMAC
THIRD CORPS   FIRST DIVISION
SECOND BRIGADE
Brig. Gen. J. H. Hobart Ward
Col. Hiram Berdan
20th Indiana   3d 4th Maine
86th 124th New York   99th Penna. Infantry
1st   2D   (8 Cos.) U. S. Sharpshooters

July 1. Arrived after sunset and bivouacked for the night.

July 2. The Corps having relieved Second Division Twelfth Corps in the morning the Brigade took position on the left of the Division and extended to the base of Little Round top. Between 2 and 3 P. M. advanced with the Division to the line from the Peach Orchard to Devil's Den occupying the left of the line to the west base of Little Round Top. The 1st U. S. Sharpshooters and 3D Maine were engaged in a reconnaissance into the woods in front of the Peach Orchard from noon until about 2 P. M. and then served with First Brigade at the Peach Orchard. The 6th New Jersey and 40th New York were sent to Brig. Gen. Ward and supported his left. Between 4 and 5 P. M. the Brigade was fiercely attacked by Brig. Gen. Robertson's and Brig. Gen. Benning's Brigades Major Gen. Hood's Division and after a prolonged conflict was forced back.

July 3. In reserve.

Casualties   Killed 12 Officers 117 Men   Wounded 33 Officers 449 Men Captured or Missing 6 Officers 164 Men   Total 781

No. 28U   Tablet on Granite Pedestal located—Sickles Avenue, Above Devil's
Den

───────

ARMY OF THE POTOMAC
THIRD CORPS   FIRST DIVISION
THIRD BRIGADE
Col. P. Regis De Trobriand
17th Maine   3D   5th Michigan   40th New York
110th   (6 Cos.) Pennsylvania Infantry

July 2. Arrived at 10 A. M. On the advance of the Division between 2 and 3
P. M. the Brigade took position in column between First and Second
Brigades for support to either. The Third Michigan was sent to support
First Brigade. The 17th Maine moved across the Wheatfield to the stone
wall on the south. The 40th New York was sent to the gorge between the
Devil's Den and Little Round Top. The 5th Michigan and 110th Penna.
held the summit commanding a ravine in front and east of the Rose
buildings until relieved by two Brigades of Fifth Corps when they retired
through the Wheatfield where being joined by 17th Maine they held back
a superior Confederate force until the arrival of First Division Second
Corps when ammunition being exhausted this portion of the Brigade
retired and at night was joined by the other regiments.

July 3. In reserve.

Casualties   Killed 4 Officers 71 Men   Wounded 28 Officers 366 men
Captured or Missing 21 Men   Total 490

No. 29U   Tablet on Granite Pedestal located—Sickles Avenue, Wheatfield

───────

ARMY OF THE POTOMAC
THIRD CORPS   FIRST DIVISION
FIRST BRIGADE
Brig. Gen. Charles K. Graham
Col. Andrew H. Tippin
57th   (8 Cos.) 63d   68th   105th   114th   141st
Pennsylvania Infantry

July 1. Arrived between 5 and 6 P. M.

July 2. The Corps having relieved Second Division Twelfth Corps in the
morning the Brigade took position on the right of the Division connecting
with Second Division on the right. Between 2 and 3 P. M. advanced to

the Emmitsburg Road and took position at the Peach Orchard supported by 3D Maine 3d Michigan 2D New Hampshire and 7th New Jersey. About 3 P. M. artillery opened on the Confederate columns moving to the left and soon thereafter the Confederate artillery replied and later the Brigade was attacked by Major Gen. McLaws's Division and forced back by superior numbers in front and on the flanks and at sunset it fell back with the Division. Brig. Gen. Graham was wounded and captured at the Peach Orchard.

July 3. The Brigade was in reserve during the day.

Casualties   Killed 6 Officers 61 Men   Wounded 45 Officers 463 Men Captured or Missing 6 Officers 159 Men   Total 740

No. 30U   Tablet on Granite Pedestal located—Emmitsburg Road, south of United States Avenue

---

ARMY OF THE POTOMAC
THIRD CORPS
SECOND DIVISION
Brig. General Andrew A. Humphreys

First Brigade   Brig. Gen. Joseph B. Carr
Second Brigade   Col. William R. Brewster
Third Brigade   Col. George C. Burling

July 2. Arrived about 1 A. M. and bivouacked for the night. In the morning took position between Birney's Division on the left and the Second Corps facing Emmitsburg Road. Between 2 and 3 P. M. advanced to the Emmitsburg Road. Carr's Brigade at first in line along the road Brewster's Brigade in reserve. Burling's Brigade at first in reserve and then except the 5th New Jersey sent to Gen. Birney. The Division was attacked by McClaws' and Anderson's Divisions and by sunset was compelled to retire to the first position occupied where it reformed on the left of Second Corps and drove back the Confederate forces beyond the Emmitsburg Road and recovered the artillery that had been abandoned and captured many prisoners and held the position during the night.

July 3. About sunrise moved to the rear and left and was supplied with rations and ammunition. Burling's Brigade joined the Division moved to different points in rear of the First Second Fifth and some Sixth Corps in support of threatened positions. Suffered some loss in the afternoon from Confederate artillery.

Casualties   Killed 28 Officers 286 Men   Wounded 140 Officers 1422 Men   Captured or Missing 2 Officers 214 Men   Total 2092

No. 31U   Tablet on Granite Marker located—Sickles Avenue, intersection Emmitsburg Road

Note: A second tablet for this division is located on Emmitsburg Road at the Peach Orchard.

———

ARMY OF THE POTOMAC
THIRD CORPS
SECOND DIVISION
Brigadier General Andrew A. Humphreys

July 1. This Division was at Emmitsburg. Shortly after 3 P. M. marched by indirect route about two miles west of main road to Gettysburg leaving Burling's Brigade.

July 2. Arrived at 1 A. M. and massed on Cemetery Ridge between Birney's Division on the left and 2D Corp. Burling's Brigade rejoined. Between 2 and 3 P. M. formed line of battle along the Emmitsburg Road to resist attack on Union left its right opposite left of Caldwell's Division 2D Corps its left joining Birney's Division. Carr's Brigade on the right Brewster's Brigade massed on the left centre Burling's Brigade in Reserve until sent to General Birney. The Confederates made demonstrations on the Division front which remained in position after the 5th and 6th Corps had arrived on the Union left until about 6 P. M. when McLaws' Division following the Confederate oblique order of battle broke Birney's line at the Peach Orchard uncovering the left of Humphreys who changed front to connect with 2D and 5th Corps troops in the Wheatfield. That line enfiladed by the enemy fell back across Plum Run while Humphreys outflanked by McLaws' Division and pressed by Anderson's Division Hill's Corps gradually retired to Cemetery Ridge reformed on 2D Corps left and drove the Confederates beyond the Emmitsburg Road recovering abandoned artillery capturing many prisoners and holding the advanced position during the night.

July 3. Division moved to different points in the rear of the 1st 2D 5th and 6th Corps supporting threatened positions.

Casualties   Killed 28 Officers 286 Men   Wounded 140 Officers 1422 Men   Captured or Missing 2 Officers 214 men   Total 2092

No. 32U   Tablet on Granite Marker located—Emmitsburg Road, Peach Orchard

———

ARMY OF THE POTOMAC
THIRD CORPS SECOND DIVISION
THIRD BRIGADE
Col. George C. Burling
2D New Hampshire 5th 6th 8th New Jersey
115th Pennsylvania Infantry

July 2. Arrived between 9 and 10 A. M. and joined the Division. Between 2 and 3 P. M. advanced with the Division and was placed in reserve in rear of Second Brigade and soon thereafter ordered to First Division except that the 5th New Jersey supported Battery K 4th U. S. on the Emmitsburg Road. The 2D New Hampshire and 7th New Jersey reported to Brig. Gen. C. K. Graham and supported batteries in the Peach Orchard the 63D Penna. on the left. The 6th New Jersey went to the support of the Second Brigade First Division on its left in Plum Run Gorge near Devil's Den. The 8th New Jersey and 115 Penna. were sent to the Wheatfield to support the right of Second Brigade First Division. The regiments of the Brigade were severely engaged where assigned and retired at the close of the day with the organizations with which they served.

July 3. In the morning rejoined the Division and was placed in reserve where apparently needed.

Casualties Killed 6 Officers 53 Men Wounded 43 Officers 333 Men Captured or Missing 78 Men Total 513

No. 33U Tablet on Granite Pedestal located—the Loop, Wheatfield

---

ARMY OF THE POTOMAC
THIRD CORPS SECOND DIVISION
FIRST BRIGADE
Brig. Gen. Joseph B. Carr
1st 11th 16th Massachusetts
12th New Hampshire 11th New Jersey
26th 84th Pennsylvania Infantry

July 2. Arrived about 1 A. M. and bivouacked for the night. Early in the afternoon formed on the right of the Division connecting with Second Corps on the right. Between 3 and 4 P. M. advanced 300 yards to the Emmitsburg Road connecting with First Division. The Brigade with the support of 5th New Jersey on the left and 15th Mass. and 82D New York on the right held the front line Second Brigade in reserve until the line on the left gave way when the Brigade with the Division changed front to the left. The Brigade then retired with the Corps by order of Major Gen.

D. B. Birney commanding to the main line in the rear where it formed and forced back the pursuing forces regained the lost ground capturing many prisoners and held the position until morning.

July 3. The Confederate artillery opened fire at daylight which continued over an hour. At 6 A. M. the Brigade was ordered to join the Corps in the rear and then to support the Fifth Corps and at 3 P. M. to support the Second Corps. The Brigade lying in close column suffered severely from the artillery fire.

Casualties   Killed 10 Officers 111 Men   Wounded 45 Officers 559 Men
Captured or Missing 2 Officers 63 Men   Total 790

No. 34U   Tablet on Granite Pedestal located—Sickles Avenue, intersection Emmitsburg Road

---

ARMY OF THE POTOMAC
THIRD CORPS SECOND DIVISION
SECOND BRIGADE
Col. William R. Brewster
70th   71st   72D   73D   120th New York Infantry

July 2. Arrived about 1 A. M. and bivouacked for the night. Near 1 P. M. formed in rear of First Brigade the 73D being advanced to the crest of the hill in front. The Brigade advanced between 2 and 3 P. M. the 71st and 72D to the left of First Brigade the 70th and 120th in reserve. Later the 73D was sent to the support of First Brigade First Division. Fiercely attacked toward sunset and the forces on the left having fallen back the Brigade retired and after sunset again advanced and captured the colors of the 8th Florida and thirty prisoners and recaptured guns that had been left on the field. Again retired and formed in rear of a Brigade of Second Corps and bivouacked for the night.

July 3. Moved further to the rear and was supplied with rations and ammunition. About 3 P. M. moved to support batteries in front.

Casualties   Killed 12 Officers 120 Men   Wounded 50 Officers 523 Men
Captured or Missing 73 Men   Total 778

No. 35U   Tablet on Granite Pedestal located—Sickles Avenue, south of U.S. Avenue

---

ARMY OF THE POTOMAC
FIFTH CORPS
Major General George Sykes

First Division	Brigadier General James Barnes
Second Division	Brigadier General Romeyn B. Ayres
Third Division	Brigadier General Samuel W. Crawford
Artillery Brigade	Captain Augustus P. Martin

July 2. Arrived in the morning and went into position on the right of 12th Corps. Later crossed Rock Creek via Baltimore Pike and was massed in the field until late in the afternoon. Moved to the left between 4 and 5 P. M. Barnes's and Ayres's Divisions taking possession of Little Round Top and re-inforcing the 3D Corps line Crawford's Division in reserve. All Brigades of the Corps except Fisher's were engaged at intervals until night.

July 3. Barnes's Division except Tilton's Brigade north of Little Round Top with Wright's Division 6th Corps on the right, left and rear. Ayres's and Crawford's Divisions and Tilton's Brigade on the Round Tops. These positions were held during the day.

July 4. In same positions except reconnaissances from each Division were made in front during the day.

Casualties   Killed 28 Officers 337 Men   Wounded 129 Officers 1481 Men   Captured or Missing 1 Officer 210 Men   Total 2186

No. 36U   Tablet on Granite Marker located—Sykes Avenue, Little Round Top

———

ARMY OF THE POTOMAC
FIFTH CORPS
FIRST DIVISION
Brig. General James Barnes

First Brigade	Col. Wm. S. Tilton
Second Brigade	Col. J. B. Sweitzer
Third Brigade	Col. Strong Vincent
	Col. Jas. C. Rice

July 2. Crossed Rock Creek in the morning and was massed on Baltimore Pike with the Corps until between 4 and 5 P. M. then moved to the left by command of Gen. Sykes to the support of Third Corps line. The Third

Brigade in the advance hastened to take possession of Little Round Top. The First and Second Brigades crossed Plum Run and the Wheatfield to the further edge of the woods beyond near the Rose House. First Brigade was formed on the right of Second. These Brigades were more or less engaged until after sundown when with other troops on the line were compelled to retire to a line extending north from the summit of Little Round Top.

July 3. The Third Brigade was relieved by the First Brigade and joined Second Brigade north of Little Round Top. Remained in these positions until the close of the battle except reconnaissance to the front.

Casualties Killed 14 Officers 153 Men Wounded 55 Officers 539 Men Captured or Missing 1 Officer 142 Men Total 904

No. 37U Tablet on Granite Marker located—Sickles Avenue, near intersection Weatfield Road

————————

ARMY OF THE POTOMAC
FIFTH CORPS   FIRST DIVISION
THIRD BRIGADE
Col. Strong Vincent   Col. James C. Rice
20th Maine   16th Michigan   44th New York
83D Pennsylvania Infantry

July 2. After 4 P.M. moved with the Division left in front to the support of the Third Corps line. The Brigade was detached and took position on Little Round Top advancing to the crests at the south and southwest. The 20th Maine 83D Penna. 44th New York and 16th Michigan took position from left to right. They were immediately attacked by Brig. Gen. Law's Brigade and the contest raged for over two hours and until dark when the attack was repulsed with great loss in killed wounded and prisoners. Over 500 prisoners including 15 commissioned officers were captured. The 20th Maine and the 83D Penna. extended their lines after dark to the summit of Round Top.

July 3. Took position about noon with Second Brigade near the left centre of the main line of battle and remained in reserve through the day exposed to severe shelling but without loss.

July 4. Made a reconnaissance to the front without finding any Confederate forces in positions occupied by them the previous day.

Casualties Killed 6 Officers 83 Men Wounded 17 Officers 236 Men Captured or Missing 11 Men Total 352

No. 38U Tablet on Granite Pedestal located—Sykes Avenue, Little Round Top

Note: Numbers inscribed for killed, wounded and captured or missing total 353, not 352.

————

ARMY OF THE POTOMAC
FIFTH CORPS   FIRST DIVISION
FIRST BRIGADE
Col. William S. Tilton
18th   22D Massachusetts   1st Michigan
118th Pennsylvania Infantry

July 2. In position in column with the Division and Corps on the Baltimore Pike near Rock Creek until after 4 P. M. then moved with the Division left in front to the support of Third Corps line the Third Brigade having been detached to occupy Little Round Top. The Brigade preceded by Second Brigade crossed Plum Run and the Wheatfield and went into position on the high ground on the edge of woods facing westerly and southerly toward the Rose House Second Brigade on the left. The Brigade was sharply attacked by Brig. Gen. Kershaw's Brigade and in compliance with orders from Brig. Gen. J. Barnes it retired to the rear and right to the woods across the Wheatfield Road and later to a line extending northerly from Little Round Top.

July 3. Relieved Third Brigade on Little Round Top.

July 4. Remained in position until close of battle except a reconnaissance in front.

Casualties   Killed 2 Officers 10 Men   Wounded 12 Officers 90 Men
Captured or Missing 11 Men   Total 125

No. 39U   Tablet on Granite Pedestal located—Sickles Avenue, west end of Wheatfield

————

ARMY OF THE POTOMAC
FIFTH CORPS   FIRST DIVISION
SECOND BRIGADE
Col. Jacob B. Sweitzer
9th   32D Massachusetts   4th Michigan
62D Pennsylvania Infantry

July 2. After 2 P. M. moved from the Baltimore Pike near Rock Creek with the Division left in front to support of Third Corps line. Third Brigade was detached to occupy Little Round Top and the Brigade crossed Plum Run followed by First Brigade and went into position on the edge of woods west of the Wheatfield facing partly towards the Rose House First Brigade on the right. Brig. Gen. Kershaw's Brigade supported by Brig. Gen. Semmes's Brigade having attacked this position and First Brigade having retired the Brigade retired across the Wheatfield Road and formed on the north side of the woods facing the road when by order of Brig. Gen. J. Barnes the Brigade advanced to the support of First Division Second Corps and engaged Brig. Gen. Anderson's Brigade at the stone wall at the south end of the Wheatfield but the supports on the right having given away the Brigade was attacked on the right and rear and it retired under a heavy fire to a line north of Little Round Top and there remained until the close of the battle.

Casualties   Killed 6 Officers 61 Men   Wounded 26 Officers 213 Men Captured or Missing 1 Officer 120 Men   Total 427

No.40U   Tablet on Granite Pedestal located—the Loop, intersection Sickles Avenue

---

ARMY OF THE POTOMAC
FIFTH CORPS
SECOND DIVISION
Brig. General Romeyn B. Ayres

First Brigade   Col. Hannibal Day
Second Brigade   Col. Sidney Burbank
Third Brigade   Brig. Gen. S. H. Weed
                          Col. Kenner Garrard

July 2. Moved from the Baltimore Pike near Rock Creek about 3 P. M. left in front to the support of the Third Corps line preceded by the First Division. The Third Brigade halted at Little Round top and occupied the summit and north slope just in time to repel an attack on the right of the Third Brigade First Division. Here Gen. Weed fell mortally wounded. The First and Second Brigades crossed Plum Run to the hill beyond and formed in two lines. The First Brigade in rear fronting the Wheatfield through which the First Division Second Corps was advancing at right angle. About sunset the troops in front and on the right retired before a fierce assault on the front and flank and these two Brigades were compelled to retire with heavy losses to Little Round top pursued by Wofford's Georgia Brigade and portions of Semmes's Kershaw's and Anderson's Brigades. Later the First and Second Brigades took position in the woods in rear of the Third Brigade.

July 3. Remained in same position.

July 4. The First Brigade made a successful reconnaissance.

Casualties   Killed 10 Officers 154 Men   Wounded 56 Officers 746 Men
Captured or Missing 63 Men   Total 1029

No. 41U   Tablet on Granite Marker located—between Crawford and Ayres Avenues

---

ARMY OF THE POTOMAC
FIFTH CORPS   SECOND DIVISION
THIRD BRIGADE
Brig. Gen. Stephen H. Weed
Col. Kenner Garrard
140th   146th New York
91st   155th Pennsylvania Infantry

July 2. Arrived early in the morning and lay on the Baltimore Pike near Rock Creek until late in the day. Moved hastily to the left leading the Division and took position on Little Round Top on the right of Third Brigade First Division in time for the 140th New York to repel an attack at that point. The other regiments having moved to the right to the support of Battery I 5th U. S. and Third Corps line were brought back and went into position on the right of the 140th New York. Brig. Gen. Weed commanding Brigade and Col. P. H. O'Rorke commanding 140th New York were mortally wounded.

July 3. Remained in position until the close of the battle.

Casualties   Killed 2 Officers 38 Men   Wounded 11 Officers 131 Men
Captured or Missing 18 Men   Total 200

No. 42U   Tablet on Granite Pedestal located—Sykes Avenue, Little Round Top

---

ARMY OF THE POTOMAC
SECOND CORPS
Major General Winfield S. Hancock
Brigadier General John Gibbon

First Division   Brigadier General John C. Caldwell
Second Division   Brigadier General John Gibbon
                        Brigadier General John Harrow

Third Division	Brigadier General Alexander Hays
Artillery Brigade	Captain John G. Hazard

July 2. Arrived between 6 and 8 A. M. on Taneytown Road and went into position on Cemetery Ridge on right of 5th Corps and at the left of the cemetery relieving a part of 1st Corps. Caldwell's Division on the left Gibbon in centre and Hays on the right of line from Cemetery Hill to Round Top. Between 5 and 6 P. M. Caldwell's Division was sent to the support of 3D Corps and was engaged until sunset. It returned to its first position.

July 3. At 1 P. M. the Confederate artillery opened a heavy fire all along Hill's Corps and the left of Longstreet's Corps for two hours when an assault under the command of General Longstreet was made by a force of about 15,000 which was repulsed with great loss in killed wounded and prisoners.

Casualties   Killed 66 Officers 731 Men   Wounded 270 Officers 2924 Men   Captured or Missing 10 Officers 365 Men   Total 4369

No. 43U   Tablet on Granite Marker located—Hancock Avenue

ARMY OF THE POTOMAC
SECOND CORPS
FIRST DIVISION
Brig. General John C. Caldwell

First Brigade	Col. Edward E. Cross
	Col. H. B. McKeen
Second Brigade	Col. Patrick Kelly
Third Brigade	Brig. Gen. Samuel K. Zook
	Lieut. Col. John Fraser
Fourth Brigade	Col. J. R. Brooke

July 2. Arrived about 7 A. M. and went into position on the right of the Third Corps on the line between the Cemetery and Round Top. The Second Division on the right. Between 5 and 6 P. M. went to the Wheatfield subject to orders of Gen. Sykes in support of Third line. The line previously occupied by Third Brigade First Division Third Corps. Was engaged with Anderson's Brigade Hood's Division until sunset with heavy losses including Col. Cross and Gen. Zook killed early in the engagement. Returned to former position in Second Corps line.

July 3. The Division formed in single line threw up breastworks and remained in position until close of the battle.

Casualties   Killed 18 Officers 169 Men   Wounded 82 Officers 798 Men
Captured or Missing 6 Officers 202 Men   Total 1275

No. 44U   Tablet on Granite Marker located—South Hancock Avenue

---

ARMY OF THE POTOMAC
SECOND CORPS   FIRST DIVISION
FIRST BRIGADE
Col. Edward E. Cross   Col. H. Boyd McKeen
5th New Hampshire   61st New York
81st   148th Pennsylvania Infantry

July 2. Arrived about 7 A. M. and was massed in woods at left and rear of the line of Corps and at 10 A. M. took position forming the left of Division in column of regiments. Between 5 and 6 P. M. moved with Division to the support of Third Corps forming line of battle along a stone wall at the rear and east of the Wheatfield and advanced against the Confederate forces in the Wheatfield and in the woods at left forcing them back to the farther end of the Wheatfield and taking many prisoners when the ammunition being exhausted the Brigade was relieved by part of Second Division Fifth Corps and Second Brigade First Division Fifth Corps and retired to the stone wall and finally with Division to former position in line with Corps. Col. Cross fell mortally wounded early in the engagement.

July 3. Constructed breastworks early in the morning which gave protection from the cannonade in the afternoon. Remained in position until the close of the battle.

Casualties   Killed 2 Officers 55 Men   Wounded 22 Officers 238 Men
Captured or Missing 13 Men   Total 330

No. 45U   Tablet on Granite Pedestal located—Ayres Avenue

ARMY OF THE POTOMAC
SECOND CORPS   FIRST DIVISION
SECOND BRIGADE
Col. Patrick Kelly
28th Massachusetts
63D (2 Cos.)   69th (2 Cos.)   88th (2 Cos.) New York
116th (4 Cos.) Pennsylvania Infantry

July 2. Arrived at 7 A. M. and took position on line from Cemetery Hill to Round Top at right of First Brigade. Between 5 and 6 P. M. went with

Division to left First Brigade on the left Third Brigade on right. Engaged the Confederate forces including Brig. Gen. Anderson's Brigade Major Gen. Hood's Division in the Wheatfield and forced them through the field southerly into woods beyond capturing many prisoners. The Fourth Brigade having advanced on the left this Brigade held its position until the Division being flanked on right and left retired and resumed former position in line of the Corps.

July 3. Constructed breastworks and remained entrenched until the close of the battle.

Casualties   Killed 1 Officer 26 Men   Wounded 4 Officers 105 Men Captured or Missing 2 Officers 60 Men   Total 198

No. 46U   Tablet on Granite Pedestal located—Sickles Avenue

ARMY OF THE POTOMAC
SECOND CORPS   FIRST DIVISION
THIRD BRIGADE
Brig. Gen. Samuel K. Zook
Lieut. Col. John Fraser
52D   57th   66th New York
140th Pennsylvania Infantry

July 2. Arrived early in the morning and formed on right of Second Brigade on line from Cemetery Hill to Round Top. Between 5 and 6 P. M. advanced with Division to left and entered the Wheatfield and the woods on its right in line of battle forcing the Confederates through the field and the woods to the further end. Brig. Gen. Zook fell mortally wounded in this advance the Brigade being on the right of Division it extended to an open field on the west. The line of Third Corps on the Emmitsburg Road having been forced back and the Division having been flanked by superior forces on its right and left the Brigade retired with the Division and resumed in line with Corps.

July 3. Constructed entrenchment and held the position until the close of battle.

Casualties   Killed 7 Officers 42 Men   Wounded 18 Officers 209 Men Captured or Missing 4 Officers 78 Men   Total 358

No. 47U   Tablet on Granite Pedestal located—Sickles Avenue

ARMY OF THE POTOMAC
SECOND CORPS   FIRST DIVISION
FOURTH BRIGADE
Col. John R. Brooke
27th Connecticut (2 Cos.)
2D Delaware   64th New York
53D   145th (7 Cos.) Pennsylvania Infantry

July 2. Arrived early in the morning took position on the line from Cemetery Hill to Round Top and was the right Brigade of Division. Between 5 and 6 P. M. went with Division to Wheatfield and advanced in reserve until the Division had forced back the Confederates to the further end when the Brigade advanced on the left of Third Brigade across a marsh to crest of a wooded hill. The Union line along the Emmitsburg Road having soon thereafter been forced back by Brig. Gen. Semmes's Brig. Gen. Kershaw's and Brig. Gen. Wofford's Brigades which advanced in front and on the left flank the Brigade retired with the Division and resumed its former place in Corps line.

July 3. Constructed entrenchments and remained in former position until the close of the battle.

Casualties   Killed 8 Officers 46 Men   Wounded 38 Officers 246 Men Captured or Missing 51 Men   Total 389

No. 48U   Tablet on Granite Pedestal located—the Loop

ARMY OF THE POTOMAC
FIFTH CORPS   SECOND DIVISION
SECOND BRIGADE
Col. Sidney Brubank
2D (6 Cos.)   7th (4 Cos.)   10th (3 Cos.)
11th (6 Cos.)   17th (7 Cos.) U. S. Infantry

July 2. Arrived in the morning and formed on the right of Twelfth Corps afterwards crossed Rock Creek and remained near the Baltimore Pike until late in the day then moved with the Division to the north slope of Little Round Top and soon advanced across Plum Run Valley supported by First Brigade and formed line on the hill beyond facing the Wheatfield through which First Division Second Corps was forcing the Confederate forces perpendicular to the line of the Brigade later advanced on the left of First Division Second Corps and the First Brigade in support when the Union forces on the right and front having been forced back by superior numbers the two Brigades retired in good order but with great loss under a heavy musketry fire on its front and flank to Little Round Top and in the evening to the woods on the other side in reserve.

July 3. Remained in the same position until the close of the battle.

Casualties   Killed 7 Officers 71 Men   Wounded 32 Officers 310 Men Captured or Missing 27 Men   Total 447 out of a strength of 900 muskets

No. 49U   Tablet on Granite Pedestal located—Ayres Avenue

ARMY OF THE POTOMAC
FIFTH CORPS
SECOND DIVISION   SECOND BRIGADE
SECOND U. S. INFANTRY
Six Companies
Major Arthur T. Lee and Captain Samuel A. McKee
Commanding

July 2. Arrived in the morning and took position with the Brigade at the right of the Twelfth Corps. Skirmished with the Confederates. Later moved to the left. At 5 P. M. formed line with left on north slope of Little Round Top and the right of Brigade line extending into some woods. Advanced across Plum Run and to the crest of the rocky wooded hill in front near the Wheatfield and facing left occupied the stone wall on the edge of the woods. The Confederates having opened fire on the right flank and advanced through the Wheatfield in the rear the Brigade was withdrawn under a heavy fire on both flanks and from the rear and of shot and shell from batteries and formed in line on right of Little Round Top.

July 3. Remained in same position.

Casualties   Killed 1 Officer and 5 Men   Wounded 4 Officers and 51 Men Missing 6 Men

No. 50U   Tablet on Granite Marker located—Ayres Avenue, Houck's Ridge

---

ARMY OF THE POTOMAC
FIFTH CORPS
SECOND DIVISION   SECOND BRIGADE
SEVENTH U. S. INFANTRY
Four companies
Captain David P. Hancock   Commanding

July 2. Arrived in the morning and took position with the Brigade on the right of the Twelfth Corps. Later moved with the Brigade to the left and at 5 P. M. formed line on the right of Little Round Top advanced across Plum Run and to the crest of the rocky wooded hill in front near the Wheatfield and facing to the left occupied the stone wall on the edge of the woods. The Confederates having opened fire on the right flank and advanced through the Wheatfield in the rear the Brigade was withdrawn under a deadly fire of musketry on both flanks and on the rear and of shot and shell from the batteries and formed in line on the right of Little Round Top.

July 3. Remained in same position.

July 4. Advanced nearly a mile in support of a skirmish line of the Twelfth and Fourteenth Infantry.

Casualties   Killed 1 Officer and 11 Men   Wounded 3 Officers and 42 Men

No. 51U   Tablet on Granite Marker located—Ayres Avenue, Houck's Ridge

---

ARMY OF THE POTOMAC
FIFTH CORPS
SECOND DIVISION   SECOND BRIGADE
TENTH U. S. INFANTRY
Three Companies
Captain William Clinton   Commanding

July 2. Arrived with the Brigade in the morning and took position on the right of the Twelfth Corps. Later moved to the left and at 5 P. M. the Brigade formed line with left on north slope of Little Round Top the right extending into the woods. Advanced across Plum Run and to the crest of the rocky wooded hill in front near the Wheatfield and facing left occupied the stone wall on the edge of the woods. The Confederates having opened fire on the right flank and advanced through the Wheatfield in the rear the Brigade was withdrawn under a heavy infantry fire on both flanks and from the rear and shot and shell from the batteries and was formed in line on the right of Little Round Top.

July 3. Remained in same position.

Casualties   Killed 1 Officer and 15 Men   Wounded 5 Officers and 27 Men   Missing 3 Men

No. 52U   Tablet on Granite Marker located—Ayres Avenue, Houck's Ridge

ARMY OF THE POTOMAC
FIFTH CORPS
SECOND DIVISION   SECOND BRIGADE
ELEVENTH U. S. INFANTRY
Six Companies
Major Delancey Floyd Jones   Commanding

July 2. Arrived in the morning with the Brigade and took position on the right of the Twelfth Corps. Afterwards moved to the left and at 5 P. M. formed line on the right of Little Round Top and advanced across Plum Run and to the crest of the rocky wooded hill in front under a fire of sharpshooters on the left and faced to the left with the Wheatfield on the right and rear. The Confederates having opened fire on the right flank and advancing through the Wheatfield in the rear the Regiment with the Brigade was withdrawn under a heavy fire of musketry and artillery and formed in line at the right of Little Round Top.

July 3. Remained in same position.

Present 25 Officers and 281 men

Casualties   Killed 3 Officer and 18 Men   Wounded 7 Officers and 85 Men   Missing 9 Men

No. 53U   Tablet on Granite Marker located—Ayres Avenue, Houck's Ridge

———————————

ARMY OF THE POTOMAC
FIFTH CORPS
SECOND DIVISION   SECOND BRIGADE
SEVENTEENTH U. S. INFANTRY
Seven Companies
Lieut. Colonel J. Durell Green   Commanding

July 2. Arrived in the morning and took position with the Brigade on the right of the Twelfth Corps. Later moved to the left and at 5 P. M. formed line with the Brigade at the right of Little Round Top and advanced across Plum Run to the crest of the rocky wooded hill beyond near the Wheatfield under a severe fire from the Confederate sharpshooters on the left then facing left the Regiment with the Brigade occupied the stone wall on the edge of the woods. The Confederates having opened fire on the right and advanced in the Wheatfield in the rear the Brigade was withdrawn under a heavy fire on both flanks and from the rear and formed in line on the right of Little Round Top having been engaged about two hours.

July 3. Remained in same position.

Present 25 Officers and 235 Men

Casualties   Killed 1 Officer and 24 Men   Wounded 13 Officers and 105 Men   Missing 7 Men

No. 54U   Tablet on Granite Marker located—Ayres Avenue, Houck's Ridge

---

ARMY OF THE POTOMAC
FIFTH CORPS   SECOND DIVISION
FIRST BRIGADE
Col. Hannibal Day
3D (6 Cos.)   4th (4 Cos.)   6th (5 Cos.)
12th (8 Cos.)   14th (8 Cos.) U. S. Infantry

July 2. Moved left in front with the Division late in the day from the Baltimore Pike near Rock Creek to Little Round Top and Third Corps line. Halted on north slope of Little Round Top. Third Brigade in advance went to the support of Third Brigade First Division. The Brigade preceded by Second Brigade advanced across Plum Run Valley and on to the hill beyond and formed line in rear of Second Brigade facing the Wheatfield through which First Division Second Corps was advancing perpendicular to the line of the Brigade. Later advanced supporting Second Brigade towards left when Union forces on the right and front having been driven back by superior numbers the Brigade retired under a heavy musketry fire on its front and flank to Little Round Top and at night to the woods on the east side.

July 3. Remained in same position.

July 4. Made a reconnaissance to the front supported by Second Brigade First Division Sixth Corps forcing in the Confederate pickets and drawing the fire of artillery.

Casualties   Killed 1 Officer 45 Men   Wounded 13 Officers 305 Men Captured or Missing 18 Men   Total 382

No. 55U   Tablet on Granite Pedestal located—Ayres Avenue, Houck's Ridge

---

ARMY OF THE POTOMAC
FIFTH CORPS
SECOND DIVISION   FIRST BRIGADE
THIRD U. S. INFANTRY
Six Companies
Captain Henry W. Freedly and Captain Richard C. Lay
Commanding

July 2. Arrived in the morning and took position near the line of the Twelfth Corps. The Regiment with the Brigade moved from the right to the left of the line and at 5 P. M. advanced across Plum Run near Little Round Top and supported the Second Brigade in its advance to the crest of the rocky wooded hill beyond and facing to the left engaged the Confederates but retired under a deadly fire on the left right and rear. After the Confederates had gained a position in the Wheatfield in the rear of the Brigade and took position on east slope of Little Round Top.

July 3. Remained in same position.

July 4. The Regiment with the Brigade made a reconnaissance and developed a force of the Confederate infantry and artillery in front.

Casualties   Killed 6 Men   Wounded 4 Officers and 89 Men   Missing 1 Man

No. 56U   Tablet on Granite Marker located—Ayres Avenue, Houck's Ridge

---

ARMY OF THE POTOMAC
FIFTH CORPS
SECOND DIVISION FIRST BRIGADE
FOURTH U. S. INFANTRY
Four Companies
Captain Julius W. Adams Jr.   Commanding

July 2. Arrived in the morning and took position near the line of the Twelfth Corps. The Regiment with the Brigade moved from the right to the left of the line and at 5 P. M. advanced across Plum run near Little Round Top and supported the Second Brigade in its advance to the crest of the rocky wooded hill beyond and facing to the left engaged the Confederates but retired under a deadly fire on both flanks and from the rear after the Confederates had gained a position in the Wheatfield in the rear of the Brigade.

July 3. Remained in same position.

July 4. The Regiment with the Brigade made a reconnaissance and developed a force of the Confederate infantry and artillery in front and engaged on the skirmish line well to the front.

Casualties   Killed 10 men   Wounded 2 Officers and 28 Men

No. 57U   Tablet on Granite Marker located—Ayres Avenue, Houck's Ridge

ARMY OF THE POTOMAC
FIFTH CORPS
SECOND DIVISION   FIRST BRIGADE
SIXTH U. S. INFANTRY
Five Companies
Captain Levi C. Bootes   Commanding

July 2. Arrived in the morning and took position near the line of the Twelfth Corps. The Regiment with the Brigade moved from the right to the left of the line and at 5 P. M. advanced across Plum Run near Little Round Top and supported the Second Brigade in its advance to the crest of the rocky wooded hill beyond and facing to the left engaged the Confederates but retired under a deadly fire on both flanks and from the rear after the Confederates got possession of the Wheatfield in the rear of the Brigade and took position on Little Round Top.

July 3. Remained in same position.

July 4. The Regiment with the Brigade made a reconnaissance and developed a force of the Confederate infantry and artillery in front.

Casualties   Killed 4 Men   Wounded 1 Officer and 39 Men

No. 58U   Tablet on Granite Pedestal located—Ayres Avenue, Houck's Ridge

---

ARMY OF THE POTOMAC
FIFTH CORPS
SECOND DIVISION   FIRST BRIGADE
TWELFTH U. S. INFANTRY
Eight Companies
Captain Thomas S. Dunn   Commanding

July 2. Arrived in the morning and took position with the Brigade and Division near the Twelfth Corps on the right. Moved with the Division from the right to the left of the line and at 5 P. M. with the Brigade moved across Plum Run near Little Round Top and supported the Second Brigade in its advance to the crest of the rocky wooded hill in front and facing left engaged the Confederates but retired under a heavy fire on both flanks and from the rear after the Confederates had obtained possession of the Wheatfield in the rear of the Brigade and went into position on Little Round Top.

July 3. Remained in same position.

July 4. Regiment with the 14th supported the 3D 4th and 6th U. S. Infantry in a reconnaissance and developed a force of Confederate infantry and artillery in front.

Casualties Killed 1 Officer and 7 Men Wounded 4 Officers and 87 Men
Missing 13 Men

No. 59U   Tablet on Granite Marker located—Ayres Avenue, Houck's Ridge

---

ARMY OF THE POTOMAC
FIFTH CORPS
SECOND DIVISION   FIRST BRIGADE
FOURTEENTH U. S. INFANTRY
Eight Companies
Captain Crotius R. Giddings   Commanding

July 2. Arrived in the morning and took position with the Brigade and Division near the Twelfth Corps on the right. Moved with the Division from
the right to the left of the line and at 5 P. M. with the Brigade moved
across Plum Run near Little Round Top and supported the Second Brigade in its advance to the crest of the rocky wooded hill beyond and
facing left engaged the Confederates but retired under heavy fire on
both flanks and from the rear after the Confederates had possession of
the Wheatfield in the rear of the Brigade and went into position on Little
Round Top.

July 3. Remained in same position.

July 4. The Regiment with the 12th supported the 3D 4th and 6th U. S.
Infantry in a reconnaissance and developed a force of the Confederate
infantry and artillery in front.

Casualties   Killed 16 Men   Wounded 2 Officers and 106 Men   Missing
4 Men

No. 60U   Tablet on Granite Marker located—Ayres Avenue, Houck's Ridge

---

ARMY OF THE POTOMAC
SECOND CORPS
SECOND DIVISION
Brig. General John Gibbon   Brig. General William Harrow

First Brigade	Brig. Gen. Wm. Harrow
	Col. Francis E. Heath
Second Brigade	Brig. Gen. A. S. Webb
Third Brigade	Col. N. J. Hall
	One Co. Mass. Sharpshooters

July 2. Arrived between 6 and 7 A. M. and went into position on line between Cemetery Hill and Round Top. Third Division on right and First Division on left. Second Brigade constituting the right Third Brigade the left and First Brigade in reserve. Sharp skirmishing continued through the day and artillery fire at intervals until near sunset when the Third Corps having been driven back Wright's Georgia Brigade furiously attacked the Division and was repulsed with loss including many prisoners the Twelfth Corps coming to the support of the left.

July 3. Artillery firing until 9 A. M. and sharp skirmishing during the day. At 1 P. M. Confederates concentrated the fire of over 100 guns on the Second and Third Divisions and after two hours of uninterrupted firing charged with a force of over 15,000 infantry which was repulsed with great loss of life prisoners and flags. The Division remained in position with no further engagement than skirmish firing.

Casualties including Division Staff and attached troops   Killed 25 Officers 319 Men   Wounded 105 Officers 1097 Men   Captured or Missing 6 Officers 95 Men   Total 1647

No. 61U   Tablet on Granite Marker located—Hancock Avenue

ARMY OF THE POTOMAC
SECOND CORPS   SECOND DIVISION
FIRST BRIGADE
Brig. Gen. William Harrow
Col. Francis E. Heath
19th Maine   15th Massachusetts
1st Minnesota   82D New York Infantry

July 2. Early in the morning took position in the rear of Second and Third Brigades. The 15th Mass. and 82D New York were advanced to the Emmitsburg Road on the right of Cordori House to support Third Corps the other two regiments were moved to the left on a line with the Third Brigade. The Third Corps having been forced back the advanced regiments were compelled to retire to the main line by Brig. Gen. Wright's Brigade which captured several pieces of artillery but supports coming quickly to the Union line they forced the Confederates back across the Emmitsburg Road with heavy loss and retook the captured artillery. Col. C. H. Ward 15th Mass. and Col. J. J. Huston 82D New York were mortally wounded.

July 3. At 1 P. M. a terrific cannonade was opened along the Confederate line in front which continued for about two hours followed by a charge of over 15,000 infantry its right striking Second and Third Brigades. This Brigade moved at once to the right and assisted the other two Brigades in repelling the assault and capturing a large number of prisoners and several flags.

Casualties　Killed 10 Officers 137 Men　Wounded 46 Officers 527 Men Captured or Missing 1 Officer 47 Men　Total 768

No. 62U　Tablet on Granite Pedestal located—Hancock Avenue

ARMY OF THE POTOMAC
SECOND CORPS　SECOND DIVISION
SECOND BRIGADE
Brig. Gen. Alexander S. Webb
69th　71st　72D　106th Penna. Infantry

July 2. The 69th Penna. took position along the advanced line of the stone wall at the left of the Angle. The other regiments of the Brigade in the rear of the ridge. During the day two companies of the 71st and two of the 106th Penna. were sharply engaged on the skirmish line. About sunset Brig. Gen. Wright's Brigade charged across the Emmitsburg Road to the Union line past the guns of Battery B 1st Rhode Island but was soon repulsed with the loss of many prisoners and forced back beyond the Emmitsburg Road. All the guns temporarily lost were retaken. At night the 71st and 106th Penna. except two companies on skirmish line were sent to the support of the Eleventh Corps on East Cemetery Hill. The former returned at midnight the latter remained.

July 3. At 3 P. M. after a heavy cannonading for two hours Major Gen. Pickett's Division of about 5,000 men charged the line held by this and the Third Brigade breaking through the line at the Angle. Reinforcements coming up quickly the charge was repulsed with great loss. Nearly 1,000 prisoners and six battle flags were reported captured by the Brigade.

Casualties　Killed 9 Officers 105 Men　Wounded 27 Officers 311 men Captured or Missing 5 Officers 34 Men　Total 491

No. 63U　Tablet on Granite Pedestal located—Hancock Avenue, the Angle

---

ARMY OF THE POTOMAC
SECOND CORPS　SECOND DIVISION
THIRD BRIGADE
Col. Norman J. Hall

19th   20th Massachusetts   7th Michigan
42D   59th (4 Cos.) New York Infantry

July 2. Took position on the line at the left of Second Brigade and of the copse of trees. The 19th Mass. and 42D New York were late in the day advanced to support Second Division Third Corps but retired on Second Division being forced back. The Brigade was attacked by Brig. Gen. Wright's Brigade which overrun Battery A 1st Rhode Island then in advance but was repulsed with heavy loss and forced beyond the Emmitsburg Road.

July 3. Remained in position. At 3 P. M. Longstreet's assault was made after a cannonade of two hours. The Brigade and the Second Brigade received the charge of Major Gen. Pickett's Division which was repulsed with great loss in killed wounded prisoners and flags. In this engagement the First Brigade and the other troops were rushed to support of the two Brigades engaged and contributed to the victory. The Brigade remained in its position until the close of the battle.

Casualties   Killed 6 Officers 75 Men   Wounded 29 Officers 253 Men
Captured or Missing 14 Men   Total 377

No. 64U   Tablet on Granite Pedestal located—Hancock Avenue

ARMY OF THE POTOMAC
SECOND CORPS
THIRD DIVISION
Brig. General Alexander Hays

First Brigade   Col. S. S. Carroll
Second Brigade   Col. Thos. A Smyth
                       Lieut. Col. Francis E. Pierce
Third Brigade   Col. Geo. L. Willard
                       Col. Eliakim Sherrill
                       Lieut. Col. Jas. M. Bull

July 2. About 8 A. M. took position on Cemetery Ridge relieving Second Division First Corps and at noon advanced to the stone wall in front. Late in the day the Third Brigade went to the support of the Third Corps on the left and became engaged with Barksdale's Mississippi Brigade capturing many prisoners. At dark Col. Carroll with the 4th Ohio 7th West Virginia and 14th Indiana of First Brigade went to support of Eleventh Corps on East Cemetery Hill and remained until the close of the battle.

July 3. The Bliss Barn in front occupied by sharpshooters was burned by order of Gen. A. Hays. At 1 P. M. a heavy artillery fire from the Confederate line was concentrated on the positions of Second and Third Divisions of the Corps for two hours followed by a charge of more than 15,000 infantry which was repulsed with loss the Division capturing about 1500 prisoners and 15 stand of colors. The muskets found on the field after the charge numbered about 3500.

July 4. Sharp skirmishing in front all day.

Casualties   Killed 20 Officers 218 Men   Wounded 75 Officers 912 Men Captured or Missing 1 Officer 65 Men   Total 1291

No. 65U   Tablet on Granite Marker located—North Hancock Avenue

---

ARMY OF THE POTOMAC
SECOND CORPS   THIRD DIVISION
THIRD BRIGADE
Col. George L. Willard
Col. Eliakim Sherrill
Lieut. Col. James M. Bull
39th (4 Cos.)   111th   126th New York Infantry

July 2. Took position in the morning along Cemetery Ridge at right of the Angle. Near sunset went to the left to support Third Corps. Charged Brig. Gen. Barksdale's Brigade in the wooded swale at the head of Plum Run forcing it back and capturing many prisoners. The 39th New York recaptured Battery I 5th U. S. from the 21st Miss. Col. Willard was killed and Brig. Gen. Barksdale mortally wounded. At dark the Brigade returned and was held in reserve.

July 3. Engaged on the skirmish line with much loss. At 3 P. M. after a terrific cannonade of two hours the Brigade was moved up to the line of the Second Brigade and assisted in repulsing Longstreet's assault in which Col. Sherrill was mortally wounded. A large detail from the Brigade under Capt. Armstrong of the 125th New York and the 8th Ohio on the skirmish line withdrew to the right and poured in a deadly fire upon the left of the assaulting lines and then charging captured prisoners and flags.

Casualties   Killed 11 Officers 128 Men   Wounded 26 Officers 516 Men Captured or Missing 33 Men   Total 714

No. 66U   Tablet on Granite Pedestal located—North Hancock Avenue

ARMY OF THE POTOMAC
FIFTH CORPS
THIRD DIVISION
Brig. General Samuel W. Crawford

First Brigade   William McCandless
Third Brigade   Col. Joseph W. Fisher

July 2. Moved to Little Round Top late in the day and went into position on the right of the Wheatfield Road. On the retreat of the troops from the Wheatfield in front after sunset the First Brigade was advanced against the pursuing forces and drove them across Plum Run marsh and beyond the stone wall and into the Wheatfield. The Third Brigade was sent to the left to take possession of Round Top.

July 3. The First Brigade remained in position until about 5 P. M. and then advanced across the Wheatfield and through the woods beyond and on the left capturing many prisoners. The Confederates retired to the crest of the ridge they originally formed on. These positions were held until the close of the battle.

Casualties   Killed 3 Officers 23 Men   Wounded 17 Officers 164 Men Captured or Missing 3 Men   Total 210

No. 67U   Tablet on Granite Marker located—Crawford Avenue

ARMY OF THE POTOMAC
FIFTH CORPS   THIRD DIVISION
FIRST BRIGADE
Col. William McCandless
30th   31st   42D Pennsylvania Infantry
(1st (9 Cos.) 2D 6th 13th Reserves)

July 2. Moved with the Division from the Baltimore Pike near Rock Creek late in the day to Little Round Top north of the Wheatfield Road. After sunset formed line to cover the retiring of First and Second Brigades Second Division and supported by Third Brigade Third Division Sixth Corps charged the advancing Confederates and forced them down the Hill and across into the Wheatfield. The Brigade remained at a stone wall in rear of the Wheatfield. Col. C. F. Taylor commanding 13th Penna. Reserves fell in the advance.

July 3. Advanced through the Wheatfield into the woods beyond supported by Third Brigade Third Division Sixth Corps and changing front swept southward through the woods west and south of the Wheatfield encountering a portion of Brig. Gen. Benning's Brigade and capturing about 200 prisoners and the colors of 15th Georgia. The Confederates retired to the crest of the ridge from which they advanced the previous day. In this movement one 10 pounder Parrott was recovered and about 3,000 small arms were captured from the field.

Casualties   Killed 2 Officers 18 Men   Wounded 14 Officers 118 Men Captured or Missing 3 Men   Total 155

No. 68U   Tablet on Granite Pedestal located—Ayres Avenue

ARMY OF THE POTOMAC
FIFTH CORPS   THIRD DIVISION
THIRD BRIGADE
Col. Joseph W. Fisher
34th   38th   39th   40th Penna. Infantry
(5th   9th   10th   11th   12th   (9 Cos.) Reserves)

July 2. Moved with the Division from the Baltimore Pike near Rock Creek to Little Round Top and at dusk took position in rear of Third Brigade First Division. The 5th and 12th Penna. Reserves and 20th Maine of the Third Brigade First Division took possession of the north slope of Round Top after a slight resistance and constructed a stone wall from base to summit for defense. This position was held until the close of the battle.

Casualties   Killed 1 Officer 5 Men   Wounded 3 Officers 46 Men   Total 55

No. 69U   Tablet on Granite Pedestal located—Sykes Avenue

ARMY OF THE POTOMAC
SIXTH CORPS
Major General John Sedgwick

First Division   Brigadier General Horatio G. Wright
Second Division   Brigadier General Albion P. Howe
Third Division   Major General John Newton
                        Brigadier General Frank Wheaton
Artillery Brigade   Colonel Charles H. Tompkins

The Corps being in reserve its operations were mostly by Brigades independent of each other and of different portions of the field.

July 2. Arrived in the afternoon after a march of over 30 miles. Nevin's Brigade Wheaton's Division Bartlett's Brigade Wright's Division went into action about sunset on the left centre between the divisions of 5th Corps and assisted in repulsing the Confederate assault. Russell's and Torbert's Brigades Wright's Division was sent to the extreme left of the line east of Round Top. Shaler's Brigade Wheaton's Division was held in reserve near the left centre.

July 3. The brigades of the Corps were put into position where needed at different points on the line from right to left until the close of the battle.

Casualties   Killed 2 Officers 25 Men   Wounded 14 Officers 171 Men
Captured or Missing 30 Men   Total 242 Men

No. 70U   Tablet on Granite Marker located—Sedgwick Avenue

ARMY OF THE POTOMAC
SIXTH CORPS
THIRD DIVISION
Major General John Newton Brig. General Frank Wheaton

First Brigade   Gen. Alex Shaler
Second Brigade   Col. Henry L. Eustis
Third Brigade   Col. David J. Nevin

July 2. Arrived about 2 P. M. and late in the day marched toward the north slope of Little Round Top. Third Brigade with Second Brigade First Division went into action at sunset on the right of First Brigade Third Division Fifth Corps on the northwest slope of Little Round Top and the combined force drove the advancing Confederates back down the slope across Plum Run marsh and a hundred yards up the slope beyond. First and Second Brigades were in reserve on the northeast slope of Little Round Top.

July 3. First Brigade was ordered to the left and at 8 A. M. to the support of Second Division Twelfth Corps on the right. Second Brigade was sent to the right centre to report to Gen. Newton. The Third Brigade remained under the command of Gen. Bartlett supporting First Brigade Third Division Fifth Corps in the vicinity of the Wheatfield.

Casualties   Killed 1 Officer 19 Men   Wounded 12 Officers 136 Men
Captured or Missing 28 Men   Total 196

No. 71U   Tablet on Granite Marker located—Sedgwick Avenue

ARMY OF THE POTOMAC
SIXTH CORPS   THIRD DIVISION
THIRD BRIGADE
Brig. Gen. Frank Wheaton
Col. David J. Nevin
62D New York   93D   98th   102D   139th Penna. Infantry

July 2. Arrived about 2 P. M. and late in the day moved to the north slope of Little Round Top. On the advance of Brig. Gen. Wofford's Brigade and others forcing First and Second Brigades Second Division Fifth Corps across Plum Run and up the west base of Little Round Top the Brigade with First Brigade Third Division Fifth Corps on the left countercharged forcing the Confederates down the hill and across Plum Run and marsh and 100 yards up the slope beyond and remained during the night having recaptured two Napoleon guns.

July 3. Assigned to the command of Brig. Gen. J. J. Bartlett in the morning and remained in the advanced position of the previous night. Late in the day supported First Brigade Third Division Fifth Corps at an interval of 200 yards in advance through the Wheatfield and the woods on the south encountering a detachment of Brig. Gen. Benning's Brigade and the combined forces captured about 200 prisoners of that Brigade and the colors of the 15th Georgia. At dark the line was recalled to a position of a few hundred yards in advance of the original line. The Brigade sustained some loss in this movement. One Napoleon and three caissons belonging to 9th Mass. Battery recaptured.

Casualties   Killed 2 Men   Wounded 7 Officers 44 Men   Total 53

No. 72U   Tablet on Granite Pedestal located—field north of Valley of Death

———

ARMY OF THE POTOMAC
SIXTH CORPS
FIRST DIVISION
Brig. General Horatio G. Wright

First Brigade   Brig. Gen. Alfred T. A. Torbert
Second Brigade   Brig. Gen. Joseph J. Bartlett
Third Brigade   Brig. Gen. David A. Russell

July 2. Arrived about 4 P. M. and 6 P. M. the Second Brigade with the Third Division moved into position. First and Third Brigades were massed and held in reserve.

July 3. The First Brigade placed in line on left centre subject to orders of Gen. Newton commanding First Corps on the right. Third Brigade was sent to the extreme left to Gen. Wright in command there. At 5 P. M. Gen. Wright with his troops moved to the support of Fifth Corps then threatened. The Brigades of the Division then remained in same position during the day and succeeding night.

July 4. The Third Brigade moved to the left of Fifth Corps and occupied the slope of Round Top.

Casualties   Killed 1 Man   Wounded 17 Men   Total 18

No. 73U   Tablet on Granite Marker located—South Sedgwick Avenue

━━━━━━━━━

ARMY OF THE POTOMAC
SIXTH CORPS   FIRST DIVISION
SECOND BRIGADE
Brig. Gen. Joseph J. Bartlett
5th Maine   121st New York
95th   96th Pennsylvania Infantry

July 2. The Brigade arrived late in the day and was formed in two lines to support Fifth Corps of which the troops in front were giving ground. The Third Brigade Third Division was formed on the left and then advanced to the front. Remained in same position during the night. The 121st New York was detached from the Brigade on its arrival and supported Battery L 1st Ohio until the close of the battle.

July 3. The Third Brigade Third Division was assigned to Brig. Gen. Bartlett's command which was in an advanced position. Late in the day the Third Brigade Third Division in a second line at an interval of 200 yards supported First Brigade Third Division Fifth Corps in an advance through the Wheatfield and the woods on the south but soon after being engaged the Third Brigade Third Division advanced to the front and the combined forces captured about 200 prisoners of Brig. Gen. Benning's Brigade and the colors of the 15th Georgia. At dark the Brigade was recalled to a line a few hundred yards in advance of the original position.

Casualties   Killed 1 Man   Wounded 4 Men   Total 5

No. 74U   Tablet on Granite Pedestal located—Wheatfield Road, north of the Valley of Death

━━━━━━━━━

ARMY OF THE POTOMAC
FIRST CORPS
THIRD DIVISION
Brig. Gen. Thos. A. Rowley   Major Gen. Abner Doubleday

July 2. At sunset sent to support of the Third Corps on its right at Emmitsburg Road and captured 80 prisoners and recaptured 4 guns.

No. 10U   Tablet on Granite Marker located—South Reynolds Avenue

Note: The complete inscription on this tablet is presented in Part II—Day One—
     Page 35.

———

ARMY OF THE POTOMAC
FIRST CORPS   THIRD DIVISION
THIRD BRIGADE
Brig. Gen. George J. Stannard
Col. Francis V. Randall
12th   13th   14th   15th   16th Vermont Infantry
The 12th and 15th were guarding Corps Trains

July 1. Arrived at dusk and took position on right of Third Corps.

July 2. Joined the Corps and went into position at the left and rear of the Cemetery. Just before dusk a detachment advanced to the Emmitsburg Road and captured about 80 prisoners and recovered 4 abandoned Union guns.

July 3. In position on left of Second Division Second Corps at the time of Longstreet's assault. The 13th and 16th advanced against Major Gen. Pickett's Division changed front forward and attacked its right throwing it into confusion and capturing many prisoners. The 16th and part of 14th then went to the left and attacked the advancing Brigades of Brig. Gen. Wilcox and Perry (Col. Lang) and captured three flags and many prisoners.

Casualties   Killed 1 Officer 44 Men   Wounded 12 Officers 262 men
Captured or Missing 32 Men   Total 351

No. 75U   Tablet on Granite Pedestal located—Hancock Avenue

———

ARMY OF THE POTOMAC
SIXTH CORPS   FIRST DIVISION
FIRST BRIGADE
Brig. Gen. Alfred T. A. Torbert
1st   2D   15th New Jersey Infantry

July 2. Arrived at 4 P. M. from Manchester Md. A distance by the route taken of about 35 miles having halted an hour only. After sunset moved to the east slope of the north side of Little Round Top and arriving there at dark was held in reserve.

July 3. Moved to a position southeast of the Weikert House and remained until the close of the battle. Not engaged except on the skirmish line.

Casualties Wounded 11 Men

No. 76U   Tablet on Granite Pedestal located—Sedgwick Avenue

ARMY OF THE POTOMAC
SIXTH CORPS   FIRST DIVISION
THIRD BRIGADE
Brig. Gen. David A. Russell
6th Maine   49th (4 Cos.)   119th Pennsylvania
5th Wisconsin Infantry

July 2. Arrived about 4 P. M. from Manchester Md. and moved to the east slope of the northern side of Little Round Top. Arriving at dark and held in reserve until morning.

July 3. Moved to the extreme left and on the east slope of Round Top and remained until late in the afternoon then went into position on the left centre in support of Fifth Corps. Not engaged.

Casualties Wounded 2 Men

No. 77U   Tablet on Granite Pedestal located—Howe Avenue

ARMY OF THE POTOMAC
SIXTH CORPS   SECOND DIVISION
SECOND BRIGADE
Col. Lewis A. Grant
2D   3D   4th   5th   6th Vermont Infantry

July 2. Arrived about 5 P. M. after a march of 33 miles from Manchester Md. Moved to the left and at dark to the extreme left with one Regiment the 5th Vermont on picket.

July 3. The Brigade advanced a short distance and took position with its right on east slope of Round Top its left on the Taneytown Road and remained until the close of the battle under no fire except that from artillery.

Casualties   Wounded 1 Man

No. 78U   Tablet on Granite Pedestal located—Wright Avenue

———

ARMY OF THE POTOMAC
SIXTH CORPS   THIRD DIVISION
SECOND BRIGADE
Col. Henry L. Eustis
7th   10th   37th Massachusetts
2D Rhode Island Infantry

July 2. Arrived about 2 P. M. from Manchester Md. and late in the day moved to the northeast slope of Little Round Top and held in reserve. Bivouacked for the night with First Brigade in the rear.

July 3. Moved to the right centre and reported to Major Gen. J. Newton and was held in reserve during the battle. Not engaged but subject to artillery fire.

Casualties   Killed 3 Men   Wounded 2 Officers 39 Men   Captured or Missing 25 Men   Total 69

No. 79U   Tablet on Granite Pedestal located—South Sedgwick Avenue

———

ARMY OF THE POTOMAC
TWELFTH CORPS
Major General Henry J. Slocum
Brigadier General Alpheus S. Williams

First Division   Brigadier General Alpheus S. Williams
                        Brigadier General Thomas H. Ruger
Second Division   Brigadier General John W. Geary
Artillery Brigade   Lieutenant Edward D. Muhlenberg
Provost Guard   Tenth Maine (Four Companies)

July 1. Marched from near Littlestown to Two Taverns by the afternoon. Hearing the 1st and 11th Corps were engaged at Gettysburg the Corps advanced on the Baltimore Pike. Williams's Division to a position east of Rock Creek Geary's Division to the left of Union line extending to the summit of Little Round Top.

July 2. In the morning the Corps took position on the right of 1st Corps on a line extending from the top of Culp's Hill southeasterly across the low meadow into McAllister's woods. Later in the day the Corps except Green's Brigade was withdrawn to support the left of the Army. Johnson's Confederate Division at night advanced under cover of darkness and took possession of the works on the Corps Line on right of Green's Brigade. About midnight the Corps returned and finding Johnson's Division in possession of the works formed line in front of that Division.

July 3. Before 1 A. M. the artillery of the Corps and Rigby's Maryland Battery from Reserve Artillery in all 26 guns were so placed as to command the line occupied by Johnson's Division and at daylight opened fire under cover of which the infantry was advanced and attacked the Confederate position and after a contest lasting seven hours recaptured the works. Many prisoners and 5,000 small arms were captured. In the afternoon the Corps was in readiness to move.

July 4. Gen. Slocum in the morning advanced with a detachment of Ruger's Division and a battery and found that the Confederates in front had retired.

Casualties   Killed 18 Officers 186 Men   Wounded 43 Officers 769 Men Captured or Missing 2 Officers 64 Men   Total 1082

No. 80U   Tablet on Granite Marker located—Slocum Avenue, south slope of Culp's Hill

---

ARMY OF THE POTOMAC
TWELFTH CORPS
FIRST DIVISION
Brig. General Alpheus S. Williams   Brig. General Thos. H. Ruger

First Brigade   Col. Archibald L. McDougall
Second Brigade   Brig. Gen. Henry H. Lockwood
Third Brigade   Brig. Gen. Thos. H. Ruger
                         Col. Silas Colgrove

July 1. Approaching Rock Creek on the Baltimore Pike the Division moved on a cross road to occupy Wolf Hill but retired at sunset and took position east of Rock Creek for the night. The First and Sixth Corps having been included in Gen. Slocum's command Gen. Williams assumed command of the Corps. Gen. Ruger of the First Division and Col. S. Colgrove of the Third Brigade.

July 2. Brig. Gen. Lockwood's Brigade joined the Corps early in the morning not having been assigned to a division was subject to the direct orders of the Corps Commander until assigned July 5th to First Division.

The Division at 8 A. M. crossed Rock Creek and formed on the right of Second Division its left on Culp's Hill the right in McAllister's Woods. Breastworks were constructed along the line. Late in the day the Division moved to support Third Corps and Johnson's Confederate Division advanced and occupied the vacant works.

July 3. At daylight attacked the Confederate Infantry and was hotly engaged with charges and countercharges at different points until 10:30 A. M. when the Confederate forces retired.

July 4. Early in the morning Gen. Slocum with a detachment of infantry and a battery made a reconnaissance in front to Gettysburg without opposition.

Casualties   Killed 6 Officers 90 Men   Wounded 27 Officers 379 Men
Captured or Missing 1 Officer 30 Men   Total 533

No. 81U   Tablet on Granite Marker located—North Slocum Avenue

———————

ARMY OF THE POTOMAC
TWELFTH CORPS   FIRST DIVISION
SECOND BRIGADE
Brig. Gen. Henry H. Lockwood
1st Maryland Potomac Home Brigade
1st Maryland Eastern Shore
150th New York Infantry

July 2. The 1st Maryland Potomac Home Brigade and 150th New York arrived at 8 A. M. and went into position between Rock Creek and the Baltimore Pike on right of Division. Brig. Gen. Lockwood receiving orders direct from the General Commanding Corps. Late in the day the Brigade went with Division to support Third Corps line and advanced over the ground from which the Corps had previously been forced. The 150th New York drew off 3 abandoned guns of 9th Mass. Battery and returned about midnight.

July 3. Took part in the recapture of works which Major General Johnson's Division took possession of during the absence of Division the previous night. At about 8 A. M. 1st Maryland Eastern Shore arrived and joined Brigade. Ordered in the afternoon to Second Corps line near Cemetery to render support where needed. The Brigade was not assigned to the Division until July 5th.

Casualties   Killed 3 Officers 32 Men   Wounded 3 Officers 118 Men
Captured or Missing 18 Men   Total 174

No. 82U   Tablet on Granite Pedestal located—South Slocum Avenue

───────────

ARMY OF THE POTOMAC
TWELFTH CORPS   FIRST DIVISION
FIRST BRIGADE
Col. Archibald L. McDougall
5th   20th Connecticut   3D Maryland
123D   145th New York   46th Penna. Infantry

July 1. Marched from Littlestown and when within two miles of Gettysburg advanced on Wolf Hill then occupied by a Confederate force. Retired and bivouacked until morning.

July 2. Crossed Rock Creek in the morning and formed in two lines on Culp's Hill to the right of Second Division. The rear line behind a stone wall the front line forty yards in front where breastworks were immediately constructed. Late in the day went to support of Third Corps line and after dark returned and found the works and woods in rear in possession of Major Gen. Johnson's Confederate Division.

July 3. At daylight the Brigade with the artillery and infantry of the Corps attacked Major Gen. Johnson's Division which had been reinforced from Major Gen. Early's and Major Gen. Rodes's Divisions and at 10.30 A. M. recaptured the works after a fierce contest. In the afternoon sent to the support of Second Corps.

July 4. The 123D New York 5th Conn. and 46th Penna. with the regiments of Third Brigade and a battery made a reconnaissance in the morning in front and to the town of Gettysburg under Col. S. Colgrove and Major Gen. H. W. Slocum and found no Confederate forces.

Casualties   Killed 1 Officer 11 Men   Wounded 4 Officers 56 Men   Captured or Missing 1 Officer 7 Men   Total 80

No. 83U   Tablet on Granite Pedestal located—South Slocum Avenue

───────────

ARMY OF THE POTOMAC
TWELFTH CORPS   FIRST DIVISION
THIRD BRIGADE
Brig. Gen. Thomas H. Ruger
Col. Silas Colgrove
27th Indiana   2D Mass.   13th New Jersey
107th New York   3d Wisconsin Infantry

July 1. Arrived with the Division and bivouacked for the night east of rock Creek.

July 2. After sharp skirmishing in front crossed Rock Creek and went into position. The left on Culp's Hill the right in McAllister's Woods a swale between. Breastworks were constructed. At sunset went to support of the left of the Army and returned and found the works on left of swale occupied by Confederates. Those on the right were unoccupied and immediately re-possessed.

July 3. The 2D Mass. and 27th Indiana in the morning charged across the open swale to get possession of a stone wall and woods on the left but were repulsed with great loss the 27th Indiana falling back in a direct line the 2D Mass. towards the left. A Confederate counter-charge was made across the swale but receiving a front and enfilading fire it was quickly repulsed and the Confederate force left the works and retired across Rock Creek.

July 4. The Brigade with a battery and three regiments of First Brigade made a reconnaissance in front and around through the town the Confederate forces having withdrawn to Seminary Hill.

Casualties   Killed 2 Officers 47 Men   Wounded 20 Officers 205 Men Captured or Missing 5 Men   Total 279

No. 84U   Tablet on Granite Pedestal located—South Slocum Avenue

---

ARMY OF THE POTOMAC
TWELFTH CORPS
SECOND DIVISION
Brig. General John W. Geary

First Brigade   Col. Charles Candy

Second Brigade   Col. Geo. A. Cobham Jr.
                               Brig. Thos. L. Kane

Third Brigade   Brig. Gen. Geo. S. Greene

July 1. Arrived on the Baltimore Pike and went into position about 5 P. M. the First and Third Brigades on the line from Cemetery Ridge to Little Round Top Second Brigade on the left of Baltimore Pike.

July 2. In the morning the First and Third Brigades took position on the right of First Corps on Culp's Hill connecting with First Division on the right. Breastworks were thrown up along the entire front. At 7 P. M. the First and Third Brigades on the Baltimore Pike moved off intending to support

Third Corps. Brig. Gen. Greene extended the Third Brigade over the line of the Second Brigade refusing his right. Being reinforced by about 750 men from the left he held his position against the attacks of Johnson's Confederate Division.

July 3. At 3 A. M. an attack by infantry and artillery was made on Johnson's Division and after a contest of seven hours the Confederate forces were driven from their position losing heavily in killed wounded and prisoners also three battle-flags and over 5,000 small arms.

Casualties   Killed 12 Officers 96 Men   Wounded 16 Officers 381 Men Captured or Missing 1 Officer 34 Men   Total 540

No. 85U   Tablet on Granite Marker located—South Slocum Avenue

Note: The inscription on this tablet is in error. The First and Second Brigades moved on July 2 to support the Third Corps rather than the First and Third as described.

ARMY OF THE POTOMAC
TWELFTH CORPS   SECOND DIVISION
THIRD BRIGADE
Brig. Gen. George S. Greene
60th   78th   102D   137th   149th New York Infantry

July 1. Arrived about 5 P. M. and took position on the left of the First Corps on Cemetery ridge.

July 2. At 6 A. M. took position on Culp's Hill on the right of the First Corps with Second Brigade on right. Breastworks were constructed. At 6.30 P. M. the First and Second Brigades were ordered to follow the First Division to support the left of the Army leaving the Brigade to occupy the entire Corps line. The 137th New York was moved into the position of the Second Brigade when the line was attacked by Major Gen. Johnson's Division which made four distinct charges and at 8 P. M. occupied the works that the First Division had vacated but were successfully repulsed from the line held by the Brigade the 137th New York having changed front to face the attack. The Brigade was reinforced by about 750 men from the First and Eleventh Corps.

July 3. At daylight Major Gen. Johnson having been reinforced advanced and a fierce engagement ensued for seven hours when after suffering great losses he was forced back from the entire line.

Casualties   Killed 6 Officers 61 Men   Wounded 10 Officers 202 Men Captured or Missing 1 Officer 23 Men   Total 303

No. 86U   Tablet on Granite Pedestal located—North Slocum Avenue

━━━━━━━━━━

ARMY OF THE POTOMAC
TWELFTH CORPS
SECOND BRIGADE
Col. George A. Cobham Jr.
Brig. Gen. Thomas L. Kane
29th   109th   111th Pennsylvania Infantry

July 1 Arrived late in the afternoon and took position in support of a section of Battery K 5th U. S. on the left of the Baltimore Pike.

July 2. In the morning took position on Culp's Hill connecting with the right of Third Brigade and constructed breastworks. Near sunset moved out on Baltimore Pike and returned at dusk and found the breastworks in possession of Major Gen. Johnson's Division. Entered the woods in rear of Third Brigade and took position perpendicular to and nearly at right angles with it.

July 3. At 3.30 A. M. the artillery opened fire over the Brigade and Major Gen. Johnson's Division advanced and attacked in force exposing its line in front and enfilading fires from infantry and to a destructive fire for seven hours with great loss. Brig. Gen. Steuart's Brigade was immediately in front. No further firing except by skirmishers and sharpshooters.

Casualties   Killed 2 Officers 21 Men   Wounded 1 Officer 65 Men   Captured or Missing 9 Men   Total 98

No. 87U   Tablet on Granite Pedestal located—North Slocum Avenue

Note: The parent division of this brigade—Second Division—is not inscribed on the tablet.

━━━━━━━━━━

ARMY OF THE POTOMAC
TWELFTH CORPS SECOND DIVISION
FIRST BRIGADE
Col. Charles Candy
5th   7th   66th Ohio
28th   147th Pennsylvania Infantry

July 1. Arrived at 5 P. M. and took position on the left of Third Brigade between the First Corps and the Round Tops. The 5th Ohio and 147th Penna. occupied Little Round Top during the night as skirmishers.

July 2. Moved to Culp's Hill in the morning and took position as a reserve in rear of Third Brigade. At 7 P. M. moved to the rear on Baltimore Pike across Rock Creek. Returned at midnight and formed on the right of Third Brigade perpendicular to its line.

July 3. At daylight the artillery opened on the Confederate line. The 147th Penna. advanced and captured a stone wall. The 5th Ohio held its position on the right of the Brigade under a heavy fire. The other regiments were in reserve and at intervals relieved the regiments of Second and Third Brigades. The 66th Ohio advanced beyond the breastworks and poured an enfilading fire on the Confederates occupying the works on the right. At 10.30 A. M. Major Gen. Johnson's forces were forced from the works. Skirmishing continued all day.

Casualties   Killed 4 Officers 14 Men   Wounded 5 Officers 114 Men Captured or Missing 2 Men   Total 139

No. 88U   Tablet on Granite Pedestal located—North Slocum Avenue

---

ARMY OF THE POTOMAC
FIRST CORPS   FIRST DIVISION
FIRST BRIGADE
Brig. Gen. Solomon Meredith
Col. William W. Robinson

July 2. Repulsed without loss a sharp attack at right. About sunset the 6th Wisconsin went to the support of the Third Brigade Second Division Twelfth Corps and assisted in repelling attacks during the night.

No. 8U   Tablet on Granite Pedestal located—Meredith Avenue

Note: The complete inscription for this tablet is presented in Part II—First Day Battle—Pages 33–34.

ARMY OF THE POTOMAC
FIRST CORPS   FIRST DIVISION
SECOND BRIGADE
Brig. Gen. Lysander Cutler

July 2. At night the 84th and 147th New York went to the support of Third Brigade Second Division Twelfth Corps and was actively engaged remaining through the night.

No. 9U   Tablet on Granite Pedestal located—North Reynolds Avenue

Note: The complete inscription on this tablet is presented in Part II—First Day Battle—Page 34.

ARMY OF THE POTOMAC
ELEVENTH CORPS
FIRST DIVISION
Brig. Gen. Francis C. Barlow   Brig. Gen. Adelbert Ames

July 2. About 8 P. M. was attacked by Hoke's and Hays's Brigades which swept up among the batteries at the top. The attack was repulsed about 9.30 P. M. with the aid of First Brigade Third Division Corps.

No. 20U   Tablet on Granite Marker located—East Howard Avenue, Barlow Knoll

Note: The complete inscription on this tablet is presented in Part II—First Day Battle—Pages 41–42.

ARMY OF THE POTOMAC
ELEVENTH CORPS   FIRST DIVISION
SECOND BRIGADE
Brig. Gen. Adelbert Ames
Col. Andrew L. Harris

July 2. Remained under a hot sharpshooters fire from houses in town until sunset when Brig. Gen. Hays's Brigade charged penetrating the line left open by the removal of 17th Conn. to the right shortly before and reached the batteries on the hill where after a hand to hand conflict the attack was repulsed with heavy loss including the colors of the 8th Louisiana captured by 107th Ohio.

No. 22U   Tablet on Granite Pedestal located—East Howard Avenue

Note: The complete inscription on this tablet is presented in Part II—First Day Battle—Page 43.

ARMY OF THE POTOMAC
ELEVENTH CORPS   FIRST DIVISION
FIRST BRIGADE
Col. Leopold Von Gilsa

July 2. Remained in position all day engaged as skirmishers. An attack in the evening on Cemetery Hill on the left was repulsed with the aid of First Brigade Third Division Second Corps.

No. 21U   Tablet on Granite Pedestal located—Cemetery Hill

Note: The complete inscription on this tablet is presented in Part II—First Day Battle—Pages 42–43.

ARMY OF THE POTOMAC
ELEVENTH CORPS
SECOND DIVISION
Brig. General Adolph Von Steinwehr

July 2. Heavy artillery firing from 4 to 6 P. M. Between 8 and 9 P. M. the Division was attacked by Hays's Louisiana Brigade which penetrated to Battery I First New York Light Artillery and was repulsed with great loss.

No. 23U   Tablet on Granite Marker located—Cemetery Hill, Baltimore Pike

Note: The complete inscription on this tablet is presented in Part II—First Day Battle—Pages 43–44.

ARMY OF THE POTOMAC
ELEVENTH CORPS   SECOND DIVISION
FIRST BRIGADE
Col. Charles R. Coster

July 2. In same position during the day under fire of artillery and sharp-shooters. At 8 P. M. Brig. Gen. Hays's Brigade charged the position and was repulsed with heavy loss. The 27th Penna. bore a conspicuous part in repelling this attack. Battery I 1st New York was temporarily captured but was immediately recovered.

No. 24U   Tablet on Granite Pedestal located—Coster Avenue, Gettysburg

Note: The complete inscription on this tablet is presented in Part II—First Day Battle—Pages 44–45.

SECOND DAY TABLET INSCRIPTIONS
ARMY OF NORTHERN VIRGINIA

ARMY OF NORTHERN VIRGINIA
General Robert E Lee
Commanding

July 2. McLaw's and Hood's Divisions, Longstreet's Corps, arrived on the field about 3 P. M. and formed facing the Union left. An assault was made by the two divisions assisted by Anderson's Division, Hill's Corps. The Union troops were dislodged from Emmitsburg Road and Peach Orchard, engagement lasting until night; losses heavy. Pickett's Division, Longstreet's Corps, on the march. Johnson's Division, Ewell's Corps, about dusk advanced to the assault of Culp's Hill in connection with Early's Division, Ewell's Corps. Rodes's Division, Ewell's Corps held position west of town; not engaged. Heth's and Pender's Divisions, Hill's Corps, occupied Seminary Ridge facing Union line; not engaged. Stuart's Cavalry on left flank of Confederate Army.

No. 1C   Tablet on Granite Marker located—West Confederate Avenue

Note: The complete inscription on this tablet is presented in Part II—First Day Battle—Page 46.

ARMY OF NORTHERN VIRGINIA
FIRST ARMY CORPS
Lieutenant General James Longstreet

McLaws's Division   Major General Lafayette McLaws

Pickett's Division   Major General George E. Pickett

Hood's Division   Major General John B. Hood
                        Brigadier General E. M. Law

Artillery Reserve
  Ten Batteries   Colonel J. B. Walton

126

July 1. McLaws's Division encamped about four miles from Gettysburg a little after dark. Hood's Division reached the same distance about 12 P. M. Law's Brigade on picket at New Guilford. Pickett's Division guarding trains at Chambersburg.

July 2. Moved that portion of the command which was up to gain the Emmitsburg Road on Union left. Delayed attack until 3.30 P. M. when Law's Brigade joined from New Guilford. McLaws's Division in position facing Union left. About 4 P. M. Hood's Division moved further to the right and took position partially enveloping Union left. The batteries opened about 4 P. M. upon Union troops on Emmitsburg Road Hood's Division pressing on left and McLaws's in front the Union troops were dislodged. The engagement lasted until nearly night with heavy losses. The ground gained on the front was held. The left was withdrawn to first Union position at Peach Orchard.

July 3. Pickett's Division reached the field at 9 A. M. Pickett's Heth's and part of Pender's Divisions were ordered to form column of assault on Union centre on Cemetery Hill. The batteries opened about 1 P. M. About 3 P. M. Pickett advanced in good order under a severe fire and was repulsed at the stone wall losing heavily. McLaws's and Hood's Divisions were not seriously engaged during the day and night.

July 4. The Corps took up the line of march during the night.

Casualties   Killed 910   Wounded 4339   Captured or Missing 2290
Total 7539

No. 24C   Tablet on Granite Marker located—intersection of West Confederate Avenue and Millerstown Road

C. S. A.
ARMY OF NORTHERN VIRGINIA
FIRST ARMY CORPS
HOOD'S DIVISION
Maj. Gen. J. B. Hood   Brig. Gen. E. M. Law

Law's Brigade	Brig. Gen. E. M. Law
	Col. James L. Sheffield
Robertson's Brigade	Brig. Gen. J. B. Robertson
Anderson's Brigade	Brig. George T. Anderson
	Lieut. Col. William Luffman
Benning's Brigade	Brig. Gen. Henry L. Benning
Artillery Battalion	
Four Batteries	Major M. W. Henry

July 1. On the march to Gettysburg. Encamped about four miles from the field with the exception of Law's Brigade left on picket at New Guilford.

July 2. Law's Brigade joined from New Guilford about noon. The Division was formed on extreme right of the Army and then directed to drive in and envelop the Union left. About 4 P. M. the batteries opened and soon after the Division moved forward. After a severe struggle the Union line retired to the ridge in rear. The ground fought over was obstructed by stone fences and very difficult. The movement was partially successful the battle continuing until nearly dark. The advance gained was held.

July 3. Occupied the ground gained and with the exception of resisting a Cavalry charge and heavy skirmishing was not engaged.

July 4. The Division took up the line of march during the night.

Casualties   Killed 343   Wounded 1504   Missing 442   Total 2289

No. 25C   Tablet on Granite Marker located—South Confederate Avenue

---

C. S. A.
ARMY OF NORTHERN VIRGINIA
LONGSTREET'S CORPS   HOOD'S DIVISION
LAW'S BRIGADE
4th   15th   44th   47th   48th Alabama Infantry

July 2. Left New Guilford 25 miles distant at 3 A. M. Arrived and formed line 50 yards west of this about 4 P. M. and advanced against the Union positions. The 4th 15th and 47th Regiments attacked Little Round Top and continued the assault until dark. The 44th and 48th assisted in capturing Devil's Den and 3 guns of the 4th New York Battery.

July 3. Occupied the breastworks on west slope of Round Top. The 4th and 15th Regiments assisted at 5 P. M. in repulsing cavalry led by Brig. Gen. E. J. Farnsworth in Plum Run Valley.

July 5. About 5 A. M. began the march to Hagerstown Md.

Present about 1500   Losses about 550

No. 26C   Tablet on Granite Pedestal located—South Confederate Avenue

---

ARMY OF NORTHERN VIRGINIA
LONGSTREET'S CORPS   HOOD'S DIVISION
LAW'S BRIGADE
4th   15th   44th   47th   48th Alabama Infantry

July 2. Arrived on the field about 4 P. M. and advanced against the Union positions. The 4th 15th and 47th Regiments attacked Little Round Top and continued the assault until dark. The 44th and 48th assisted in capturing Devil's Den and 3 guns of Smith's 4th New York Battery.

No. 27C   Advance Position Cast Iron Tablet located—Warren Avenue

---

C. S. A.
ARMY OF NORTHERN VIRGINIA
LONGSTREET'S CORPS   HOOD'S DIVISION
ROBERTSON'S BRIGADE
1st   4th   5th Texas and 3D Arkansas Infantry

July 2. Arrived after a march of several miles and formed line 50 yards west of this at 4 P. M. Advanced against the Union positions. The 4th and 5th Texas joined in the attack on Little Round Top which continued until dark. The 1st and 3D Arkansas attacked and assisted in taking Devil's Den and Rocky Ridge with a number of prisoners and 3 guns of the 4th New York Battery.

July 3. At 2 A. M. the 1st Texas and 3D Arkansas were moved to the right and joined the 4th and 5th Texas on the northwest spur of Big Round Top. Three regiments occupied the breastworks there all day skirmishing hotly with Union sharpshooters. Early in the day the 1st Texas was sent to confront the Union Cavalry threatening the right flank. After night the Brigade took position near here.

July 5. About 5 A. M. began the march to Hagerstown Md.

Present about 1100   Losses about 540

No. 28C   Tablet on Granite Pedestal located—South Confederate Avenue

---

ARMY OF NORTHERN VIRGINIA
LONGSTREET'S CORPS   HOOD'S DIVISION
ROBERTSON'S BRIGADE
1st   4th   5th Texas and 3D Arkansas

July 2. Arrived on the field about 4 P. M. Advanced against the Union positions. The 4th and 5th Texas joined in the attack on Little Round Top which continued until dark. The 1st Texas and 3D Arkansas attacked and assisted in taking the Devil's Den and Rocky Ridge with a number of prisoners and 3 guns of Smith's 4th New York Battery.

No. 29C   Advance Position Cast Iron Tablet located—Sickles Avenue

━━━━━━━━━━

C. S. A.
ARMY OF NORTHERN VIRGINIA
LONGSTREET'S CORPS   HOOD'S DIVISION
BENNING'S BRIGADE
2nd   15th   17th   20th Georgia Infantry

July 2. Arrived and formed line about 4 P. M. in rear of Law's and Robertson's
Brigades and moving forward in support of these took prominent part in
the severe conflict which resulted in the capture of Devil's Den together
with a number of prisoners and three guns of the 4th New York Battery.

July 3. Held Devil's Den and the adjacent crest of rocky ridge until late in
the evening when under orders the Brigade retired to position near here.
Through mistake of orders the 15th Georgia did not retire directly but
moved northward encountered a superior Union force and suffered considerable loss.

July 4. Occupied breastworks near here facing southward until midnight.

July 5. About 5 A. M. began the march to Hagerstown Md.

Present about 1500   Losses 509

No. 30C   Tablet on Granite Pedestal located—South Confederate Avenue

━━━━━━━━━━

ARMY OF NORTHERN VIRGINIA
LONGSTREET'S CORPS   HOOD'S DIVISION
BENNING'S BRIGADE
2nd   15th   17th   20th Georgia Infantry

July 2. Formed in line about 4 P. M. in rear of Law's and Robertson's Brigades and moving forward in support took active part in the conflict that
resulted in the capture of Devil's Den together with a number of prisoners and 3 guns of Smith's 4th New York Battery.

No. 31C   Advance Position Cast Iron Tablet located—Sickles Avenue, western
side Devil's Den

━━━━━━━━━━

C. S. A.
ARMY OF NORTHERN VIRGINIA
LONGSTREET'S CORPS   HOOD'S DIVISION
ANDERSON'S BRIGADE
7th   8th   9th   11th   59th Georgia Infantry

July 2. After march of several miles formed line about 4 P. M. 100 yards west of this. The Seventh regiment was sent southward to watch Union Cavalry. The others charged into the woods south of Wheatfield and dislodged the Union line from stone fence there but flanked on the left retired to crest of Rose Hill. Reinforced later by parts of other brigades they again advanced. The wounding of Gen. G. T. Anderson caused a brief halt and some confusion but they advanced a third time and after a struggle occupied the woodland to its border on Plum Run Valley.

July 3. The Brigade was sent down Emmitsburg Road and assisted in repulsing and holding in check Union Cavalry which sought to flank the Division.

July 4. Assisted in constructing works to protect the flank.

July 5. About 5 A. M. began the march to Hagerstown Md.

Present about 1800   Losses 671

No. 32C   Tablet on Granite Pedestal located—West Confederate Avenue

---

ARMY OF NORTHERN VIRGINIA
LONGSTREET'S CORPS   HOOD'S DIVISION
ANDERSON'S BRIGADE
7th   8th   9th   11th   59th Georgia Infantry

July 2. Reached the field about 4 P. M. and formed line. The 7th Regiment was sent southward to watch the Union Cavalry. The others charged into the woods south of Wheatfield and dislodged the Union line from the stone fence. Being outflanked on left retired to crest of Rose Hill. Reinforced by parts of other Brigades they again advanced. The brigades advanced a third time and after a struggle occupied the woodland to its border in Plum Run Valley.

No. 33C   Advance Position Cast Iron Tablet located—The Loop

ARMY OF NORTHERN VIRGINIA
FIRST ARMY CORPS
McLAWS'S DIVISION
Maj. Gen. Lafayette McLaws

Kershaw's Brigade   Brig. Gen. J. B. Kershaw
Barksdale's Brigade   Brig. Gen. William Barksdale
                      Col. B. G. Humphreys

Semmes's Brigade	Brig. Gen. P. J. Semmes
	Col. George Bryan
Wofford's Brigade	Brig Gen. W. T. Wofford
Artillery Battalion	
Four Batteries	Col. H. C. Cabell

July 1. The Division reached Marsh Creek four miles from Gettysburg after dark.

July 2. The Division was placed in position facing the Union line on the Emmitsburg Road. About 4 P. M. the batteries opened on the position the Division pressing to the front and the Union troops retiring to the hill in rear. The battle continued until nearly night when a strong Union force met the supporting Division which was co-operating on the left and drove one brigade back and checked the support of the other brigade exposing the left. It was thought prudent not to push further until other troops of the Corps came up. The Division was withdrawn to the first position of Union troops resting at the Peach Orchard the conflict to be renewed in the morning when other orders were received.

July 3. With the exception of severe skirmishing the Division was not engaged and after night disposition were made to withdraw.

July 4. The Division took up the line of march during the night.

Casualties Killed 313 Wounded 1538 Captured or Missing 327 Total 2178

No. 34C   Tablet on Granite Marker located—West Confederate Avenue

━━━━━━━━━━

C. S. A.
LONGSTREET'S CORPS   McLAWS'S DIVISION
KERSHAW'S BRIGADE
2nd   3rd   7th   8th   15th Regiments and 3D Battalion South Carolina Infantry

July 2. Arrived at 3.30 P. M. and formed line here. Advanced about 4.30 to battle. The 8th and 2D Regiments and 3DBattalion shared in the attack on Peach Orchard and batteries near there on Wheatfield Road. The 7th and 3D Regiments were engaged in the long and severe conflict at and around the Loop. The 15th Regiment fought on Rose Hill and in the ravine and forest beyond. Late in the evening the Brigade took part in the general advance by which the Union forces were forced from the Wheatfield and across Plum Run Valley. At dark under orders it retired to Peach Orchard.

July 3. At Peach Orchard until noon then sent farther to front. At 1 P. M. under orders resumed position here extending line to right and keeping in touch with Hood's Division on left.

July 4. About midnight began the march to Hagerstown Md.

Present about 1800   Losses 630

No. 35C   Tablet on Granite Pedestal located—West Confederate Avenue

———

ARMY OF NORTHERN VIRGINIA
LONGSTREET'S CORPS   McLAWS'S DIVISION
KERSHAW'S BRIGADE
2nd   3rd   7th   8th   15th Regiments and 3D Battalion South Carolina Infantry

July 2. Arrived on the field at 3.30 P. M. Formed line and advanced about 4.30 o'clock. The 8th and 2D Regiments and 3D Battalion shared in the attack on the Peach Orchard and batteries near there on Wheatfield Road. The 7th and 3D Regiments were engaged at and around the Loop. The 15th Regiment fought on Rose Hill and in the ravine and forest beyond. Late in the evening the Brigade took part in the advance by which the Union forces were forced from the Wheatfield and across Plum Run Valley. At dark under orders the Brigade retired to and occupied the Peach Orchard.

No. 36C   Advance Position Cast Iron Tablet located—the Loop, Rose Woods

———

C. S. A.
ARMY OF NORTHERN VIRGINIA
LONGSTREET'S CORPS   McLAWS'S DIVISION
BARKSDALE'S BRIGADE
13th   17th   18th   21st Mississippi Infantry

July 2. Arrived about 3 P. M. and formed line here. Advanced at 5 P. M. and took part in the assault on the Peach Orchard and adjacent positions vigorously pursuing the Union forces as they retired. The 21st Regiment pushed on past the Trostle House and captured but were unable to bring off 9th Mass. Battery and I Battery 5th U. States. The other Regiments inclining more to the left pressed forward to Plum Run where they encountered fresh troops and a fierce conflict ensued in which Brig. Gen. Wm. Barksdale fell mortally wounded.

July 3. Supported artillery on Peach Orchard Ridge. Withdrew from the front late in the afternoon.

July 4. In position near here all day. About midnight began the march to Hagerstown.

Present 1598   Killed 105   Wounded 550   Missing 92   Total 747

No. 37C   Tablet on Granite Pedestal located—West Confederate Avenue, north of Millerstown Road

---

ARMY OF NORTHERN VIRGINIA
LONGSTREET'S CORPS   McLAWS'S DIVISION
BARKSDALE'S BRIGADE
13th   17th   18th   21st Mississippi Infantry

July 2. Arrived about 3 P. M. and formed in line. Advanced at 5 o'clock and took part in the assault on the Peach Orchard and adjacent position pursuing the Union forces as they retired. The 21st Regiment pushed beyond the Trostle House and captured but were unable to bring off Bigelow's and Watson's Batteries. The other Regiments inclining to the left pressed forward to Plum Run where they encountered Union troops and a fierce conflict ensued in which Brig. Gen. Wm. Barksdale fell mortally wounded.

No.38C   Advance Position Cast Iron Tablet located—west side Emmitsburg Road, Peach Orchard

---

C. S. A.
ARMY OF NORTHERN VIRGINIA
LONGSTREET'S CORPS   McLAWS'S DIVISION
SEMMES'S BRIGADE
10th   50th   51st   53rd Georgia Infantry

July 2. Arrived about 3.30 P. M. and formed line 50 yards west of this. Advanced about 5 P. M. in support of Kershaw and Anderson and took a prominent part in the severe and protracted conflict on Rose Hill and in the ravine and forest east of there and in the vicinity of the Loop. Participated also in the general advance late in the evening by which the Union forces were forced out of the Wheatfield and across Plum Run Valley. Brig Gen. Paul J. Semmes fell mortally wounded in the ravine near the Loop.

July 3. During the afternoon Anderson's Brigade being withdrawn for duty elsewhere the Brigade was left in the occupancy of the woodland south of the Wheatfield. At 1 P. M. under orders it resumed its original position near here.

July 4. About midnight began the march to Hagerstown Md.

Present about 1200   Losses 430

No. 39C   Tablet on Granite Pedestal located—West Confederate Road, south of Millerstown Road intersection

---

ARMY OF NORTHERN VIRGINIA
LONGSTREET'S CORPS   McLAWS'S DIVISION
SEMMES'S BRIGADE
10th   50th   51st   53rd Georgia Infantry

July 2. Arrived on the field about 3.30 P. M. Advanced about 5 o'clock in support of Kershaw's and Anderson's Brigades and took an active part in the conflict on Rose Hill and in the ravine and forest east of there in the vicinity of the Loop. Participated in the general advance late in the evening by which the Union forces were forced out of the Wheatfield and across Plum Run Valley. Brig. Gen. J. Semmes fell mortally wounded in the ravine near the Loop.

No. 40C   Advance Position Cast Iron Tablet located—the Loop, Rose Woods

---

C. S. A.
ARMY OF NORTHERN VIRGINIA
LONGSTREET'S CORPS   McLAWS'S DIVISION
WOFFORD'S BRIGADE
16th   18th   24th Regiments Cobb's and Phillips's Legions Georgia Infantry

July 2. Arrived at 4 P. M. and formed line 100 yards west of this. Ordered to the front about 6 P. M. and advanced soon afterward along Wheatfield Road flanked the Union forces assailing the Loop and aided the Confederates thereby relieved in forcing them back through the Wheatfield to the foot of Little Round Top. Assailed there by a strong body of fresh troops and receiving at the same moment an order to withdraw the Brigade fell back at sunset to the grove west of the Wheatfield.

July 3. One regiment was left on outpost duty in that grove. The others supported artillery on Peach Orchard Ridge. All withdrew late in the afternoon.

July 4. In line here all day. At midnight began march to Hagerstown.

Present about 1350   Killed 36   Wounded 207   Missing 112   Total 355

No. 41C   Tablet on Granite Pedestal located—West Confederate Avenue, north of Millerstown Road intersection

---

ARMY OF NORTHERN VIRGINIA
LONGSTREET'S CORPS   MCLAWS'S DIVISION
WOFFORD'S BRIGADE
16th   18th   24th Regiments Cobb's and Phillip's Legions Georgia Infantry

July 2. Arrived at 4 P. M. and formed line 500 yards west of here ordered to the front about 6 o'clock. Advanced soon afterwards along Wheatfield Road struck the Union line near the Loop and joined Kershaw's Brigade in driving the Union forces through the Wheatfield to the base of Little Round Top. Assailed by Union reinforcements and receiving orders to withdraw the Brigade fell back at sunset to the cover of the woods west of the Wheatfield.

July 3. One regiment was left on outpost duty in that grove. The others supported artillery on Peach Orchard Ridge. All withdrew late in the afternoon.

July 4. In line 500 yards west of here all day. At midnight began the march to Hagerstown.

Present about 1355   Killed 36   Wounded 207   Missing 112   Total 355

No. 42C   Advance Position Cast Iron Tablet located—west side Emmitsburg Road, Peach Orchard

---

ARMY OF NORTHERN VIRGINIA
THIRD ARMY CORPS
Lieutenant General Ambrose P. Hill

July 2. Anderson's Division extended to the right along the crest of hills facing Cemetery Ridge Pender's Division occupying the crest from the Seminary and joining Anderson's Division with Heth's Division in Reserve the artillery in position on Seminary Ridge. The First Corps ordered to attack the left of Union forces the Third Corps to co-operate. General Anderson moved forward three brigades connecting with left of McLaws's Division and drove the Union forces from their position. Anderson's right becoming separated from McLaws's left and no support coming to these brigades they returned to their former lines.

No. 2C   Tablet on Granite Marker located—West Confederate Avenue

Note: The complete inscription on this tablet is presented in Part II—First Day Battle—Pages 47–48.

ARMY OF NORTHERN VIRGINIA
THIRD ARMY CORPS
ANDERSON'S DIVISION
Major Gen. R. H. Anderson

Wilcox's Brigade	Brig. Gen. Cadmus M. Wilcox
Mahone's Brigade	Brig. Gen. William Mahone
Wright's Brigade	Gen. A. R. Wright
	Col. William Gibson
Perry's Brigade	Col. David Lang
Posey's Brigade	Brig. Gen. Carnot Posey
Artillery Battalion	
Three Batteries	Major John Lane

July 1. Anderson's Division on the march to Gettysburg was directed about dark to occupy the position vacated by Heth's Division and to send a brigade and battery a mile or more to the right.

July 2. In the morning a new line of battle formed extending further to the right. About noon Longstreet's Corps placed on the right nearly at right angles to the line directed to assault the Union left the Division to advance as the attack progressed to keep in touch with Longstreet's left. The Union troops were forced from the first line and a portion of the ridge beyond. Union reinforcements pressing on the right flank which had become disconnected from McLaws's left made the position gained untenable. The brigades withdrew to their position in line.

July 3. The Division remained in position until 3.30 P. M. Orders were given to support Lieut. Gen. Longstreet's attack on the Union centre Wilcox and Perry moved forward. The assault failed the order to advance was countermanded.

July 4. The Division after dark took up the line of march.

Casualties   Killed 147   Wounded 1128   Missing 840   Total 2115

No. 43C   Tablet on Granite Marker located—West Confederate Avenue

---

C. S. A.
ARMY OF NORTHERN VIRGINIA
HILL'S CORPS   ANDERSON'S DIVISION
WILCOX'S BRIGADE
8th   9th   10th   11th   14th Alabama Infantry

July 2. Formed line here in forenoon. The 10th and 11th Regiments taking position on the right after a severe skirmish with the Union outpost. Advanced at 6 P. M. and broke the Union line on Emmitsburg Road capturing two guns and pursuing rapidly took many prisoners and six more guns. At Plum Run was met by a heavy fire of artillery and fresh infantry and being unsupported after severe losses fell back without being able to bring off the captured guns.

July 3. Took position west of Emmitsburg Road in support of artillery. Soon after Longstreet's column started an order was received to advance and support it but smoke hiding the oblique course of Pickett's Division the Brigade moving straight forward found itself engaged in a separate and useless conflict and was promptly withdrawn.

July 4. In line here all day and at dark began the march to Hagerstown.

Present 1777   Killed 51   Wounded 469   Missing 261   Total 781

No. 44C   Tablet on Granite Pedestal located—West Confederate Avenue

────────

ARMY OF NORTHERN VIRGINIA
HILL'S CORPS   ANDERSON'S DIVISION
WILCOX'S BRIGADE
8th   9th   10th   11th   14th Alabama Infantry

July 2. Formed line in forenoon the 10th and 11th Regiments taking position on the right after a severe skirmish with a Union outpost. Advanced at 6 P. M. and broke the Union line on Emmitsburg Road capturing two guns and pursuing rapidly took many prisoners and six guns. At Plum Run was met by a heavy fire of artillery and infantry and being unsupported after severe loss fell back without being able to bring off the captured guns.

No. 45C   Advance Position Cast Iron Tablet located—Emmitsburg Road

────────

C. S. A.
HILL'S CORPS   ANDERSON'S DIVISION
PERRY'S BRIGADE
2nd   5th   8th Florida Infantry

July 2. Formed line in forenoon in the eastern border of these woods. Advanced at 6 P. M. and assisted in forcing the Union line on the Emmitsburg Road and by rapid pursuit compelled the temporary abandonment of several guns. At the foot of the slope met fresh Union forces and the line on its right retiring it also fell back. The color-bearer of the 8th Florida fell and its flag was lost.

July 3. Ordered to join Wilcox's Brigade on its left and conform to its movements. Supported artillery until Longstreet's column started and then advanced in aid of his assault. But dense smoke hiding his oblique course the Brigade moved directly forward. In the gap caused thereby a strong force struck its left flank capturing about half of the 2nd Florida and its colors.

July 4. In line here and at dark began the march to Hagerstown.

Present 700   Killed 33   Wounded 217   Missing 205   Total 455

No. 46C   Tablet on Granite Pedestal located—West Confederate Avenue

---

ARMY OF NORTHERN VIRGINIA
HILL'S CORPS   ANDERSON'S DIVISION
PERRY'S BRIGADE
2nd   5th   8th Florida Infantry

July 2. Formed line in forenoon in the western border of these woods. Advanced at 6 P. M. and assisted in driving back the Union lines on Emmitsburg Road and by rapid pursuit compelled the temporary abandonment of several guns. At the foot of the slope met Union infantry and the line on the right retiring also fell back. The color bearer of the 8th Florida fell and its flag was lost.

No. 47C   Advance Position Cast Iron Tablet located—Emmitsburg Road

---

C. S. A.
HILL'S CORPS   ANDERSON'S DIVISION
WRIGHT'S BRIGADE
3rd, 22nd, 48th Regiments and 2D Battalion Georgia Infantry

July 2. Formed line here in the forenoon. Advanced at 6 P. M. and dislodged Union troops posted near the Codori House capturing several guns and many prisoners. Pushing on broke the Union line at the stone wall south of the Angle and reached the crest of the ridge beyond capturing more guns. The supports on the right being repulsed and those on the left not coming up with both flanks assailed and converging columns threatening its rear it withdrew fighting its way out with heavy losses and unable to bring off the captured guns.

July 3. Advanced 600 yards to cover the retreat of Pickett's Division. Afterward was moved to the right to meet a threatened attack.

July 4. In line here all day. At dark began the march to Hagerstown.

Present 1450   Killed 146   Wounded 394   Missing 333   Total 873

No. 48C   Tablet on Granite Pedestal located—West Confederate Avenue

---

ARMY OF NORTHERN VIRGINIA
HILL'S CORPS   ANDERSON'S DIVISION
WRIGHT'S BRIGADE
3rd   22nd   48th Regiments and 2D Battalion Georgia Infantry

July 2. Formed line in forenoon. Advanced at 6 P. M. and dislodged Union troops posted near the Codori House capturing several guns and many prisoners. Pursuing on broke the Union line at the stone wall south of the angle reached the crest of the ridge beyond capturing more guns. The supports on the right being repulsed and those on the left not coming up with both flanks assailed and converging columns threatening its rear it withdrew fighting its way out with heavy losses and unable to bring off the captured guns.

No. 49C   Advance Position Cast Iron Tablet located—Emmitsburg Road

---

C. S. A.
ARMY OF NORTHERN VIRGINIA
HILL'S CORPS   ANDERSON'S DIVISION
POSEY'S BRIGADE
12th   16th   19th   48th Mississippi Infantry

July 2. Arrived and took position here in the morning. Through some misunderstanding of orders instead of the Brigade advancing in compact ranks in support of the troops on its right in their assault on the Union lines the regiments were ordered forward at different times. Deployed as skirmishers and fighting in detachments they pushed back the Union outposts and drove some artillerists for awhile from their guns but did not join in the attack upon the Union position on Cemetery Ridge.

July 3. Was held in reserve here supporting artillery in its front.

Present 1150 Killed 12 Wounded 71 Total 83

No. 50C Tablet on Granite Pedestal located—West Confederate Avenue

---

C. S. A.
ARMY OF NORTHERN VIRGINIA
HILL'S CORPS ANDERSON'S DIVISION
MAHONE'S BRIGADE
6th 12th 16th 41st 61st Virginia Infantry

July 2. Arrived and took position here in the forenoon under orders to support the artillery. A strong skirmish line was sent out which was constantly engaged and did effective service.

July 3. Remained here in support of the artillery. Took no active part in the battle except by skirmishers.

July 4. In line here all day. At dark began the march to Hagerstown.

Present 1500 Killed 8 Wounded 55 Missing 39 Total 102

No. 51C Tablet on Granite Pedestal located—West Confederate Avenue

---

ARMY OF NORTHERN VIRGINIA
SECOND ARMY CORPS
Lieutenant General Richard S. Ewell

July 2. In the early morning Johnson's Division was ordered to take possession of a wooded hill on the left. Skirmishers were advanced and a desultory fire kept up until 4 P. M. when the artillery from Benner's Hill opened the firing continued for two hours. The batteries were withdrawn much crippled. The Division about dusk was advanced to the assault in connection with Early's Division on the right the battle continuing until after dark. A partial success was made by a portion of each division but not being supported on the right was withdrawn to the former positions.

No. 13C Tablet on Granite Marker located—North Confederate Avenue

Note: The complete inscription on this tablet is presented in Part II—Day One—
Pages 54–55.

ARMY OF NORTHERN VIRGINIA
SECOND ARMY CORPS
JOHNSON'S DIVISION
Maj. Gen. Edward Johnson

Steuart's Brigade   Brig. Gen. Geo. H. Steuart
Stonewall Brigade   Brig. Gen. James A. Walker
Nicholl's Brigade   Col. J. M. Williams
Jones Brigade   Lieut. Col. R. H. Duncan
Artillery Battalion
    Four Batteries   Maj. J. W. Latimer
                           Capt. C. L. Raine

July 1. The Division arrived on the field too late to participate in the engagement of the day. Moved to the northeast of town during the night to take possession of wooded hill that commanded Cemetery Ridge.

July 2. Early in the morning skirmishers advanced and a desultory fire kept up. The artillery was posted on hill in rear of line and opened fire about 4 P. M. the infantry advanced to assault at dusk up the steep hill. Steuart's Brigade captured a line of works on the left. Firing continued at close range during night.

July 3. The assault was renewed in early morning. An attempt was made by the Union forces to retake the works occupied the night before and was repulsed. The Division being reinforced by four brigades two other assaults were made and repulsed. Retired at 10.30 A. M. to former position of July 2 which was held until 10 P. M. when the Division was withdrawn to the ridge northwest of town.

July 4. The Division took up the line of march during the day.

Casualties   Killed 229   Wounded 1269   Missing 375   Total 1873

No. 52C   Tablet on Granite Marker located—East Confederate Avenue

━━━━━━━━━━━━━━━━

C. S. A.
ARMY OF NORTHERN VIRGINIA
EWELL'S CORPS   JOHNSON'S DIVISION
JONES'S BRIGADE
21st   25th   42nd   44th   48th   50th Virginia Infantry

July 1. Arrived near nightfall and took position east of Rock Creek and north of Hanover road with pickets advanced to the front.

July 2. About 4 P. M. moved forward to support artillery on Benner's Hill. Crossed Rock Creek at 6 P. M. and assailed the Union position on the summit of Culp's Hill charging up to the Union breastworks and continuing the struggle until dark.

July 3. In line near here all day sometimes skirmishing heavily. About midnight moved with the Division and Corps to Seminary Ridge northwest of the town.

July 4. Occupied Seminary Ridge. About 10 P. M. began the march to Hagerstown.

Present 1600   Killed 58   Wounded 302   Missing 61   Total 421

No. 53C   Tablet on Granite Pedestal located—East Confederate Avenue

---

C. S. A.
ARMY OF NORTHERN VIRGINIA
EWELL'S CORPS   JOHNSON'S DIVISION
NICHOLL'S BRIGADE
1st   2nd   10th   14th   15th Louisiana Infantry

July 1. Arrived near nightfall and took position east of Rock Creek north of Hanover road and on the right of the Division.

July 2. About 6 P. M. changing to left of Jones's Brigade crossed the creek attacked Union forces on Culp's Hill drove in their outposts and reached and held a line about 100 yards from their breastworks against which a steady fire was maintained for hours and some vigorous but unsuccessful assaults made.

July 3. At dawn the Brigade reopened fire and continued it for many hours then retired to line near the creek whence about midnight it moved with Division and Corps to Seminary Ridge.

July 4. Occupied Seminary Ridge. About 10 P. M. began the march to Hagerstown.

Present about 1100   Killed 43   Wounded 309   Missing 36   Total 388

No. 54C   Tablet on Granite Pedestal located—East Confederate Avenue

---

C. S. A.
ARMY OF NORTHERN VIRGINIA
EWELL'S CORPS   JOHNSON'S DIVISION
STEUART'S BRIGADE
1st Maryland Battalion   1st and 3rd North Carolina   10th   23rd and 37th Virginia Infantry

July 1. Arrived about nightfall and took position near Hanover Road about a mile east of Rock Creek with left wing at edge of woods.

July 2. Crossing Rock Creek at 6 P. M. the 3D N. C. and 1st Md. attacked the lesser summit of Culp's Hill. Reinforced later by the other regiments the Union breastworks thinly manned at some points were occupied to the southern base of the main summit but only after a vigorous and desperate conflict.

July 3. The Union troops reinforced the conflict at dawn and it raged fiercely until 11 A. M. when this Brigade and the entire line fell back to the base of the hill and from thence moved about midnight to Seminary Ridge northwest of the town.

July 4. Occupied Seminary Ridge. About 10 P. M. began the march to Hagerstown.

Present about 1700   Killed 83   Wounded 409   Missing 190   Total 682

No. 55C   Tablet on Granite Pedestal located—East Confederate Avenue

─────────────

C. S. A.
ARMY OF NORTHERN VIRGINIA
EWELL'S CORPS   JOHNSON'S DIVISION
WALKER'S BRIGADE
2nd   4th   5th   27th   33rd Virginia Infantry

July 2. Guarded Division all day on its flank from Union forces in woods near by skirmishing with them sharply at times and finally driving them away. After dark crossed Rock Creek and rejoined the Division which had crossed about 6 P. M. and occupied part of the Union breastworks.

July 3. Took part in the unsuccessful struggle lasting from daybreak until near noon and then retired to the foot of the hill and from thence about midnight moved with the Division and Corps to Seminary Ridge.

July 4. Occupied Seminary Ridge. About 10 P. M. began the march to Hagerstown.

Present about 1450   Killed 35   Wounded 208   Missing 87   Total 330

No. 56C   Tablet on Granite Pedestal located—East Confederate Avenue

─────────────

C. S. A.
ARMY OF NORTHERN VIRGINIA
SECOND ARMY CORPS
EARLY'S DIVISION
Maj. Gen. Jubal A. Early

July 2. In the early morning Hays's and Hoke's Brigades took position to front and left of town. Gordon's Brigade in reserve moved to the rear of the Brigades. Smith's Brigade remained in this position until nearly dusk when Hays's and Hoke's Brigades advanced on Cemetery Hill. The Brigades reached the crest of hill but not being supported on the right were forced to retire. Gordon's Brigade advanced to support the attack.

No. 20C   Tablet on Granite Marker located—East Confederate Avenue

Note: The complete inscription on this tablet is presented in Part II—Day One—Pages 59–60.

C. S. A.
ARMY OF NORTHERN VIRGINIA
EWELL'S CORPS   EARLY'S DIVISION
HAYS'S BRIGADE

July 2. Moved forward early into the low ground here with its right flank resting on Baltimore St. and skirmished all day. Enfiladed by artillery and exposed to musketry fire in front it pushed forward over all obstacles scaled the hill and planted its colors on the lunettes capturing several guns. Assailed by fresh troops and with no supports it was forced to retire but brought off 75 prisoners and 4 stand of colors.

No. 22C   Tablet on Granite Pedestal located—East Confederate Avenue

Note: The complete inscription on this tablet is presented in Part II—Day One—Pages 60–61.

C. S. A.
ARMY OF NORTHERN VIRGINIA
EWELL'S CORPS   EARLY'S DIVISION
HOKE'S BRIGADE

July 2. Skirmished all day at 8 P. M. with Hays's Brigade charged East Cemetery Hill. Severely enfiladed on the left by artillery and musketry it pushed on over infantry line in front scaled the hill planted its colors on the lunettes and captured several guns. But assailed by fresh forces and having no supports it was soon compelled to relinquish what it had gained and withdraw. Its commander Col. Isaac E. Avery was mortally wounded leading the charge.

No. 23C   Tablet on Granite Pedestal located—East Confederate Avenue

Note: The complete inscription on this tablet is presented in Part II—Day One— Page 61.

━━━━━━━━━━

C. S. A.
ARMY OF NORTHERN VIRGINIA
EWELL'S CORPS   EARLY'S DIVISION
GORDON'S BRIGADE
13th   26th   31st   38th   60th   61st Georgia Infantry

July 2. After participating in the operations of July 1st at Barlow Knoll and elsewhere it took position in the afternoon between the town and Rock Creek. When the assault was made at 8 P. M. on East Cemetery Hill the Brigade advanced to its support but was halted here because the expected re-enforcements were unable to cooperate and it was evident that the assault would fail.

July 3. Remained here skirmishing with sharpshooters and exposed to artillery fire.

July 4. The Brigade was withdrawn and moved to Seminary Ridge. After midnight began the march to Hagerstown.

Present about 1500   Killed 71   Wounded 270   Missing 39   Total 380

No. 57C   Tablet on Granite Pedestal located—East Confederate Avenue

Note: The inscription on a cast iron tablet for this brigade, located on East Howard Avenue, is included in Part II.

**PART
IV**

The Third Day
July 3, 1863

THIRD DAY BATTLE SUMMARY

The two armies were still in place to resume the fight when dawn broke on July 3, 1863. The ever-cautious General Meade convened his senior commanders and called for a vote on what the Army of the Potomac should do. The decision was to stay but take no offensive action. The Union divisions and brigades that had been sent to threatened parts of the line the day before had returned to their assigned sector, and reinforcements were sent to plug gaps in the line. The Union line was intact with no immediate threat except for the far right where Johnson's Confederates were entrenched within striking distance of Baltimore Pike and the Union rear. But even there the situation was not desperate. Slocum's Twelfth Corps, returning to Culp's Hill at midnight to find that Johnson's men had occupied their breastworks, established a line between the Confederates and the Baltimore Pike.

Unlike Meade, General Lee did not call his senior lieutenants together to decide what action the Army of Northern Virginia would take. With Confederate lodgments on both flanks of the Union line, he was convinced that the line could be broken with a strong assault into its center. Lee selected a very reluctant Longstreet to lead the assault with Maj. Gen. George Pickett's fresh division, which had arrived the night before. Six brigades from Heth's and Pender's Divisions, which were heavily engaged the first day of the battle but not the second day, were selected to support Pickett on the left. Two brigades from Anderson's Division would support the right, even though both had seen severe action the day before. The main attack was to be supported with heavy skirmishing by Hood's and McLaws' Divisions on the Union left and a vigorous showing from Ewell's Corps on the Union right. Maj. Gen. J. E. B. Stuart's Cavalry Division, which had finally reached Gettysburg, would threaten Meade's lines of communication and participate in the Union rout, should Longstreet's assault succeed.

Lee was in no hurry to launch the main attack that day. Pickett's Division was not ordered from its bivouac position west of Spangler's Woods during the night and would need considerable time to get into position to attack. Thorough preparation was more important to the Confederate army commander than a hasty attack. Though displaying confidence that the attack would succeed, Lee knew that it would be the last—win or lose.

CONTINUATION OF BATTLE ON CULP'S HILL

The combatants on Culp's Hill did not wait for Lee's main attack. Given the closeness of the lines on the main summit of Culp's Hill, the resumption of the fight at first light was inevitable. Johnson's Division, having been reinforced by Smith's Brigade from Early's Division, and Daniel's and O'Neal's Brigades from Rodes' Division, renewed its assault on the summit. A fierce fight raged there for seven hours but Greene's line held.

Further down the hill, the Twelfth Corps was the first to start the fight at daylight. Even though a decision had been made to avoid offensive action, Meade authorized Slocum to retake the breastworks that his corps vacated the evening before in order to remove the threat to the Baltimore Pike and the Union rear. At daylight the Twelfth Corps launched an hour-long artillery assault from 26 guns on the Confederates in the abandoned breastworks. But the Confederates were the first to surge out of the trenches in an infantry assault on the Union line along the Baltimore Pike. The assault was repulsed, as were two other Confederate assaults, during that seven hours of savage charge and countercharge. In the end, Johnson's Confederates could not overcome a determined Union force with an overwhelming artillery presence. Suffering heavy casualties, Johnson withdrew his Confederates to the base of the hill in front of Rock Creek at about 10:30 A.M. Slocum, having accomplished his objective of retaking the lost breastworks, did not pursue the retiring Confederates. The battle for Culp's Hill had ended.

LONGSTREET'S ASSAULT

Pickett's three-brigade division arrived on the field about 9 A.M. and took position behind Seminary Ridge just south of the center of the Confederate line. Heth's Division, supported by two brigades from Pender's Division, was already positioned behind the ridge to the north of Pickett's assembly area, directly in front of the small stand of trees on Cemetery Ridge which Lee had selected as the guiding point for the assault. The two brigades from Anderson's Division were also in position to the south; but the assembled attackers would have about six hours to wait for the assault. First, Lee would soften up the objective with a furious artillery assault from more than 140 guns.

The attackers waited while the artillery was positioned on the high ground running north from the Peach Orchard for about two miles. The greatest cannonade of the war started about 1 P.M. and continued for most of two hours. The Union infantrymen, hugging the ground behind the stone walls below the

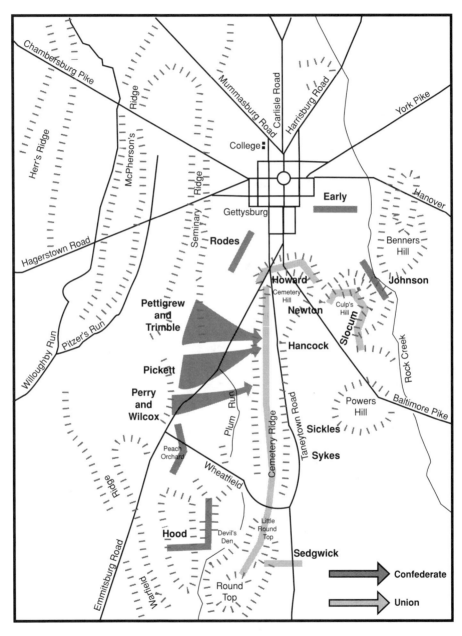

Battle of Gettysburg, third day

Positions as of 3 p.m.

crest of the ridge, were not greatly affected by the cannonade. As the trails of the Confederate guns dug in, causing the tubes to elevate, the shells crept up the hill until they burst either on the Union artillery on the crest or on the rear-area elements on the reverse slope, including Meade's Headquarters. The Confederate gunners, blinded by the smoke from their own guns, could not see the target to correct their aim.

Brig. Gen. Henry Hunt, the Union army chief of artillery, wanting to conserve the artillery for the infantry attack that was sure to follow the Confederate bombardment, directed that counterfire only be fired by batteries on Little Round Top and Cemetery Hill. General Hancock, whose Second Corps was the focus of the Confederate bombardment, had other ideas. To provide encouragement to his infantry, he ordered his artillery to respond. The Union batteries brought effective fire on the rebel gunners and caused considerable damage to the awaiting attackers behind the Confederate guns. By 2:45 P.M., the Second Corps batteries, heavily damaged and out of long-range ammunition, were being moved to the rear. This was the sign that the Confederates were looking for to start their attack.

Pickett's Division formed for the assault about 1:30 P.M. in an open field east of Spangler's woods. Brig. Gen. J. L. Kemper's Brigade formed the right of the forward line with Brig. Gen. R. B. Garnett's Brigade on the left. Brig. Gen. L. A. Armistead's Brigade formed a second line behind Kemper and Garnett. To the north of Pickett, Heth's Division, now commanded by General Pettigrew, formed a line of four brigades: Archer, Pettigrew, Davis, and Brockenbrough, from right to left. Two brigades from Pender's Division, now commanded by Maj. Gen. I. R. Trimble, formed a line to the right rear of Pettigrew, Scales on the right and Lane the left.

There were about 15,000 men in the 11 brigades that formed Longstreet's assault line. All six of the brigades from Heth's and Pender's Divisions had suffered heavy losses on the first day of the battle. Wilcox's and Perry's Brigades from Anderson's Division, which formed a line on Pickett's right flank, had also sustained heavy losses in the previous day's fighting. The eight brigades selected to add weight to the assault could provide no more than double the number of attackers that Pickett had in his three brigades. Most debilitating was the heavy loss of leaders in the brigades. Scales' Brigade, for example, had only one field officer remaining.

The three Union divisions occupying the section of the ridge that Lee planned to attack were also depleted from previous fights. Brigadier General Gibbons' Second Corps Division held the center with three brigades under Cols. William Harrow, Alexander Webb, and Norman Hall. Brig. Gen. Alexander Hays' Second Corps Division held the right with two brigades under Cols. Thomas Smyth and Eliakim Sherrill. Hays' other brigade under Col. Samuel Carroll was posted farther to the right on Cemetery Hill. Maj. Gen. Abner Doubleday's First Corps Division held the line to the left of

Gibbon. Two of Doubleday's brigades under Cols. Chapman Biddle and George Stannard were positioned to engage the attackers.

At about 3 P.M., General Longstreet gave the nod to start the assault. Trimble's and Pettigrew's Divisions were the first to appear from the woods in a half mile long line in front of the awestruck Union troops. Even without many of their leaders, they advanced straight ahead in near parade ground order. Pickett's line of three brigades soon came over the rise in front of Spangler's Woods on an oblique course, which would join with Pettigrew's line beyond the Emmitsburg Road. They too advanced at a deliberate pace with well-dressed ranks.

Wilcox's Brigade, with Perry's Brigade on its left, was ordered forward about 30 minutes after the assault started. Unable to see Pickett's oblique movement because of dense smoke, the brigades moved straight ahead, creating a wide gap between their line and Pickett's. As the brigades approached the Union line, two regiments from Stannard's Brigade attacked through the gap, striking the left flank of Perry's Brigade, capturing about half of the 2nd Florida Infantry and its colors. Finding themselves in a separate and useless engagement, Wilcox and Perry withdrew.

Immediately upon the appearance of the Confederate assault line, the Union artillery began its deadly task of reducing the advancing ranks. Brockenbrough's and Davis' Brigades on the left were particularly hard hit by the Union artillery firing into their flank from Cemetery Hill. The 8th Ohio from Carroll's Brigade struck the left flank of Brockenbrough's Brigade after it advanced beyond Emmitsburg Road, taking many prisoners and four stands of colors. Suffering heavy losses, Brockenbrough's Brigade withdrew. Davis' Brigade continued on to the stone wall south of the Brian Barn where, with regiments reduced to companies and further effort useless, it too was forced to withdraw.

The remaining brigades from Heth's and Pender's Divisions merged with Pickett's at Emmitsburg Road to form a blunt triangle, now surging at double time toward the Union line. The attackers encountered a deadly musket fire on the front from the Union infantry behind their stone walls, and heavy fire from the reserve artillery that moved forward to replace the direct support batteries damaged by the Confederate cannonade. The vulnerable flanks of the attackers were hit by Stannard's Brigade on the south and regiments from Smyth's and Willlard's Brigades on the north. The Union double envelopment boxed in the Confederate advance and quickened the already rapid depletion of their ranks. The charge by Archer's and Pettigrew's Brigades faltered in front of the stone wall at the Angle and the high wall running north and 80 yards further east. A few men leaped over the wall but were quickly killed or captured. Lane's and Scales' Brigades pushed forward to aid in the final struggle, but the charge was spent. The brigades on Pickett's left, reduced to skeleton regiments, withdrew without penetrating the Union line.

Pickett's lead brigades pushed forward from Emmitsburg Road, but their shattered ranks also faltered in front of the stone wall at the Angle. Two of his brigade commanders fell in front of the wall; General Garnett was killed and General Kemper wounded, later to be captured. Armistead's Brigade, with fewer casualties, pushed forward to the wall. General Armistead leaped over the wall and led many of his men and some from the other brigades into the angle. Armistead fell mortally wounded upon reaching the disabled and abandoned guns of Battery A 4th U.S. Artillery. The small number of men that went over the wall with him were repulsed. Pickett's charge was broken. The Confederate survivors retreated from Cemetery Ridge, and the Union defenders were content to let them go.

CAVALRY BATTLES

As General Lee was personally attempting to rally his troops retreating from Cemetery Ridge, the first of two violent but inconsequential cavalry engagements that would end the battle of Gettysburg had already reached its climax. The first engagement took place in the Union right rear, off Hanover Road about three miles from Gettysburg, on what is now called East Cavalry Field. The second engagement started on the left flank of the Union line about an hour after the retreat from Cemetery Ridge.

The first engagement resulted from General Stuart's move to position his cavalry in order to carry out his instructions to assail the Union rear. At about noon Stuart was moving four of his brigades onto Cress Ridge, which controlled the open ground toward Hanover, when he spotted Union cavalry in the open fields to the front. Keeping three brigades under Brig. Gens. Wade Hampton, Fitzhugh Lee, and Col. J. R. Chambliss screened from view in the woods, Stuart ordered Jenkins' Brigade, under Col. M. J. Ferguson, to form a dismounted line of sharpshooters in front of the Rummel Barn. Stuart's plan was to draw the Federals into a fight with the sharpshooters, setting them up for an attack from the other brigades.

Brig. Gen. David Gregg commanded the Union cavalry that Stuart spotted. He had with him the First Brigade of his Second Cavalry Division, under Col. John McIntosh, and Brig. Gen. George Custer's Second Brigade of the Third Cavalry Division. Gregg took Stuart's bait, sending McIntosh to engage the Confederate dismounted line. Ferguson's dismounted troopers were in trouble almost as soon as the fight started. Through an oversight, they had brought to the field only about ten rounds of ammunition each. Chambliss' Brigade was sent in to save the dismounted line.

Hampton's and F. Lee's Brigades emerged from the woods about 3 P.M. to join the fight but were too far away to gain surprise. McIntosh disengaged and fell back to form a line to meet the charging Confederates but Custer wouldn't wait. He led his four Michigan regiments in a head-on countercharge. The violent collision and ensuing hand-to-hand fight stopped the Confederate

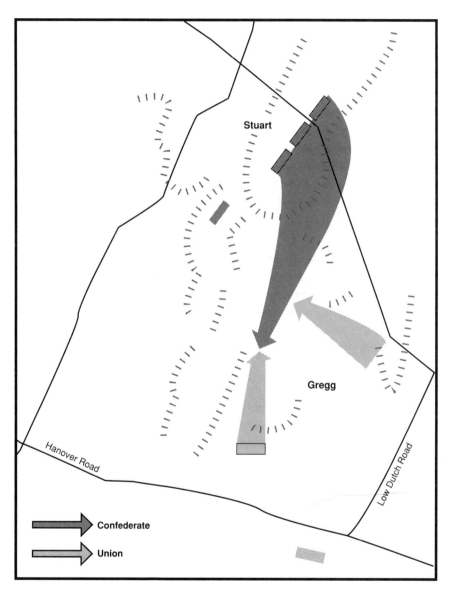

Battle of Gettysburg, cavalry battle

charge. Gregg quickly took advantage of the situation, sending McIntosh to strike the flanks of the gray brigades. The conflict was soon over. Having lost the initiative, Stuart withdrew his brigades back to Cress Ridge. The Union troopers were content to let them go. An artillery exchange would go on until dark, but the cavalry fight on the Union right rear was over.

The commander of the Union Third Cavalry Division, Brig. Gen. Judson Kilpatrick, started the second cavalry engagement. He had taken position at about 1 P.M. on the extreme left of the Union line with his remaining brigade under Brig. Gen. Elon Farnsworth. Brig. Gen. Wesley Merritt's Reserve Cavalry Brigade also arrived on the Union left in the afternoon and was driving the Confederate flank-guard detachments back along Emmitsburg Road to their main battle line. Perhaps emboldened by Merritt's arrival and the repulse of Longstreet's assault—or just plain foolishly—Kilpatrick ordered Farnsworth to attack the rebel flank. The objective of the attack was the main body of Confederate infantry deployed at the base of the Round Tops. Farnsworth's troopers first had to go through a strong skirmish line of Texas regiments from Hood's Division, hidden in the boulder-strewn woods between them and the objective. At 5:30 P.M. Farnsworth, leading three of his regiments already blooded by previous skirmishing, charged into the woods. By concentrating his troopers, Farnsworth penetrated the rebel skirmish line; but upon reaching Plum Run Valley, ran into two Alabama regiments which, being forewarned, had turned to stop them. The mission of the Union troopers soon changed to one of survival. Turning to find an exit from the trap they found themselves in, the troopers ran a gauntlet of Confederate infantry and artillery back to the Union line. Their losses were heavy, including General Farnsworth killed. The repulse of Farnsworth's Brigade ended Kilpatrick's attack. The Union Reserve Cavalry Brigade's advance was also checked by the movement of G. T. Anderson's Brigade of Confederates down Emmitsburg Road; but they continued to fight until stopped by a heavy rain.

Expecting a counterattack following the failure of Longstreet's assault on Cemetery Ridge, General Lee moved quickly to prepare his army for defense. The retreating rebels were collected and consolidated with the few reserves that were held back behind Seminary Ridge. McLaws and Law were ordered to pull back to the line that they had attacked from the day before. This was to position their divisions to support the weakened center. But there would be no attack from the Union side. Even though he still had the mostly uncommitted Sixth Corps with which to counterattack, General Meade had lost a fourth of his army and a large number of its most able leaders. He was not prepared to risk turning a clear victory into a defeat. Other than skirmishing between the lines as they separated and artillery exchanges, the battle of Gettysburg had ended.

Culp's Hill

Showing effects of bullets and cannon, date unknown.

Courtesy USAMHI-MOLLUS

Culp's Hill, 1998

Looking toward summit from East Confederate Avenue.

Photograph by Author

View from Little Round Top, 1885
Looking along Union line to Cemetery Hill.

Courtesy USAMHI-MOLLUS

View from Little Round Top, 1998

Photograph by Author

View from Cemetery Ridge, circa 1885

Looking toward Round Tops. Stand of trees used as guiding point in Longstreet's assault is on the right.

Courtesy USAMHI-MOLLUS

View from Cemetery Ridge, 1998

Photograph by Author

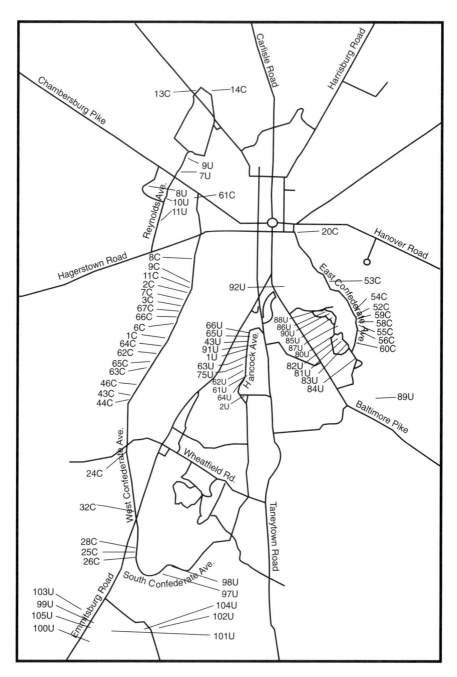

Third day tablet locations

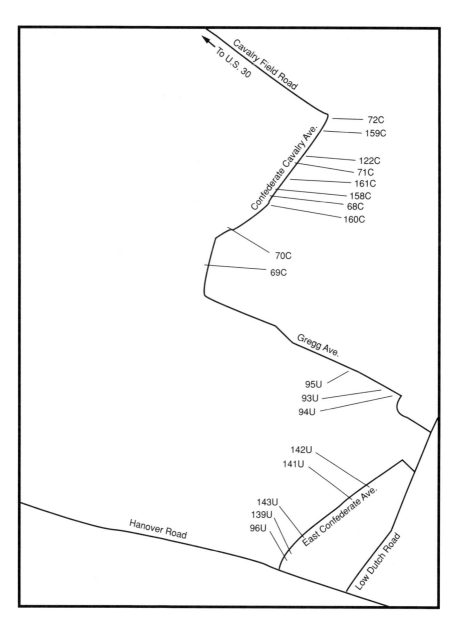

Cavalry battle tablet locations

THIRD DAY TABLET INSCRIPTIONS
ARMY OF THE POTOMAC

━━━━━━━━━━━━━━━━━━━

ARMY OF THE POTOMAC
Major General George G. Meade
Commanding

July 3. The Twelfth Corps having by order vacated a large part of its line on Culp's Hill on the night of the 2D and Johnson's Division of Ewell's Corps having occupied the works. The Twelfth Corps in the morning attacked and regained the lines it had previously vacated. Hill's Corps and Pickett's Division of Longstreet's Corps in the afternoon attacked the line of the Second Corps and were repulsed with great loss. Stuart's Confederate Cavalry in the afternoon attacked the Second Cavalry Division and the Second Brigade Third Cavalry Division and was repulsed.

No. 1U   Tablet on Granite Marker located—Hancock Avenue

Note: The complete inscription on this tablet is presented in Part II—Day One— Pages 28–29.

━━━━━━━━━━━━━━━━━━━

ARMY OF THE POTOMAC
TWELFTH CORPS
Major General Henry J. Slocum
Brigadier General Alpheus S. Williams

July 3. Before 1 A. M. the artillery of the Corps and Rigby 's Maryland Battery from Reserve Artillery in all 26 guns were so placed as to command the line occupied by Johnson's Division and at daylight opened fire under cover of which the infantry was advanced and attacked the Confederate position and after a contest lasting seven hours recaptured the works. Many prisoners and 5,000 small arms were captured. In the afternoon the Corps was in readiness to move.

No. 80U   Tablet on Granite Marker located—Slocum Avenue, south slope of Culp's Hill

Note: The complete inscription on this tablet is presented in Part III—Day Two—Pages 116–17.

ARMY OF THE POTOMAC
TWELFTH CORPS
SECOND DIVISION
Brig. General John W. Geary

July 3. At 3 A. M. an attack by infantry and artillery was made on Johnson's division and after a contest of seven hours the Confederate forces were driven from their position losing heavily in killed wounded and prisoners also three battle-flags and over 5,000 small arms.

No. 85U   Tablet on Granite Marker located—South Slocum Avenue

Note: The complete inscription on this tablet is presented in Part III—Day Two—Pages 120–21.

ARMY OF THE POTOMAC
TWELFTH CORPS   SECOND DIVISION
THIRD BRIGADE
Brig. Gen. George S. Greene

July 3. At daylight Major Gen. Johnson having been reinforced advanced and a fierce engagement ensued for seven hours when after suffering great losses he was forced back from the entire line.

No. 86U   Tablet on Granite Pedestal located—North Slocum Avenue

Note: The complete inscription on this tablet is presented in Part III—Day Two—Pages 121–22.

ARMY OF THE POTOMAC
TWELFTH CORPS   SECOND DIVISION
FIRST BRIGADE
Col. Charles Candy

July 3. At daylight the artillery opened on the Confederate Line. The 147th Penna. advanced and captured a stone wall. The 5th Ohio held its position on the right of the Brigade under a heavy fire. The other regiments were in reserve and at intervals relieved the regiments of Second and

Third Brigades. The 66th Ohio advanced beyond the breastworks and poured an enfilading fire on the Confederates occupying the works on the right. At 10.30 A. M. Major Gen. Johnson's forces were forced from the works. Skirmishing continued all day.

No. 88U   Tablet on Granite Pedestal located—North Slocum Avenue

Note: The complete inscription on this tablet is presented in Part III—Day Two— Pages 122–23.

━━━━━━━━━━━

ARMY OF THE POTOMAC
TWELFTH CORPS
SECOND BRIGADE
Col. George A. Cobham Jr.
Brig. Gen. Thomas L. Kane

July 3. At 3.30 A. M. the artillery opened over the Brigade and Major Gen. Johnson's Division advanced and attacked in force exposing its line in front and enfilading fires from infantry and to a destructive fire for seven hours with great loss. Brig. Gen. Steuart's Brigade was immediately in front. No further firing except for skirmishers and sharpshooters.

No. 87U   Tablet on Granite Pedestal located—North Slocum Avenue

Note: The complete inscription on this tablet is presented in Part III—Day Two— Page 122. The parent division of this brigade—Second Division—is not inscribed on the tablet.

━━━━━━━━━━━

ARMY OF THE POTOMAC
SIXTH CORPS   SECOND DIVISION
THIRD BRIGADE
Brig. Gen. Thomas H. Neill
7th Maine (6 Cos.)   43D   49th   77th New York
61st Pennsylvania Infantry

July 2. Arrived after a march of 33 miles from Manchester Md. and about 6 P. M. was detached from the Corps and ordered by Major Gen. G. G. Meade to hold Powers Hill. Later was ordered by Major Gen. H. W. Slocum to support the front line but at midnight was ordered to Powers Hill.

July 3. The Brigade by order of Major Gen. Slocum crossed Rock Creek and took position on the extreme right of the Army making connection with the Cavalry pickets and encountered and checked the advancing

Confederate sharpshooters and skirmishers and remained until the close of the battle.

Casualties   Killed 1 Officer 1 Man   Wounded 11 Men   Captured or Missing 2 Men   Total 15

No. 89U   Tablet on Granite Pedestal located—Neill Avenue east of Rock Creek on Wolf Hill behind the Baker farmhouse, north side of Baltimore Pike

Note: This tablet can only be reached by crossing private property. Visitors should obtain permission before crossing.

ARMY OF THE POTOMAC
SIXTH CORPS   THIRD DIVISION
FIRST BRIGADE
Brig. Gen. Alexander Shaler
65th   67th   122D New York
23D   82D Pennsylvania Infantry

July 2. Arrived about 2 P. M. from Manchester Md. and late in the day moved to the northeast slope of Little Round Top and held in reserve bivouacking for the night near Taneytown Road in rear of Second Brigade.

July 3. Ordered to the left and at 8 A. M. to the right to the support of Second Division Twelfth Corps. Took position in rear of woods on Culp's Hill beyond which action was progressing and was engaged under command of Brig. Gen. J. W. Geary from 9 until 11 A. M. when the original line of the Twelfth Corps was regained. At 3 P. M. returned and under terrific fire of artillery was ordered by Major Gen. G. G. Meade to remain in rear of Third Corps and to report to Major Gen. J. Newton. At 7 P. M. moved half a mile to the right in reserve and remained during the night. Rejoined the Division the next morning.

Casualties   Killed 1 Officer 14 Men   Wounded 3 Officers 53 Men   Captured or Missing 3 Men   Total 74

No. 90U   Tablet on Granite Pedestal located—South Slocum Avenue

---

ARMY OF THE POTOMAC
TWELFTH CORPS
FIRST DIVISION
Brig. General Alpheus S. Williams   Brig. General Thos. H. Ruger

July 3. At daylight attacked the Confederate infantry and was hotly engaged with charges and counter-charges at different points until 10.30 A. M. when the Confederate forces retired.

No. 81U   Tablet on Granite Marker located—Slocum Avenue

Note: The complete inscription on this tablet is presented in Part III—Day Two—Pages 117–18.

ARMY OF THE POTOMAC
TWELFTH CORPS   FIRST DIVISION
FIRST BRIGADE
Col. Archibald L. McDougall

July 3. At daylight the Brigade with the artillery and infantry of the Corps attacked Major Gen. Johnson's Division which had been reinforced from Major Gen. Early's and Major Gen. Rodes's Divisions and at 10.30 A. M. recaptured the works after a fierce contest. In the afternoon sent to the support of Second Corps.

No. 83U   Tablet on Granite Pedestal located—Slocum Avenue

Note: The complete inscription on this tablet is presented in Part III—Day Two—Page 119.

ARMY OF THE POTOMAC
TWELFTH CORPS   FIRST DIVISION
THIRD BRIGADE
Brig. Gen. Thomas H. Ruger
Col. Silas Colgrove

July 3. The 2D Mass. and 27th Indiana in the morning charged across the open swale to get possession of a stone wall and woods on the left but were repulsed with great loss the 27th Indiana falling back in a direct line the 2D Mass. towards the left. A Confederate counter-charge was made across the swale but receiving a front and enfilading fire it was quickly repulsed and the Confederate force left the works and retired across Rock Creek.

No. 84U   Tablet on Granite Pedestal located—South Slocum Avenue

Note: The complete inscription on this tablet is presented in Part III—Day Two—Pages 119–20.

ARMY OF THE POTOMAC
TWELFTH CORPS   FIRST DIVISION
SECOND BRIGADE
Brig. Gen. Henry H. Lockwood

July 3. Took part in the recapture of works which Major General Johnson's Division took possession of during the absence of Division the previous night. At about 8 A. M. 1st Maryland Eastern Shore arrived and joined Brigade. Ordered in the afternoon to Second Corps line near Cemetery to render support where needed.

No. 82U   Tablet on Granite Pedestal located—South Slocum Avenue

Note: The complete inscription on this tablet is presented in Part III—Day Two— Pages 118–19.

ARMY OF THE POTOMAC
FIRST CORPS
FIRST DIVISION

Brig. General James S. Wadsworth

July 2 & 3. Entrenched on Culp's Hill and repulsed attacks made in the evening of second and morning of third.

No. 7U   Tablet on Granite Marker located—North Reynolds Avenue

Note: The complete inscription on this tablet is presented in Part II—Day One— Page 33.

ARMY OF THE POTOMAC
FIRST CORPS   FIRST DIVISION
FIRST BRIGADE
Brig. Gen. Solomon Meredith
Col. William W. Robinson

July 3. Repulsed a sharp attack in the morning without loss.

No. 8U   Tablet on Granite Pedestal located—Meredith Avenue

Note: The complete inscription on this tablet is presented in Part II—First Day— Pages 33–34.

ARMY OF THE POTOMAC
FIRST CORPS   FIRST DIVISION
SECOND BRIGADE
Brig. Gen. Lysander Cutler

July 3. Repulsed an attack in the morning and remained in position until the close of the battle.

No. 9U   Tablet on Granite Pedestal located—North Reynolds Avenue

Note: The complete inscription on this tablet is presented in Part II—First Day— Page 34.

———

ARMY OF THE POTOMAC
SECOND CORPS
Major General Winfield S. Hancock
Brigadier General John Gibbon

July 3. At 1 P. M. the Confederate artillery opened a heavy fire all along Hill's Corps and the left of Longstreet's Corps for two hours when an assault under the command of General Longstreet was made by a force of about 15,000 which was repulsed with great loss in killed wounded and prisoners.

No. 43U   Tablet on Granite Marker located—Hancock Avenue

Note: The complete inscription on this tablet is presented in Part III—Day Two— Pages 93–94.

———

ARMY OF THE POTOMAC
SECOND CORPS
SECOND DIVISION
Brig. General John Gibbon   Brig. General William Harrow

July 3. Artillery firing until 9 A. M. and sharp skirmishing during the day. At 1 P. M. Confederates concentrated the fire of over 100 guns on the Second and Third Divisions and after two hours of uninterrupted firing charged with a force of over 15,000 infantry which was repulsed with great loss of life prisoners and flags.

No. 61U   Tablet on Granite Marker located—Hancock Avenue

Note: The complete inscription on this tablet is presented in Part III—Day Two— Pages 104–5.

ARMY OF THE POTOMAC
SECOND CORPS   SECOND DIVISION
SECOND BRIGADE
Brig. Gen. Alexander S. Webb

July 3. At 3 P. M. after a heavy cannonading for two hours Major Gen. Pickett's Division of about 5,000 men charged the line held by this and the Third Brigade breaking through the line at the Angle. Reinforcements coming up quickly the charge was repulsed with great loss. Nearly 1,000 prisoners and six battle flags were reported captured by the Brigade.

No. 63U   Tablet on Granite Pedestal located—Hancock Avenue

Note: The complete inscription on this tablet is presented in Part III—Day Two—
    Page 106.

ARMY OF THE POTOMAC
SECOND CORPS   SECOND DIVISION
THIRD BRIGADE
Col. Norman Hall

July 3. Remained in position. At 3 P. M. Longstreet's assault was made after a cannonade of two hours. The Brigade and the Second Brigade received the charge of Major Gen. Pickett's Division which was repulsed with great loss in killed wounded prisoners and flags. In this engagement the First Brigade and the other troops were rushed to support of the two Brigades engaged and contributed to the victory. The Brigade remained in its position until the close of the battle.

No. 64U   Tablet on Granite Pedestal located—Hancock Avenue

Note: The complete inscription on this tablet is presented in Part III—Day Two—
    Pages 106–7.

ARMY OF THE POTOMAC
SECOND CORPS   SECOND DIVISION
FIRST BRIGADE
Brig. Gen. William Harrow
Col. Francis E. Heath

July 3. At 1 P. M. a terrific cannonade was opened along the Confederate line in front which continued for about two hours followed by a charge of over 15,000 infantry its right striking Second and Third Brigades. This Brigade moved at once to the right and assisted the other two Brigades in repelling the assault and capturing a large number of prisoners and several flags.

No. 62U   Tablet on Granite Pedestal located—Hancock Avenue

Note: The complete inscription on this tablet is presented in Part III—Day Two— Pages 105–6.

━━━━━━━━━

ARMY OF THE POTOMAC
SECOND CORPS
THIRD DIVISION
Brig. General Alexander Hays

July 3. The Bliss Barn in front occupied by sharpshooters was burned by order of Gen. A. Hays. At 1 P. M. a heavy artillery fire from the Confederate line was concentrated on the positions of Second and Third Divisions of the Corps for two hours followed by a charge of more than 15,000 infantry which was repulsed with loss the Division capturing about 1500 prisoners and 15 stand of colors. The muskets found on the field after the charge numbered about 3500.

No. 65U   Tablet on Granite Marker located—North Hancock Avenue

Note: The complete inscription on this tablet is presented in Part III—Day Two— Pages 107–8.

━━━━━━━━━

ARMY OF THE POTOMAC
SECOND CORPS   THIRD DIVISION
SECOND BRIGADE
Col. Thomas A. Smyth
Lieut. Col. Francis E. Pierce
14th Connecticut   1st Delaware
12th New Jersey   10th   108th New York Infantry

July 2. Took position early in the morning along a stone fence on Cemetery Ridge at the left of Ziegler's Grove supporting Battery I 1st U. S. on the right. Sharp skirmishing during the day and artillery firing at intervals in the afternoon. At night the line of the Brigade was extended to the Angle to cover the portion previously occupied by the Third Brigade.

July 3. In the afternoon the Bliss Barn having been occupied by the Confederate sharpshooters the 14th Conn. by order of Brig. Gen. A. Hays recaptured and burned the barn. At 1 P. M. a terrific cannonade was opened by the Confederates in front which continued for two hours followed by a charge of the Divisions of Major Gen. Pickett Brig. Gen. Pettigrew and Major Gen. Pender which was repulsed by the Brigade reinforced by the Third Brigade. More than 1200 prisoners and 9 stand of colors were captured by the Brigade.

July 4. The Brigade remained in position until the close of the battle with sharp skirmishing during the day.

Casualties   Killed 6 Officers 55 Men   Wounded 34   Officers 245 Men Captured or Missing 1 Officer 25 Men   Total 366

No. 91U   Tablet on Granite Pedestal located—North Hancock Avenue

━━━━━━━━━━━━━━

ARMY OF THE POTOMAC
SECOND CORPS   THIRD DIVISION
THIRD BRIGADE
Col. George L. Willard
Col. Eliakim Sherrill

July 3. Engaged on the skirmish line with much loss. At 3 P. M. after a terrific cannonade of two hours the Brigade was moved up to the line of the Second Brigade and assisted in repulsing Longstreet's assault in which Col. Sherrill was mortally wounded. A large detail from the Brigade under Capt. Armstrong of the 125th New York and the 8th Ohio on the skirmish line withdrew to the right and poured in a deadly fire upon the left of the assaulting lines and then charging captured prisoners and flags.

No. 66U   Tablet on Granite Pedestal located—North Hancock Avenue

Note The complete inscription on this tablet is presented in Part III—Day Two— Page 108.

━━━━━━━━━━━━━━

ARMY OF THE POTOMAC
SECOND CORPS   THIRD DIVISION
FIRST BRIGADE
Col. Samuel S. Carroll
14th Indiana   4th   8th Ohio
7th West Virginia Infantry

July 2. Took position in the morning on right of Corps on Cemetery Ridge between the Cemetery and Battery I 1st U. S. in Ziegler's Grove. In the afternoon the 8th Ohio was sent on the skirmish line and remained until the close of the battle. At 7 P. M. the remainder of the Brigade occupied the place on the left made vacant by the Third Brigade going to the support of Third Corps for a short time. At dark the Brigade went to relief of Eleventh Corps and was hotly engaged in support of Batteries on East Cemetery Hill until after 10 P. M.

July 3. Sharp skirmishing continued through the day the Brigade was subjected to an annoying sharpshooters fire from the houses in the town and a cross fire from artillery from the north east and west. The 8th Ohio assisted in the repulse of Longstreet's assault. The Brigade captured 252 prisoners and 4 stand of colors.

Casualties   Killed 3 Officers 35 Men   Wounded 15 Officers 151 Men Captured or Missing 7 Men   Total 211

No. 92U   Tablet on Granite Pedestal located—East Cemetery Hill

---

ARMY OF THE POTOMAC
FIRST CORPS
THIRD DIVISION
Brig. Gen. Thos. A. Rowley   Major Gen. Abner Doubleday

July 3. In position on left of Second Division Second Corps. Assisted in repulsing Longstreet's assault capturing many prisoners and three stand of colors.

No. 10U   Tablet on Granite Marker located—South Reynolds Avenue

Note: The complete inscription on this tablet is presented in Part II—Day One—Page 35.

ARMY OF THE POTOMAC
FIRST CORPS   THIRD DIVISION
FIRST BRIGADE
Col. Chapman Biddle
Brig. Gen. Thomas A. Rowley

July 3. Remained in the same position and assisted in repelling Longstreet's assault in the afternoon taking many prisoners. At 6 P. M. withdrew to former position on Taneytown Road.

No. 11U   Tablet on Granite Pedestal located—South Reynolds Avenue

Note: The complete inscription on this tablet is presented in Part II—Day One—Pages 35–36.

ARMY OF THE POTOMAC
FIRST CORPS   THIRD DIVISION
THIRD BRIGADE
Brig. Gen. George J. Stannard
Col. Francis V. Randall

July 3. In position on left of Second Division Second Corps at the time of Longstreet's assault. The 13th and 16th advanced against Major Gen. Pickett's Division changed front forward and attacked its right throwing it into confusion and capturing many prisoners. The 16th and part of 14th then went to the left and attacked the advancing Brigades of Brig. Gen. Wilcox and Perry (Col. Lang) and captured three flags and many prisoners.

No. 75U   Tablet on Granite Pedestal located—Hancock Avenue

Note: The complete inscription on this tablet is presented in Part III—Day Two— Page 114.

———————

ARMY OF THE POTOMAC
CAVALRY CORPS
Major General Alfred Pleasonton

July 3. Merritt's Brigade arrived and skirmished with Confederate right while the 6th U. S. advanced to Fairfield and became engaged. Kilpatrick with Farnsworth Brigade took position on left of battle line and made a charge in the afternoon on the Confederate right but was repulsed with loss including General Farnsworth killed. Gregg's Division on the right was attacked by Stuart's Cavalry in the afternoon but with the aid of Custer's Brigade Kilpatrick's Division the attack was repulsed.

No. 2U   Tablet on Granite Marker located—Pleasonton Avenue

Note: The complete inscription on this tablet is presented in Part II—Day One— Pages 29–30.

———————

ARMY OF THE POTOMAC
CAVALRY CORPS
SECOND DIVISION
Brig. General David McM. Gregg

First Brigade	Col. John B. McIntosh
Second Brigade	Col. Pennock Huey
Third Brigade	Col. J. Irvin Gregg

July 2. Gen. Gregg with two Brigades left Hanover and took position about noon at the junction of the Hanover Road with the Low Dutch Road First Brigade on the right Third on the left connecting with the infantry pickets (the Second Brigade having been sent to Westminster). Took and held Brinkerhoff Ridge after a sharp skirmish with the 2D Virginia Infantry. About 10 P. M. the two Brigades withdrew and bivouacked for the night on the Baltimore Pike a mile East of Rock Creek Bridge.

July 3. Took position with the right on Hanover Road. The Second Brigade Third Cavalry Division on the right. Gen. Custer having received an order from Gen. Pleasonton to rejoin his Division was relieved about 2 P. M. by the First Brigade. A large force of Confederate Cavalry under Gen. Stuart screened from view by woods having been discovered Gen. Gregg ordered Custer to remain in support of McIntosh until Confederate Cavalry could be driven back. Custer and McIntosh and the Batteries of Randol and Pennington were soon hotly engaged with the Confederate Cavalry and Artillery. About 3 P. M. Stuart made a charge with his reserves under Hampton and Fitzhugh Lee which was repulsed. This closed operations on the field.

Casualties   Killed 6 Men   Wounded 7 Officers 31 Men   Captured or Missing 1 Officer 11 Men   Total 56

No. 93U   Tablet on Granite Marker located—Gregg Avenue, East Cavalry Field

---

ARMY OF THE POTOMAC
CAVALRY CORPS   SECOND DIVISION
FIRST BRIGADE
Col. John B. McIntosh

1st MD. (11 Cos.)   Purnell Legion   1st Mass. Co. A
1st New Jersey   1st   3rd Penna. Cavalry
Section Battery H   3rd Penna. H. Artillery

July 2. After an exhausting march took position about noon on Hanover Road near intersection with Low Dutch Road Third Brigade on left. During the afternoon there was a skirmish between 3D Penna. Purnell Legion 1st New Jersey and Section Battery H Penna. H. A. and 2D Virginia Infantry for the possession of Brinkerhoff Ridge. About 10 P. M. the line was withdrawn and with third Brigade bivouacked on Baltimore Pike nearly a mile east of Rock Creek Bridge. 1st Mass. with Sixth Corps.

July 3. Returning in the morning and finding Second Brigade Third Division in position of the day before the Brigade formed on left of Second Brigade Third Division and soon after noon relieved it. About 2 P. M. a large

Confederate force having been observed Brig. Gen. D. McM. Gregg ordered Second Brigade Third Division to return and the Brigade with Second Brigade Third Division was soon engaged with Major Gen. Stuart's command. About 3 P. M. Brig. Gen. Hampton's and Brig. Gen. Fitzhugh Lee's Brigades the reserves which had been concealed on the Stallsmith Farm emerged from the woods in front and charged but were repulsed with the aid of Artillery.

Casualties Wounded 7 Officers 19 Men Captured or Missing 9 Men Total 35

No. 94U Tablet on Granite Pedestal located—Gregg Avenue, East Cavalry Field

---

ARMY OF THE POTOMAC
CAVALRY CORPS THIRD DIVISION
SECOND BRIGADE
Brig. Gen. George A. Custer
1st 5th 6th 7th (10 Cos.) Michigan Cavalry

June 30. Skirmished with Major Gen. Stuart's Cavalry at Hanover. Supported Battery M 2D U. S.

July 1. Not engaged.

July 2. Engaged with Brig. Gen. Hampton's Brigade of Major Gen. Stuart's Cavalry at Hunterstown and with the aid of Battery M 2D U. S. forced it from the field. The 7th Michigan dismounted as skirmishers.

July 3. Marched to Two Taverns arriving at daylight and at 8 A. M. moved to the right under orders to report to Brig. Gen. D. McM. Gregg. Took position north of the Hanover road and West of the Low Dutch Road Second Division coming up and connecting on the left. Soon after noon was ordered to join the Division on the extreme left but about 2 P. M. Major Gen. Stuart's Division and Brig. Gen. Jenkins' Brigade of Cavalry having been discovered on the right and front Brig. Gen. Custer under orders from Brig. Gen. D. McM. Gregg turned back his Brigade and with First Brigade Second Division was immediately engaged with the Confederate forces which were repulsed and forced from the field. Late in the day moved to the extreme left and rejoined the Division.

Casualties Killed 1 Officer 31 Men Wounded 13 Officers 134 Men Captured or Missing 78 Men Total 257

No. 95U Tablet on Granite Pedestal located—Gregg Avenue, East Cavalry Field

ARMY OF THE POTOMAC
CAVALRY CORPS SECOND DIVISION
THIRD BRIGADE
Col. J. Irvin Gregg
1st Maine (10 Cos.)   10th New York
4th 16th Pennsylvania Cavalry

July 2. Arrived and took position on Hanover Road 2 miles from Gettysburg in proximity to Lieut. Gen. Ewell's Corps about 11 A. M. Two regiments of infantry from Eleventh Corps were in front as skirmishers. They were withdrawn about 3 P. M. and 10th New York deployed in their place. Confederate sharpshooters from hill and woods in front were annoying. Fifty dismounted men were ordered to drive them back but were themselves met by a superior force until checked and forced back by First Brigade.

July 3. Took position in morning on Baltimore Pike and moved to the right near Hanover Road. Not engaged in Cavalry fight except one section of Batteries E & G 1st U. S. Lieut. J. Chester. Ordered to the left to meet a threatened attack.

July 4. Made a reconnaissance to Hunterstown and forced in Confederate pickets.

Casualties Killed 6 Men Wounded 12 Men Captured or Missing 1 Officer 2 Men Total 21

No. 96U Tablet on Granite Pedestal located—East Cavalry Avenue, East Cavalry Field

---

ARMY OF THE POTOMAC
CAVALRY CORPS
THIRD DIVISION
Brig. General Judson Kilpatrick

First Brigade   Brig. Gen. Elon J. Farnsworth
                         Col. Nathaniel P. Richmond

Second Brigade   Brig. General George A. Custer

Headquarters Guard,
  Co. C 1st Ohio   Capt. S. N. Stanford

June 30. The First Brigade was attacked by Stuart's Confederate Cavalry at Hanover and was repulsed.

July 1. Marched to Berlin to intercept Stuart without success.

July 2. Arrived on the field of Gettysburg at 2 P. M. Moved over the road from Gettysburg to Abbottstown and was attacked at sundown near Hunterstown by Stuart's Cavalry which was driven from the field after an engagement of two hours.

July 3. Moved to attack the Confederate right and rear. The Second Brigade reported to Gen. Gregg and was engaged on the extreme right. Gen. Farnsworth arrived on the extreme left at 1 P. M. and became engaged with the Confederate skirmishers and was supported by the Reserve Brigade on his left. About 5.30 P. M. the First and Reserve Brigades advanced Gen. Farnsworth with the 1st West Virginia and 18th Pennsylvania through woods and across stone walls occupied by superior forces of Confederate infantry and artillery and was repulsed with heavy loss and Gen. Farnsworth killed.

July 4. Moved to Emmitsburg.

Casualties   Killed 4 Officers 49 Men   Wounded 19 Officers 162 Men Captured or Missing 1 Officer 120 Men   Total 355

No. 97U   Tablet on Granite Marker located—South Confederate Avenue, Bushman Woods

---

ARMY OF THE POTOMAC
CAVALRY CORPS   THIRD DIVISION
FIRST BRIGADE
Brig. Gen. Elon J. Farnsworth
Col. Nathaniel P. Richmond

5th New York   18th Pennsylvania
1st Vermont   1st (10 Cos.) West Virginia Cavalry

June 30. Arrived at Hanover about noon and was attacked by Major Gen. Stuart's Cavalry and Horse Artillery which first encountered the 18th Penna. in the rear of the column. Later the Brigade was engaged and Major Gen. Stuart having been repulsed from the town retired with the loss of a battle-flag and over 70 men.

July 1 & 2. Not engaged.

July 3. Moved to the left to attack the Confederate right and rear arriving about 1 P. M. and engaged with Confederate skirmishers being supported at 3 P. M. by the Reserve Cavalry Brigade on the left. At 5.30 P. M. the 18th Pa. 1st Vt. and 1st West Virginia charged the Confederate left through the woods and among stone fences held by superior forces of Infantry and Artillery but were repulsed with heavy loss including Brig. Gen. Farnsworth killed.

Casualties   Killed 3 Officers 18 Men   Wounded 6 Officers 28 Men
Captured or Missing 1 Officer 42 Men   Total 98

No. 98U   Tablet on Granite Pedestal located—South Confederate Avenue

---

ARMY OF THE POTOMAC
CAVALRY CORPS   FIRST DIVISION
RESERVE BRIGADE
Brig. Gen. Wesley Merritt

6th Pennsylvania
1st 2D 5th 6th United States Cavalry

July 1. Engaged in picketing and patrolling the roads through the mountains detachments scouting the country about Hagerstown Cavetown and other points.

July 2. Marched to Emmitsburg Md.

July 3. At noon marched four miles on the road to Gettysburg met Confederate detachments and for more than a mile drove them from stone fences barricades and other positions being engaged four hours and until the operations were brought to a close by heavy rain. The 6th United States under Major S. H. Starr was detached and marched towards Fairfield to intercept a Confederate wagon train supposed to be in that vicinity but encountered a superior force and was compelled to fall back with heavy loss.

Casualties   Killed 1 Officer 27 Men   Wounded 12 Officers 104 Men
Captured or Missing 6 Officers 268 Men   Total 418

No. 99U   Tablet on Granite Pedestal located—Emmitsburg Road, South Cavalry Field

---

ARMY OF THE POTOMAC
CAVALRY CORPS
RESERVE BRIGADE   FIRST DIVISION
FIRST U. S. CAVALRY
Captain Robert S. C. Lord Commanding

Detachment at Headquarters Army of the Potomac

July 3. Moved with the Brigade at 12 M under Brig. General W. Merritt from Emmitsburg and attacked the Confederate right and rear and was engaged for 4 hours until the action was brought to a close by a heavy rain.

Casualties   Killed 1 Man   Wounded 9 Men   Missing 5 Men

No. 100U   Tablet on Granite Pedestal located—east of Emmitsburg Road, South Cavalry Field

---

ARMY OF THE POTOMAC
CAVALRY CORPS
RESERVE BRIGADE   FIRST DIVISION
SECOND U. S. CAVALRY
Captain Theo. P. Rodenbough Commanding

Detachment at Headquarters Army of the Potomac

July 3. Moved with the Brigade at 12 M. under Brig. General W. Merritt from Emmitsburg and attacked the Confederate right and rear and was engaged for four hours until the action was brought to a close by a heavy rain.

Casualties   Killed 3 Men   Wounded 1 Officer and 6 Men   Missing 1 Officer and 6 Men

No. 101U   Tablet on Granite Marker located—east of Emmitsburg Road, South Cavalry Field

---

POSITION OCCUPIED
By
DETACHMENTS
OF THE
1ST & 2D REGIMENTS
UNITED STATES CAVALRY
DURING JULY 3D 1863

No. 102U   Tablet on Granite Pedestal located—east of Ridge Road, South Cavalry Field

---

POSITION OCCUPIED
By
DETACHMENTS
OF THE
1ST & 2D REGIMENTS
UNITED STATES CAVALRY
DURING JULY 3D 1863

No. 103U Tablet on Granite Pedestal located—west of Emmitsburg Road, South Cavalry Field

━━━━━━━━━━

ARMY OF THE POTOMAC
CAVALRY CORPS
RESERVE BRIGADE FIRST DIVISION
FIFTH U. S. CAVALRY
Captain Julius W. Mason Commanding

Detachment at Headquarters Army of the Potomac

July 3. Moved with the Brigade at 12 M. under Brig. General W. Merritt from Emmitsburg and attacked the Confederate right and rear and was engaged for four hours until the action was brought to a close by a heavy rain.

Casualties Wounded 4 Men Missing 1 Man

No. 104U Tablet on Granite Marker located—west of Ridge Road, South Cavalry Field

━━━━━━━━━━

ARMY OF THE POTOMAC
CAVALRY CORPS
RESERVE BRIGADE FIRST DIVISION
SIXTH U. S. CAVALRY
Major Samuel H. Starr Commanding

Detachment at Headquarters Army of the Potomac

July 3. Moved at 12 M. with the Brigade from Emmitsburg to attack the Confederate right and rear but was detached from the Brigade to intercept the Confederate wagon train supposed to be near Fairfield or Millerstown. Engaged a superior force of the Confederate Cavalry near Millerstown and withdrew after heavy loss.

Casualties Killed 6 Men Wounded 5 Officers and 23 Men Missing 5 Officers and 203 Men

No. 105U Tablet on Granite Marker located—east of Emmitsburg Road, South Cavalry Field

THIRD DAY TABLET INSCRIPTIONS
ARMY OF NORTHERN VIRGINIA

ARMY OF NORTHERN VIRGINIA
General Robert E. Lee
Commanding

July 3. Pickett's Division Longstreet's Corps reached the field in the morning. Assaulted the Union line on Cemetery Ridge about 3 P. M. assisted by Hill's Corps. The assault failed with great loss. An attack made on the left by Johnson's Division, Ewell's Corps, reinforced by three brigades of the Corps, failed. Stuart's Cavalry Division engaged with 2d Union Cavalry Division and 2d Brigade 3d Cavalry Division on the Confederate left about 1 P. M.

No. 1C   Tablet on Granite Marker located—West Confederate Avenue

Note: The complete inscription on this tablet is presented in Part II—Day One—Pages 46–47.

ARMY OF NORTHERN VIRGINIA
SECOND ARMY CORPS
Lieutenant General Richard S. Ewell

July 3. Early in the morning an attack was made by Johnson's Division having been reinforced by three brigades from the Corps two other assaults were made but failed. Early's Division was withdrawn and occupied its former position in the town and not engaged. At night the Corps fell back to the range of hills west of the town.

No. 13C   Tablet on Granite Marker located—North Confederate Avenue

Note: The complete inscription on this tablet is presented in Part II—Day One—Pages 54–55.

181

ARMY OF NORTHERN VIRGINIA
SECOND ARMY CORPS
JOHNSON'S DIVISION
Maj. Gen. Edward Johnson

July 3. The assault was renewed in early morning. An attempt was made by the Union forces to retake the works occupied the night before and was repulsed. The Division being reinforced by four brigades two other assaults were made and repulsed. Retired at 10.30 A. M. to former position of July 2 which was held until 10 P. M. when the Division was withdrawn to the ridge northwest of town.

No. 52C   Tablet on Granite Marker located—East Confederate Avenue

Note: The complete inscription on this tablet is presented in Part III—Day Two— Page 142.

———

C. S. A.
ARMY OF NORTHERN VIRGINIA
EWELL'S CORPS   JOHNSON'S DIVISION
JONES'S BRIGADE

July 3. In line near here all day sometimes skirmishing heavily. About midnight moved with the Division and Corps to Seminary Ridge northwest of the town.

No. 53C   Tablet on Granite Pedestal located—East Confederate Avenue

Note: The complete inscription on this tablet is presented in Part III—Day Two— Pages 142–43.

———

C. S. A.
ARMY OF NORTHERN VIRGINIA
EWELL'S CORPS   JOHNSON'S DIVISION
NICHOLL'S BRIGADE

July 3. At dawn the Brigade reopened fire and continued it for many hours then retired to line near the creek whence about midnight it moved with Division and Corps to Seminary Ridge.

No. 54C   Tablet on Granite Pedestal located—East Confederate Avenue

Note: The complete inscription on this tablet is presented in Part III—Day Two— Page 143.

———

C. S. A.
ARMY OF NORTHERN VIRGINIA
EWELL'S CORPS   JOHNSON'S DIVISION
STEUART'S BRIGADE

July 3. The Union troops reinforced the conflict at dawn and it raged fiercely until 11 A. M. when this Brigade and the entire line fell back to the base of the hill and from thence moved about midnight to Seminary Ridge northwest of the town.

No. 55C   Tablet on Granite Pedestal located—East Confederate Avenue

Note: The complete inscription on this tablet is presented in Part III—Day Two— Pages 143–44.

C. S. A.
ARMY OF NORTHERN VIRGINIA
EWELL'S CORPS   JOHNSON'S DIVISION
WALKER'S BRIGADE

July 3. Took part in the unsuccessful struggle lasting from daybreak until near noon and then retired to the foot of the hill and from thence about midnight moved with the Division and Corps to Seminary Ridge.

No. 56C   Tablet on Granite Pedestal located—East Confederate Avenue

Note: The complete inscription on this tablet is presented in Part III—Day Two— Page 144.

C. S. A.
ARMY OF NORTHERN VIRGINIA
SECOND ARMY CORPS
RODES'S DIVISION
Maj. Gen. R. E. Rodes

July 3. The Brigades of Daniel and O'Neal were ordered to report to Gen. E. Johnson on the left early in the morning and joined in the attack on Culp's Hill. The remainder of the Division held the position of day before and at night retired to Seminary Ridge.

No. 14C   Tablet on Granite Marker located—rear of Peace Memorial, Oak Hill

Note: The complete inscription on this tablet is presented in Part II—Day One— Pages 55–56.

C. S. A.

ARMY OF NORTHERN VIRGINIA

EWELL'S CORPS   RODES'S DIVISION

DANIEL'S BRIGADE

32nd 43rd 45th 53rd Regiments and 2nd Battalion North Carolina Infantry

July 3. After taking part in the battles of the First and Second days elsewhere on the field the Brigade marched about 1.30 A. M. from its position in the town to Culp's Hill to reinforce Johnson's Division. Arriving
about 4 A. M. it fought at different points wherever ordered through the
long and fierce conflict its main position being in the ravine between the
two summits of Culp's Hill. At the close of the struggle near noon it was
withdrawn by Gen. Johnson with the rest of the line to the base of the hill
from whence it moved during the night to Seminary Ridge west of the
town and there rejoined Rodes's Division.

July 4. Occupied Seminary Ridge. Late at night began the march to
Hagerstown.

Present 2100   Killed 165   Wounded 635   Missing 116   Total 916

No. 58C   Tablet on Granite Pedestal located—East Confederate Avenue

---

C. S. A.

ARMY OF NORTHERN VIRGINIA

EWELL'S CORPS   RODES'S DIVISION

O'NEAL'S BRIGADE

3rd   5th   6th   12th   26th Alabama Infantry

July 3. After taking part in the battle of the First and Second Days elsewhere on the field the Brigade leaving the 5th Regiment on guard marched
at 2 A. M. from its position in town to Culp's Hill to reinforce Johnson's
Division. Arrived at daybreak and was soon under fire but not actively
engaged until 8 A. M. when it advanced against breastworks on the
eastern slope of the main summit of the Hill gaining there a position near
the Union works and holding it under a terrific fire for three hours until
withdrawn by Gen. Johnson with his entire line to the base of the hill
near the creek. From thence it moved during the night to Seminary Ridge
west of the town and rejoined Rodes's Division.

July 4. Occupied Seminary Ridge. Late at night began the march to
Hagerstown.

Present 1650   Killed 73   Wounded 430   Missing 193   Total 696

No. 59C   Tablet on Granite Pedestal located—East Confederate Avenue

━━━━━━━━━━

C. S. A.
ARMY OF NORTHERN VIRGINIA
SECOND ARMY CORPS
EARLY'S DIVISION
Maj. Gen. Jubal A. Early

July 3. At daylight Smith's Brigade was ordered to support of Johnson's Division on the left. Hays's and Hoke's Brigades formed line in town holding the position of previous day. Gordon's Brigade held the line of the day before. The Division not further engaged.

No. 20C   Tablet on Granite Marker located—East Confederate Avenue

Note: The complete inscription on this tablet is presented in Part II—Day One— Pages 59–60.

━━━━━━━━━━

C. S. A.
ARMY OF NORTHERN VIRGINIA
EWELL'S CORPS   EARLY'S DIVISION
SMITH'S BRIGADE
31st   49th   52nd Virginia Infantry

July 3. The Brigade having been detached two days guarding York Pike and other roads against the reported approach of Union Cavalry was ordered to Culp's Hill to reinforce Johnson's Division. Arriving early formed in line along this stone wall receiving and returning fire of Infantry and sharpshooters in the woods opposite and being subjected to heavy fire of Artillery. It repulsed the charge of the 2nd Massachusetts and 27th Indiana Regiments against this line and held its ground until the Union forces regained their works on the hill. It then moved to a position further up the creek and during the night marched to Seminary Ridge where it rejoined Early's Division.

July 4. Occupied Seminary Ridge. After midnight began the march to Hagerstown.

Present about 800   Killed 12   Wounded 113   Missing 17   Total 142

No. 60C   Tablet on Granite Pedestal located—East Confederate Avenue

━━━━━━━━━━

ARMY OF NORTHERN VIRGINIA
EWELL'S CORPS
RODES'S EARLY'S AND JOHNSON'S DIVISIONS

July 4. Having withdrawn under orders from its previous positions the Corps formed line about daybreak on this ridge with its right a short distance south of the Hagerstown Road its left near the Mummasburg Road and its center near here. Rodes was on the right Johnson on the left and Early on a supporting line in their rear. The breastworks of stone here and the old earthworks beyond the railroad are remains of defenses then thrown up and indicate the position of the front line.

July 5. The three divisions left here at different hours but all were on the march to Hagerstown early in the morning of this day.

No. 61C   Cast Iron Position Tablet located—Seminary Avenue, south of Chambersburg Pike

---

ARMY OF NORTHERN VIRGINIA
FIRST ARMY CORPS
Lieutenant General James Longstreet

July 3. Pickett's Division reached the field at 9 A. M. Pickett's Heth's and part of Pender's Division were ordered to form column of assault on Union centre on Cemetery Hill. The batteries opened about 1 P. M. About 3 P. M. Pickett advanced in good order under a severe fire and was repulsed at the stone wall losing heavily. McLaws's and Hood's Divisions were not seriously engaged during the day and night.

No. 24C   Tablet on Granite Marker located—intersection of West Confederate Avenue and Millerstown Road

Note: The complete inscription on this tablet is presented in Part III—Day Two— Pages 126–27.

ARMY OF NORTHERN VIRGINIA
FIRST ARMY CORPS
PICKETT'S DIVISION
Maj. Gen. Geo. E. Pickett

Garnett's Brigade	Brig. Gen. R. B. Garnett
	Major C. S. Peyton
Armistead's Brigade	Brig. Gen. L. A. Armistead
	Lieut. Col. William White

Kemper's Brigade   Brig. Gen. J. L. Kemper
                             Col. Joseph Mayo Jr.

Artillery Battalion,
  Four Batteries   Major James Dearing

July 1. Guarding trains at Chambersburg.

July 2. On march to Gettysburg.

July 3. Reached the field about 9 A. M. Near 12 M. took position beyond crest of hill on which the artillery was placed. About 1.30 P. M. Division was formed in an open field east of Spangler's Woods the right near a barn facing the Union line on Cemetery Ridge. At 3 P. M. moved forward to assault across the field about three fourths of a mile under severe fire losing many officers and men only a few reaching the salient. The Division being separated from its support on the right and left and the assault having failed returned to its former position on the ridge.

July 4. The Division took up the line of march during the night.

Casualties   Killed 232   Wounded 1157   Missing 1499   Total 2888

No. 62C   Tablet on Granite Marker located—West Confederate Avenue

---

C. S. A.
LONGSTREET'S CORPS PICKETT'S DIVISION
KEMPER'S BRIGADE
1st   3rd   7th   11th   24th Virginia Infantry

July 2. Arrived about sunset and bivouacked on the western border of Spangler's Woods.

July 3. In the forenoon formed line in the field east of the woods with right flank near Spangler's Barn. At the close of the cannonade advanced and took part in Longstreet's assault upon the Union position in the vicinity of the Angle. Exposed to a severe fire of artillery and vigorously assailed beyond the Emmitsburg Road by infantry on the right flank with ranks thinned and much disorganized by its losses especially of officers it pressed on against the Union line at the stone wall where after a fierce encounter the struggle ended. Gen. J. L. Kemper fell wounded in front of the stone wall.

July 4. Spent the day in reorganization and during the night began the march to Hagerstown.

Present 1575   Killed 56   Wounded 356   Missing 317   Total 731

No. 63C   Tablet on Granite Pedestal located—West Confederate Avenue

C. S. A.
ARMY OF NORTHERN VIRGINIA
LONGSTREET'S CORPS   PICKETT'S DIVISION
GARNETT'S BRIGADE
8th   18th   19th   28th   56th Virginia Infantry

July2. Arrived about sunset and bivouacked on the western border of Spangler's Woods.

July 3. In the forenoon formed line on Kemper's left in the field east of the woods. At the cessation of the cannonade advanced and took part in Longstreet's assault on the Union position in the vicinity of the Angle. This advance was made in good order under a storm of shells and grape and a deadly fire of musketry after passing the Emmitsburg Road. The lines were much broken in crossing the post and rail fences on both sides of that road but with shattered ranks the Brigade pushed on and took part in the final struggle at the Angle. Gen. R. B. Garnett fell dead from his saddle in front of the stone wall.

July 4. Spent the day in reorganization and during the night began the march to Hagerstown.

Present 1480   Killed 78   Wounded 324   Missing 539   Total 941

No. 64C   Tablet on Granite Pedestal located—West Confederate Avenue

―――――――――

C. S. A.
ARMY OF NORTHERN VIRGINIA
LONGSTREET'S CORPS   PICKETT'S DIVISION
ARMISTEAD'S BRIGADE
9th   14th   38th   53rd   57th Virginia Infantry

July 2. Arrived about sunset and bivouacked on the western border of Spangler's Woods.

July 3. In the forenoon formed line behind Kemper and Garnett east of the woods. When the cannonade ceased advanced to support Kemper's and Garnett's Brigades forming the right of Longstreet's Corps. Its losses being less at first than those of the other brigades it passed the Emmitsburg Road in compact ranks and as the front line was going to pieces near the stone wall pushed forward and many of its men and some from other commands responding to the call and following Gen. L. A. Armistead sprang over the wall into the Angle and continued the desperate struggle until he fell mortally wounded beyond the stone wall.

July 4. Spent the day in reorganization and during the night began the march to Hagerstown.

Present 1650   Killed 88   Wounded 460   Missing 643   Total 1191

No. 65C   Tablet on Granite Pedestal located—West Confederate Avenue

---

ARMY OF NORTHERN VIRGINIA
THIRD ARMY CORPS
Lieutenant General Ambrose P. Hill

July 3. The Corps occupied the same position. Reserve Batteries were placed facing the Union lines. The Confederate line held by Anderson's Division half of Pender's and half of Heth's the remainder of the Corps ordered to report to General Longstreet as a support in the assault to be made on the Union position on Cemetery Ridge. About 1 P. M. the artillery along the line opened fire. 3 P. M. the assault was made and failed. Anderson's Division was held in reserve. The troops fell back to former positions.

No. 2C   Tablet on Granite Marker located—West Confederate Avenue

Note: The complete inscription on this tablet is presented in Part II—Day One— Pages 47–48.

C. S. A.
ARMY OF NORTHERN VIRGINIA
THIRD ARMY CORPS   HETH'S DIVISION
Major Gen. Henry Heth   Brig. Gen. J. J. Pettigrew

July 3. The Division occupied the position of the day before and was ordered to report to Lieut. Gen. Longstreet to unite in the attack on the Union Centre. The assault was made and failed. The Division returned to its former position.

No. 3C   Tablet on Granite Marker located—West Confederate Avenue

Note: The complete inscription on this tablet is presented in Part II—Day One— Pages 48–49.

C. S. A.
ARMY OF NORTHERN VIRGINIA
HILL'S CORPS   HETH'S DIVISION

ARCHER'S BRIGADE

5th Battalion and 13th Alabama 1st 7th 14th Tennessee Infantry

July 1. Reached the field in the morning. The Battalion was ordered to watch Cavalry on the right. The four regiments advancing to Reynolds Woods were met and flanked by the 1st Brigade 1st Division First Corps and fell back across the Run losing 75 prisoners including Brig. Gen. Archer.

July 2. In the evening marched from the woods west of Willoughby Run and took position here.

July 3. In Longstreet's assault was the right Brigade of Pettigrew's Division. Advanced to the stone wall at the Angle and some of the men leaped over it. Had 13 color bearers shot four of them at the wall. Lost 4 of 5 flags and 5 of the 7 field officers with company officers and men in nearly the same proportion.

July 4. After night withdrew and began the march to Hagerstown.

Present 1048   Killed and wounded 160   Missing 517   Total 677

No. 66C   Tablet on Granite Pedestal located—West Confederate Avenue

Note: Another tablet for Archer's Brigade—No. 4C located on Meredith Avenue— is included with the activity of July 1.

C. S. A.
ARMY OF NORTHERN VIRGINIA
HILL'S CORPS   HETH'S DIVISION

PETTIGREW'S BRIGADE

July 3. In Longstreet's assault the Brigade occupied the right center of the Division and the course of the charge brought it in front of the high stone wall north of the Angle and 80 yards farther east, it advanced very nearly to that wall. A few reached it but were captured. The skeleton regiments retired led by Lieutenants and the Brigade by a Major the only field officer left.

No. 6C   Tablet on Granite Pedestal located—West Confederate Avenue

Note: The complete inscription on this tablet is presented in Part II—Day One— Page 50.

C. S. A.
ARMY OF NORTHERN VIRGINIA
HILL'S CORPS   HETH'S DIVISION
DAVIS'S BRIGADE
55th North Carolina 2nd 11th 42nd Mississippi Infantry

July 1. Formed line west of Herr's Tavern and crossing the Run at 10 A. M. dislodged 2nd Maine Battery and the 2nd Brigade 1st Division First Corps. Threatened on the right it wheeled and occupied railroad cut too deep and steep for defense whereby it lost many prisoners and a stand of colors. Joined later by the 11th Regiment previously on duty guarding trains the Brigade fought until the day's contest ended.

July 2. Lay all day west of the Run. At evening took position near here.

July 3. In Longstreet's assault the Brigade formed the left center of Pettigrew's Division and advanced to the stone wall south of Bryan Barn where with regiments shrunken to companies and field officers all disabled further effort was useless.

July 4. After night withdrew and began the march to Hagerstown.

Present on the first day about 2000   Killed 180   Wounded 717   Missing about 500   Total 1397

No. 67C   Tablet on Granite Pedestal located—West Confederate Avenue

Note: Another tablet for Davis' Brigade—No. 5C located on Reynolds Avenue—is included with the activity of July 1st.

C. S. A.
ARMY OF NORTHERN VIRGINIA
HILL'S CORPS   HETH'S DIVISION
BROCKENBROUGH'S BRIGADE

July 3. In Longstreet's assault this Brigade was on the left flank of the column and as it approached the Union position was exposed to a severe fire of musketry on the left flank and artillery and musketry in front. It pushed beyond the Emmitsburg Road but was met by a heavy front and flank fire from the Union lines north of Bryan Barn and compelled to fall back.

No. 7C   Tablet on Granite Pedestal located—West Confederate Avenue

Note: The complete inscription on this tablet is presented in Part II—Day One—Pages 50–51.

C. S. A.
ARMY OF NORTHERN VIRGINIA
THIRD ARMY CORPS
PENDER'S DIVISION
Major Gen. William D. Pender

July 3. During the morning two Brigades ordered to report to Lieut. Gen. Longstreet as a support to Gen. Pettigrew and were placed in rear of right of Heth's Division which formed a portion of the column of assault. The line moved forward one mile in view of the fortified position on Cemetery Ridge, exposed to severe fire. The extreme right reached the works but was compelled to fall back. The Division reformed where it rested before making the attack.

No. 8C   Tablet on Granite Marker located—West Confederate Avenue

Note: The complete inscription on this tablet is presented in Part II—Day One— Pages 51–52.

C. S. A.
ARMY OF NORTHERN VIRGINIA
HILL'S CORPS   PENDER'S DIVISION
SCALES'S BRIGADE

July 3. In Longstreet's assault the Brigade supported the right wing of Pettigrew's Division. With few officers to lead them the men advanced in good order through a storm of shot and shell and when the front line neared the Union works they pushed forward to aid it in the final struggle and were among the last to retire.

No. 11C   Tablet on Granite Pedestal located—West Confederate Avenue

Note: The complete inscription on this tablet is presented in Part II—Day One— Page 53.

C. S. A.
HILL'S CORPS   PENDER'S DIVISION
LANE'S BRIGADE

July 3. In Longstreet's assault the Brigade supported the centre of Pettigrew's Division advancing in good order under the storm of shot and shell and when near the Union works north of the Angle pushed forward to aid the fragments of the front line in the final struggle and was among the last to retire.

No. 9C   Tablet on Granite Pedestal located—West Confederate Avenue

Note: The complete inscription on this tablet is presented in Part II—Day One—
Page 52.

ARMY OF NORTHERN VIRGINIA
THIRD ARMY CORPS
ANDERSON'S DIVISION
Major Gen. R. H. Anderson

July 3. The Division remained in position until 3.30 P. M. Orders were given to support Lieut. Gen. Longstreet's attack on the Union centre Wilcox and Perry moved forward. The assault failed the order to advance was countermanded.

No. 43C   Tablet on Granite Marker located—West Confederate Avenue

Note: The complete inscription on this tablet is presented in Part III—Day Two—
Page 137.

C. S. A.
ARMY OF NORTHERN VIRGINIA
HILL'S CORPS   ANDERSON'S DIVISION
WILCOX'S BRIGADE

July 3. Took position west of Emmitsburg Road in support of artillery. Soon after Longstreet's column started an order was received to advance and support it but smoke hiding the oblique course of Pickett's Division the Brigade moving straight forward found itself engaged in a separate and useless conflict and was promptly withdrawn.

No. 44C   Tablet on Granite Pedestal located—West Confederate Avenue

Note: The complete inscription on this tablet is presented in Part III—Day Two—
Page 138.

C. S. A.
ARMY OF NORTHERN VIRGINIA
HILL'S CORPS   ANDERSON'S DIVISION
PERRY'S BRIGADE

July 3. Ordered to join Wilcox's Brigade on its left and conform to its movements. Supported artillery until Longstreet's column started and then advanced in aid of his assault. But dense smoke hiding his oblique course the Brigade moved directly forward. In the gap caused thereby a strong force struck its left flank capturing about half of the 2nd Florida and its colors.

No. 46C   Tablet on Granite Pedestal located—West Confederate Avenue

Note: The complete inscription on this tablet is presented in Part III—Day Two—Pages 138–39.

ARMY OF NORTHERN VIRGINIA
CAVALRY DIVISION
STUART'S DIVISION   MAJOR GENERAL J. E. B. STUART

Hampton's Brigade	Brig. Gen. Wade Hampton
	Col. L. S. Baker
Robertson's Brigade	Brig. Gen. Beverly H. Robertson
Fitz Lee's Brigade	Brig. Gen. Fitzhugh Lee
Jenkins's Brigade	Brig. Gen. A. G. Jenkins
	Col. M. J. Ferguson
Jones's Brigade	Brig. Gen. William E. Jones
W. H. F. Lee's Brigade	Col. J. R. Chambliss Jr.
Stuart's Horse Artillery	
Six Batteries	Major R. F. Beckham

Robertson's and Jones's Brigades with 3 batteries detached operating on right flank of the Army.

July 1. The Division on the march from Dover to Carlisle received information that the Confederate Army was concentrating at Gettysburg.

July 2. The advance near Gettysburg late in the afternoon engaged with Custer's Cavalry Brigade at Hunterstown on the left and rear of Early's Division.

July 3. Pursuant to order the Cavalry Division of four Brigades took position on the left in advance of Early on a ridge which controlled the open ground toward Hanover. Gregg's Union Cavalry was massed in full view. The sharpshooters were advanced and soon engaged. The battle continued until near night being hotly contested. At night the Division withdrew to the York Road.

July 4. The Division was posted on the flanks and rear of the Army.

Casualties   Killed 36   Wounded 140   Missing 64   Total 240

No. 68C   Tablet on Granite Marker located—Confederate Cavalry Avenue, East Cavalry Field

---

C. S. A.
ARMY OF NORTHERN VIRGINIA
STUART'S CAVALRY DIVISION
JENKINS'S BRIGADE
14th   16th   17th Virginia Cavalry and 34th   36th Virginia Cavalry Battalions

July 3. The Brigade had been with Ewell's Corps but rejoined the Cavalry Division here on this day about noon. It was armed with Enfield Rifles but an oversight brought to this field only about ten rounds of ammunition. While this lasted it was actively engaged mainly on foot as sharpshooters around and in front of the Rummel Barn and out-houses. It was withdrawn from the field at an early hour in the evening.

Losses not reported.

No. 69C   Tablet on Granite Pedestal located—Confederate Cavalry Avenue, East Cavalry Field

---

C. S. A.
ARMY OF NORTHERN VIRGINIA
STUART'S CAVALRY DIVISION
CHAMBLISS' BRIGADE
2nd North Carolina and 9th   10th   13th Virginia Cavalry

July 3. The Brigade reached here about noon and took an active part in the fight until it ended. Some of the men serving as sharpshooters in the vicinity of the Rummel Barn but most of the Command participating in the charges made by the Cavalry during the afternoon. It left the field after nightfall.

Losses   Killed 8   Wounded 41   Missing 25   Total 74

No. 70C   Tablet on Granite Pedestal located—Confederate Cavalry Avenue, East Cavalry Field

---

C. S. A.

ARMY OF NORTHERN VIRGINIA

STUART'S CAVALRY DIVISION

HAMPTON'S BRIGADE

1st North Carolina   1st and 2nd South Carolina Cavalry
Jeff Davis (Miss.) and Cobb's and Phillips's (Ga.) Legions

July 2. Engaged in the evening with 3rd Division Cavalry Corps near Hunterstown. Cobb's Legion led the attack and lost a number of officers and men killed and wounded.

July 3. The Brigade arrived here about noon and skirmished with Union sharpshooters. In the afternoon the 1st North Carolina and Jeff Davis' Legion advancing in support of Chambliss's Brigade drove the Union cavalry but met their reserve and were in a critical position when the Brigade went to their support and a hand to hand fight ensued in which Brig. Gen. Wade Hampton was severely wounded. The conflict ended in the failure of the Confederates in their purpose to assail the rear of the Union Army.

Losses   Killed 17   Wounded 58   Missing 16   Total 91

No. 71C   Tablet on Granite Pedestal located—Confederate Cavalry Avenue, East Cavalry Field

C. S. A.

ARMY OF NORTHERN VIRGINIA

STUART'S CAVALRY DIVISION

FITZHUGH LEE'S BRIGADE

1st Maryland Battalion and 1st   2nd   3rd   4th   5th Virginia Cavalry

July 3. The Battalion being on duty with Ewell's Corps the Brigade brought only five regiments to this field where it arrived soon after midday and took position on the left of Hampton's Brigade on the edge of the neighboring woods. It participated actively in the conflict which ensued.

Losses   Killed 5   Wounded 16   Missing 29   Total 50

No. 72C   Tablet on Granite Pedestal located—Confederate Cavalry Avenue, East Cavalry Field

C. S. A.
ARMY OF NORTHERN VIRGINIA
FIRST ARMY CORPS
HOOD'S DIVISION
Maj. Gen. J. B. Hood   Brig. Gen. E. M. Law

July 3. Occupied the ground gained and with the exception of resisting a Cavalry charge and heavy skirmishing was not engaged.

No. 25C   Tablet on Granite Marker located—South Confederate Avenue

Note: The complete inscription on this tablet is presented in Part III—Day Two— Pages 127–28.

───────

C. S. A.
ARMY OF NORTHERN VIRGINIA
LONGSTREET'S CORPS   HOOD'S DIVISION
ROBERTSON'S BRIGADE

July 3. At 2 A. M. the 1st Texas and 3rd Arkansas were moved to the right and joined the 4th and 5th Texas on the northwest spur of Big Round Top. Three regiments occupied the breastworks there all day skirmishing hotly with Union sharpshooters. Early in the day the 1st Texas was sent to confront the Union Cavalry threatening the right flank. After night the Brigade took position near here.

No. 28C   Tablet on Granite Pedestal located—South Confederate Avenue

Note: The complete inscription on this tablet is presented in Part III—Day Two— Page 129.

───────

C. S. A.
ARMY OF NORTHERN VIRGINIA
LONGSTREET'S CORPS   HOOD'S DIVISION
LAW'S BRIGADE

July 3. Occupied the breastworks on west slope of Round Top. The 4th and 5th Regiments assisted at 5 P. M. in repulsing cavalry led by Brig. Gen. Farnsworth in Plum Run Valley.

No. 26C   Tablet on Granite Pedestal located—South Confederate Avenue

Note: The complete inscription on this tablet is presented in Part III—Day Two—
Page 128.

───────────

C. S. A.
ARMY OF NORTHERN VIRGINIA
LONGSTREET'S CORPS   HOOD'S DIVISION
ANDERSON'S BRIGADE

July 3. The Brigade was sent down Emmitsburg Road and assisted in repulsing and holding in check Union cavalry which sought to flank the
Division.

No. 32C   Tablet on Granite Pedestal located—West Confederate Avenue

Note: The complete inscription on this tablet is presented in Part III—Day Two—
Pages 130–31.

PART
V

Artillery and Other
Supporting Units

ARTILLERY ORGANIZATION

The inscriptions on the narrative tablets erected by the Gettysburg National Military Park Commission to describe the activities of artillery and other supporting units are presented in this section. With some exceptions, the combat activity of the artillery in both the Union and Confederate armies was neither confined to a single phase of the battle nor to the support of a single brigade or division. Therefore, the tablet inscriptions which describe the activities of the artillery units are presented separately in the sequence that the corps to which they were assigned was most heavily engaged. Inscriptions on the tablets erected to describe the activities of units that were in the campaign but did not reach the battlefield proper or were not directly involved in the battle, are also included in this section.

The organizational structure of the artillery in the Army of the Potomac was different from that of the Army of Northern Virginia but control and employment was similar. Each army had a chief of artillery who exercised technical control but deferred tactical control to the individual corps. Each Union corps, except the cavalry corps, was organized with an artillery brigade consisting of four or more batteries; the most common number of batteries being five. The cavalry corps had two brigades of horse artillery. Union divisions did not have artillery assigned. An artillery reserve with one regular and four volunteer brigades was assigned to the Union army; however, the reserves were sent to the individual corps as needed and the corps directed their fires.

The artillery in the Army of Northern Virginia was organized into battalions of normally four to five batteries each. One battalion was assigned to each division and two were assigned to each corps as the artillery reserve. Even though the Confederate divisions had an organic artillery battalion, the battalions were not always supporting their parent division. General Heth's artillery battalion, for example, was not with the division when it became engaged on the first day of the battle and provided only limited support when it arrived late in the day.

201

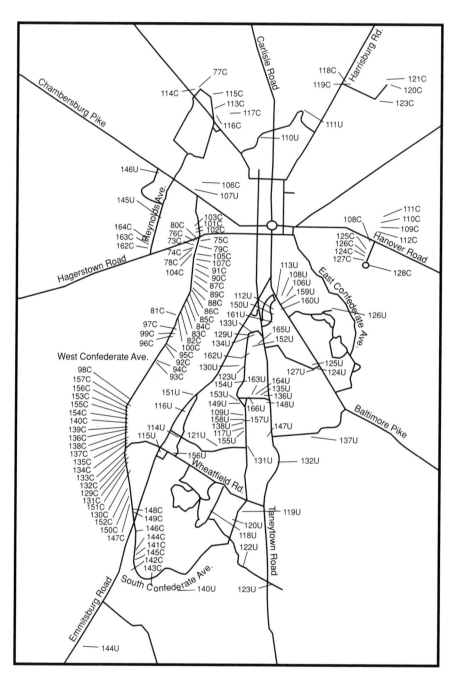

Artillery and other supporting units tablet locations

ARTILLERY UNITS TABLET INSCRIPTIONS
ARMY OF THE POTOMAC

ARMY OF THE POTOMAC
FIRST CORPS
ARTILLERY BRIGADE
Col. Charles S. Wainwright
Maine 2D Battery B   Six 3 Inch Rifles
Capt. James A. Hall
Maine 5th Battery E   Six 12 Pounders
Capt. Greenleaf T. Stevens   Lieut. Edward N. Whittier
1st New York Battery L   Four 3 Inch Rifles
Capt. Gilbert Reynolds   Lieut. George Breck
1st Penna. Battery B   Four 3 Inch Rifles
Capt. James H. Cooper
4th U. S. Battery B   Four 12 Pounders
Lieut. James Stewart

July 1. Arrived between 10 and 11 A. M. Battery B 2D Maine in advance relieved Battery A 2D U. S. on Chambersburg Pike and became hotly engaged with artillery in front and infantry on right but was compelled to retire from the ridge. About 2 P. M. the Confederates having opened with artillery from Oak Hill on right the batteries in advance were compelled to withdraw and take position on ridge in rear and on both sides of Reynolds Woods but again being flanked and enfiladed by Confederate infantry and artillery the Union forces were withdrawn to Seminary Ridge and at 4 P. M. retired through the town to Cemetery Hill. On reaching Cemetery Hill the artillery was immediately put into position for defence.

July 2. Not engaged until 4 P. M. when the Confederates opened on the position with four 20 Pounders and six 10 Pounder Perrotts but were compelled to withdraw. Battery B 1st Penna. relieved by Batteries F and C 1st Penna. At dusk the position on East Cemetery Hill was attacked by Brig. Gen. Hays's and Brig. Gen. Hoke's Brigades. They fought through Battery I 1st New York into Batteries F and C 1st Penna. spiking one gun. The cannoniers stood to their guns and with hand-spikes rammers

203

and stones and the aid of infantry that was hurried to the defence the attack was repulsed between 9 and 10 P. M.

July 3. No serious engagement.

Casualties   Killed 9 Men   Wounded 6 Officers 80 Men   Captured or Missing 11 Men   Total 106

No. 106U   Tablet on Granite Pedestal located—East Cemetery Hill

━━━━━━━━━

ARMY OF THE POTOMAC
FIRST CORPS
ARTILLERY BRIGADE
BATTERY B FOURTH U. S. ARTILLERY
Six 12 Pounders
Lieut. James Stewart Commanding

July 1. In position about 200 yards south of the Lutheran Theological Seminary until 3 P. M. when ordered to support the Second Division First Corps and took position on Seminary Ridge half of the Battery in command of Lieut. James Davison between Chambersburg Pike and railroad cut. The other half north of the cut in corner of the woods was actively engaged. The Battery afterwards retired with the troops to Cemetery Hill and went into position on the Baltimore Pike opposite Evergreen Cemetery commanding the approach from the town two guns on the Pike and two in the field two having been disabled.

Casualties   Killed 2 Men   Wounded 2 Officers and 29 Men   Missing 3 Men   Total 36

No. 107U   Tablet on Granite Marker located—Chambersburg Pike, West Side Quality Inn

━━━━━━━━━

ARMY OF THE POTOMAC
FIRST CORPS
ARTILLERY BRIGADE
BATTERY B FOURTH U. S. ARTILLERY
Six 12 Pounders
Lieut. James Stewart Commanding

July 1. In position about 200 yards south of the Seminary until 3 P. M. when ordered to the support of Brig. General J. C. Robinson's Division First

Corps and took position on Seminary Ridge one half of the Battery between Chambersburg Pike and the railroad cut. The other half north of the cut in the corner of the woods was actively engaged. The Battery afterwards retired with the troops to Cemetery Hill where it went into position on the Baltimore Pike opposite the Evergreen Cemetery commanding the approach from the town. Two guns on the Pike and two in the field two guns having been disabled.

July 2 & 3. Remained in this position.

Casualties   Killed 2 Men   Wounded 2 Officers and 29 Men   Missing 3 Men

No. 108U   Tablet on Granite Marker located—East Cemetery Hill, Baltimore Pike

Note: This tablet is essentially a duplicate of the one for this battery located off Chambersburg Pike.

———

ARMY OF THE POTOMAC
FIRST CORPS
FIRST VOLUNTEER BRIGADE
FIRST PENNA. LIGHT ARTILLERY
BATTERY B
Four 3 Inch Rifles
Captain James H. Cooper   Commanding

July 3. Moved to this position from East Cemetery Hill at 3 P. M. during a heavy cannonade and opened fire upon a Confederate battery in front. In half an hour a line of Confederate infantry approached over the hill about 1000 yards distant. The Battery in connection with batteries in line fired case shot until the Confederates reached canister range a few charges of which compelled their retreat.

Casualties   Killed 3 Men   Wounded 1 Officer and 8 Men   Total 12

No. 109U   Cast Iron Tablet located—Hancock Avenue, south of Pennsylvania Monument

Note: This battery was assigned to the First Corps Artillery Brigade.

———

ARMY OF THE POTOMAC
ELEVENTH CORPS
ARTILLERY BRIGADE
Major Thomas W. Osborn
1st New York Battery I   Six 3 Inch Rifles
Capt. Michael Wiedrich
New York 13th Battery   Four 3 Inch Rifles
Lieut. William Wheeler
1st Ohio Battery I   Six 12 Pounders
Capt. Hubert Dilger
1st Ohio Battery K   Four 12 Pounders
Capt. Lewis Heckman
4th U. S. Battery G   Six 12 Pounders
Lieut. Bayard Wilkeson   Lieut. Eugene A. Bancroft

July 1. Arrived with the Corps. All the batteries engaged except Battery I
1st New York on Cemetery Hill. The artillery retired and took position on
Cemetery Hill west of the Baltimore Pike except Battery K 1st Ohio sent
to the rear disabled and Battery I 1st New York on East Cemetery Hill.

July 2. The Brigade was reinforced in the morning by five batteries from the
Reserve Artillery.

July 3. At 1 P. M. the Confederate artillery opened a terrific front and enfilading fire from the right followed by an infantry charge and on which the
artillery of this command was concentrated with great effect. The Brigade lost one gun captured one gun disabled and two dismounted.

Casualties   Killed 1 Officer 6 Men   Wounded 3 Officers 50 Men   Captured or Missing 9 Men   Total 69   98 Horses Killed

No. 110U   Tablet on Granite Pedestal located—West Howard Avenue

ARMY OF THE POTOMAC
ELEVENTH CORPS
ARTILLERY BRIGADE
BATTERY G FOURTH U. S. ARTILLERY
Six 12 Pounders
Lieut. Bayard Wilkeson   Commanding

July 1. Arrived at Gettysburg about 11 A. M. Advanced and took position
two sections on Barlow's Knoll the left section detached near Almshouse.
Engaged Confederate infantry and artillery on right and left. Lieut.
Wilkenson fell early mortally wounded and the command devolved on
Lieut. Bancroft. The sections were compelled to change positions several
times. Retired about 4 P. M. one section relieving a section of Battery I 1st

Ohio on Baltimore Street in covering the retreat. About 5 P. M. took position on Cemetery Hill.

July 2. Moved to rear of Cemetery facing Baltimore Pike. In action at the Cemetery from 4.30 P. M. until 7 P. M.

July 3. About 2 P. M. two sections were engaged in the Cemetery until the repulse of the Confederates.

Casualties   Killed 1 Officer and 1 Man   Wounded 11 Men   Missing 4 Men

Ammunition Expended 1400 rounds   31 Horses Killed

No. 111U   Tablet on Granite Marker located—East Howard Avenue, Barlow Knoll

─────

ARMY OF THE POTOMAC
ELEVENTH CORPS
ARTILLERY BRIGADE
BATTERY G FOURTH U. S. ARTILLERY
Six 12 Pounders
Lieut. Eugene A. Bancroft   Commanding

July 1. Arrived at Gettysburg about 11 A. M. Advanced and took position two sections on Barlow's Knoll the left section detached near Almshouse. Engaged Confederate infantry and artillery on right and left. Lieut. Wilkeson fell early mortally wounded and the command devolved to Lieut. Bancroft. The sections were compelled to change positions several times. Retired about 4 P. M. one section relieving a section of Battery I 1st Ohio on Baltimore Street in covering the retreat.

July 2. Moved to rear of Cemetery facing Baltimore Pike. In action at the Cemetery from 4.30 P. M. until 7 P. M.

July 3. About 2 P. M. two sections were engaged in the Cemetery until repulse of the Confederates.

Casualties   Killed 1 Officer and 1 Man   Wounded 11 Men   Missing 4 Men

Ammunition expended 1400 Rounds   31 Horses Killed

No. 112U   Tablet on Granite Marker located—National Cemetery

Note: This tablet is a duplicate of the one for this battery located on Barlow Knoll.

ARMY OF THE POTOMAC
ELEVENTH CORPS
BATTERY I FIRST OHIO ARTILLERY
Six 12 Pounders
Captain Hubert Dilger Commanding

July 1. Arrived at Gettysburg before noon and went into position west of the Carlisle Road. Engaged with two Confederate batteries which were finally silenced with a loss of five gun carriages. A Confederate rifled battery having opened fire Wheeler's Thirteenth New York battery was added to the command of Capt. Dilger and a fierce artillery duel ensued. About 4 P. M. retired to take position on Cemetery Hill. One section was posted on Baltimore street above the square in town to cover the retreating infantry until relieved by two pieces of Battery G Fourth U. S. Artillery. At 5 P. M. took position in the cemetery next the Baltimore Pike facing westerly. Remained there until the close of the battle. One gun disabled.

Casualties   Wounded 13 Men

28 Horses killed

No. 113U   Cast Iron Tablet located—National Cemetery

———————————

ARMY OF THE POTOMAC
THIRD CORPS
ARTILLERY BRIGADE
Capt. George E. Randolph
Capt. A. Judson Clark
2D New Jersey Battery   Six 10 Pounder Parrotts
Capt. A. Judson Clark   Lieut. Robert Sims
1st New York Battery D   Six 12 Pounders
Capt. George B. Winslow
4th New York Battery   Six 12 Pounder Parrotts
Capt. James E. Smith
1st Rhode Island Battery E   Six 12 Pounders
Lieut. John K. Bucklyn   Lieut. Benjamin Freeborn
4th U. S. Battery K   Six 12 Pounders
Lieut. Francis W. Seeley   Lieut. Robert James

July 2. On the advance of the Corps between 2 and 3 P. M. the 4th New York Battery was placed near Devil's Den Battery D 1st New York in the Wheatfield 9th and 5th Mass. (E 10th New York attached) Batteries from Artillery Reserve on Wheatfield Road 2D New Jersey Battery near Peach Orchard Battery G 1st New York from Artillery Reserve in the Peach

Orchard. Along Emmitsburg Road were Batteries E 1st Rhode Island K 4th U. S. and F & K 3d U. S. from the Artillery Reserve. The artillery at Peach Orchard was reinforced by Battery I 5th U. S. 15th New York Battery and Penna. C & F from Artillery Reserve.

July 3. Not engaged except Battery K 4th U. S. early in the morning.

Casualties Killed 8 Men Wounded 3 Officers 78 Men Captured or Missing 17 Men Total 106

No. 114U Tablet on Granite Pedestal located—Sickles Avenue

ARMY OF THE POTOMAC
THIRD CORPS
ARTILLERY BRIGADE
Capt. George E. Randolph Capt. A. Judson Clark

Battery B, 1st New Jersey	Six 10 Pounders	Capt. A. Judson Clark
		Lieut. Robert Sims
Battery D, 1st New York	Six 12 Pounders	Capt. George B. Winslow
4th New York Battery	Six 10 Pounders	Capt. James E. Smith
Battery E, 1st Rhode Island	Six 12 Pounders	Lieut. John K. Bucklyn
		Lieut. Benjamin Freeborn
Battery K, 4th United States	Six 12 Pounders	Lieut. Francis W. Seeley
		Lieut. Robert James

July 2. Upon the advance of the 3D Corps between 2 and 3 P. M. the 4th N. Y. Battery was posted near Devil's Den, Battery D, 1st N. Y. in the Wheatfield. Battery B, 1st N. J. near the Peach Orchard north of Wheatfield Road; Battery E, 1st R. I. on same road near the right of First Division and Battery K, 4th U. S. near the left of Second Division.

About 3.30 P. M. Lt. Colonel F. McGilvery brought from the Artillery Reserve the 9th Mass. Battery, which was posted on the Wheatfield Road east of the Peach Orchard; 5th Mass. Battery (10th N. Y. Battery attached) within a 100 yards of 9th Mass. Battery and 15th N. Y. Battery to the east side of the Peach Orchard.

Later and during the battle, there was brought up Penna. Battery C & F, which took position at the salient in the Peach Orchard, and Battery F & K, 3D U. S. posted near the Roger House. Battery I, 5th U. S. was brought from 5th Corps and relieved Battery G, 1st New York.

Casualties Killed 8 Men Wounded 3 Officers 78 Men Captured or Missing 17 Men Total 106

No. 115U   Tablet on Granite Marker located—Emmitsburg Road, Peach Orchard

ARMY OF THE POTOMAC
THIRD CORPS
ARTILLERY BRIGADE
BATTERY K FOURTH U. S. ARTILLERY
Six 12 Pounders
Lieut. Francis W. Seeley   Commanding

July 1. Arrived at night and encamped in a field south of the town between Emmitsburg and Taneytown Roads.

July 2. Went into position at 4 P. M. on the right of Smith's log house on Emmitsburg Road with Brig. General A. A. Humphreys's Division Third Corps and soon took position on the left of the log house and at the left of an apple orchard and opened fire on the Confederate infantry as it began to advance. Hotly engaged with the Confederate infantry and artillery in front and on the left until about 7 P. M. when forced to retire and took position on the line from Evergreen Cemetery to Little Round Top. Lieut. Seeley having been wounded the command devolved on Lieut. Robert James.

July 3. Remained in the positions of the previous night.

Casualties   Killed 2 Men   Wounded 1 Officer and 18 Men   Missing 4 Men

Lost and Disabled   28 Horses

No. 116U   Tablet on Granite Marker located—Emmitsburg Road

ARMY OF THE POTOMAC
THIRD CORPS
ARTILLERY BRIGADE
NEW JERSEY LIGHT ARTILLERY
2ND BATTERY
Six 10 Pounder Parrotts
Captain A. Judson Clark   Commanding

July 2. Engaged in the action in a field near the Peach Orchard retired to the rear about 6.30 P. M. for want of support.

July 3. In line here with the Artillery Brigade during the heavy cannonading and the charge and repulse of Longstreet's assault but was not engaged.

Casualties July 2nd   Killed 1 Man   Wounded 16 Men   Missing 3 Men
Total 20

No. 117U   Cast Iron Tablet located—Hancock Avenue, South of Pennsylvania
Monument

ARMY OF THE POTOMAC
THIRD CORPS   ARTILLERY BRIGADE
FOURTH NEW YORK INDEPENDENT BATTERY
Six 10 Pounder Parrots
Capt. James E. Smith   Commanding

July 2. Arrived from Emmitsburg at 9 A. M. Four guns posted on the height
above Devil's Den at 2 P. M. Two guns in this position. After the capture
of three of the guns in the advanced position and the repulse of their
supports this section opened fire with great effect on the Confederate
forces advancing up the valley. At 6 P. M. this section was moved to the
right near Winslow's battery and subsequently to the rear.

July 3. Not engaged.

Killed 2 Men   Wounded 10 Men   Missing 1 Man
11 Horses Killed   240 Rounds of ammunition expended

No. 118U   Cast Iron Tablet located—Crawford Avenue

ARMY OF THE POTOMAC
FIFTH CORPS
ARTILLERY BRIGADE
Capt. Augustus P. Martin
Mass. 3D Battery C   Six 12 Pounders
Lieut. Aaron F. Walcott
1st New York Battery C   Four 3 Inch Rifles
Capt. Almont Barnes
1st Ohio Battery L   Six 12 Pounders
Capt. Frank C. Gibbs
5th U. S. Battery D   Six 10 Pounders
Lieut. Charles E. Hazlett   Lieut. Benjamin F. Rittenhouse
5th U. S. Battery I   Four 3 Inch Rifles
Lieut. Malbone F. Watson   Lieut. Charles C. MacConnell

July 2. Arrived on the field on the left between 5 and 6 P. M. Battery D 5th
U. S. Battery C 3D Mass. and Battery I 5th U. S. in rear of First Division

and Battery L 1st Ohio and Battery C 1st New York in rear of Second Division. Battery D 5th U. S. was placed on the summit of Little Round Top and Battery C 3D Mass. and Battery I 5th U. S. were engaged further to the right in rear of Third Corps until dark. Battery L 1st Ohio was placed on the north slope and at the base of Little Round Top.

July 3. Battery D 5th U. S. remained on Little Round Top Battery I 5th U. S. being unserviceable was sent from the field. The position of Battery L 1st Ohio remained nearly the same. At 3 A. M. Battery C 1st New York and Battery C 3D Mass. moved to the extreme left and not engaged.

Casualties   Killed 1 Officer 7 Men   Wounded 1 Officer 32 Men   Captured or Missing 2 Men   Total 43

No. 119U   Tablet on Granite Pedestal located—Sykes Avenue, Little Round Top

---

ARMY OF THE POTOMAC
FIFTH CORPS
ARTILLERY BRIGADE
BATTERY D FIFTH U. S. ARTILLERY
Six Rifled 10 Pounders
Lieut. Charles E. Hazlett   Commanding

July 2. Marched to the left of the Union line about 4.30 P. M. and in rear of Brig. General J. Barnes's First Division Fifth Corps. Immediately upon taking position here at 5.45 opened fire upon the Confederates who were engaging the Division. The Battery kept up a continuous fire until after dark. Lieut. Hazlett was mortally wounded and the command devolved upon Lieut. Benjamin F. Rittenhouse.

July 3. Remained in position and in the afternoon did effective service on the lines of infantry engaged in Longstreet's assault.

Casualties   Killed 1 Officer and 6 Men   Wounded 6 Men

No. 120U   Tablet on Granite Marker located—Little Round Top

ARMY OF THE POTOMAC
FIFTH CORPS
ARTILLERY BRIGADE
BATTERY I FIFTH U. S. ARTILLERY
Four 3 Inch Rifles
Lieut. Malbone F. Watson   Commanding

July 2. About 4.30 P. M. arrived and took position north of Little Round Top 5.30 moved to the front at the Peach Orchard. On the advance of the Confederates driving back the infantry the Battery was retired across Plum Run near the Trostle House and fired shell and canister at the approaching Confederates until the Battery disabled by loss of men and horses was captured by the 21st Mississippi Infantry. It was almost immediately recaptured with the assistance of the 39th New York Infantry and being unserviceable was taken to the Artillery Brigade.

Casualties   Killed 1 Man   Wounded 1 Officer and 18 Men   Missing 2 Men

No. 121U   Tablet on Granite Marker located—field north of United States Avenue, East of Trostle House

―――――――

ARMY OF THE POTOMAC
FIFTH CORPS   ARTILLERY RESERVE
BATTERY C
MASSACHUSETTS LIGHT ARTILLERY
Six 12 Pounders
Lieut. A. F. Walcott   Commanding

July 3. At 3 A. M. moved to and occupied this position until the close of the battle.

No. 122U   Cast Iron Tablet located—Wright Avenue

―――――――

ARMY OF THE POTOMAC
FIFTH CORPS ARTILLERY RESERVE
BATTERY C
FIRST NEW YORK LIGHT ARTILLERY
Four 3 Inch Rifles
Capt. Almont Barnes   Commanding

July 3. At 3 A. M. moved to and occupied this position until the close of the battle.

No. 123U   Cast Iron Tablet located—Howe Avenue

―――――――

ARMY OF THE POTOMAC
TWELFTH CORPS
ARTILLERY BRIGADE
Lieut. Edward D. Muhlenberger

1st New York Battery M	Four 10 Pounders	Lieut. Charles E. Winegar
Penna. Battery E	Six 10 Pounders	Lieut. Charles A. Atwell
4th U. S. Battery F	Six 10 Pounders	Lieut. Sylvanus T. Rugg
5th U. S. Battery K	Four 10 Pounders	Lieut. David H. Kinzie

July 1. About noon two batteries moved from Two Taverns with First Division toward the Hanover Road to within a mile and a half of Gettysburg. The other two batteries moved with Second Division and encamped for the night the same distance from town.

July 2. In the afternoon three guns of Battery E Penna. and two of Battery K 5th U. S. were placed on the summit of Culp's Hill and were engaged at once with the Confederate artillery. At night Battery E Penna. and Battery M 1st New York were placed on Powers's and McAllister's Hills. Battery F 4th U. S. and Battery K 5th U. S. at the base of Powers's Hill.

July 3. Battery F 4th U. S. and Battery K 5th U. S. in rear of the centre of the Corps. Battery E Penna. and Battery A Maryland six 3 inch rifles from the Reserve Artillery on Powers's Hill all commanding the valley of Rock Creek. At daylight the artillery (26) guns opened on the position occupied by Major Gen. Johnson's Division and fired for about 15 minutes then ceased to allow the infantry to advance. Began firing again at 5.30 and continued at intervals until 10.30 A. M. when the Confederates were forced from their position along the entire line.

Casualties   9 men wounded   3 mortally

No. 124U   Tablet on Granite Pedestal located—Hunt Avenue near Baltimore Pike

━━━━━━━━━━

ARMY OF THE POTOMAC
TWELFTH CORPS
ARTILLERY BRIGADE
BATTERY F FOURTH U. S. ARTILLERY
Six 12 Pounders
Lieut. Sylvanus T. Rugg   Commanding

July 1. Approached Gettysburg on the Baltimore Pike to Two Taverns and took position to counteract any movements of the Confederates from towards Hanover. At noon moved to the Hanover Road and marched to within one and one half miles of Gettysburg.

July 2. Took position so as to command a gap between the First and Second Corps.

July 3. At 1 A. M. posted opposite the centre of the line of the Twelfth Corps and at 4.30 opened fire on the Confederates who had taken possession of a portion of the line of the Twelfth Corps the preceding night. Continued firing until after 10 A. M. when the Confederates were driven from the line. In the afternoon the Battery was exposed to severe shelling which passed over Cemetery Hill.

Casualties   Wounded 1 Man

No. 125U   Tablet on Granite Marker located—Hunt Avenue near Baltimore Pike

---

ARMY OF THE POTOMAC
TWELFTH CORPS
BATTERY K FIFTH U. S. ARTILLERY
Four 12 Pounders
Lieut. David H. Kinzie   Commanding

July 1. Marched to within a mile and half of Gettysburg.

July 2. At daylight took position to command a gap between the First and Twelfth Corps. At 5 P. M. one section was placed on the summit of Culp's Hill and assisted in silencing Confederate batteries on Benner's Hill. At 6 P. M. rejoined the Battery at the foot of Powers's Hill.

July 3. At 1 A. M. posted with Lieut. S. T. Rugg's Battery F 4th U. S. Artillery on the south side of Baltimore Pike opposite the centre of the line of the Twelfth Corps. At 4.30 A. M. opened fire on the Confederates in possession of the line vacated by the Twelfth Corps the preceding night. Firing continued at intervals until after 10 A. M. when the Confederates were driven out. Remained in the same position exposed to the severe shelling which came over Cemetery Hill in the afternoon.

Casualties   Wounded 5 Men

No. 126U   Tablet on Granite Marker located—Summit Culp's Hill

---

ARMY OF THE POTOMAC
TWELFTH CORPS
BATTERY K FIFTH U. S. ARTILLERY
Four 12 Pounders
Lieut. David H. Kinzie   Commanding

July 1. Marched to within a mile and half of Gettysburg.

July 2. At daylight took position to command a gap between the First and Twelfth Corps. At 5 P. M. one section was placed on the summit of

Culp's Hill and assisted in silencing Confederate batteries on Benner's Hill. At 6 P. M. rejoined the Battery at the foot of Powers's Hill.

July 3. At 1 A. M. posted with Battery F 4th U. S. Artillery on the south side of Baltimore Pike opposite the centre of the line of the Twelfth Corps. At 4.30 A. M. opened fire on the Confederates in possession of the line vacated by the Twelfth Corps the preceding night. Firing continued at intervals until after 10 A. M. when the Confederates were driven out. Remained in the same position exposed to the severe Shelling which came over Cemetery Hill in the afternoon.

Casualties   Wounded 5 Men

No. 127U   Tablet on Granite Marker located—Hunt Avenue near Baltimore Pike

Note: This tablet is a duplicate of the one for this battery located on Culp's Hill.

ARMY OF THE POTOMAC
SECOND CORPS
ARTILLERY BRIGADE
Capt. John G. Hazard
1st New York Battery B   Four 10 Pounders
Lieut. Albert S. Sheldon   Capt. James M. Rorty   Lieut. Robert E. Rogers
1s Rhode Island Battery A   Six 3 Inch Rifles
Capt. William A. Arnold
1st Rhode Island Battery B   Four 12 Pounders
Lieut. T. Frederick Brown   Lieut. Wm. S. Perrin
1st U. S. Battery I   Six 12 Pounders
Lieut. George A. Woodruff   Lieut. Tully McCrea
4th U. S. Battery A   Six 3 Inch Rifles
Lieut. Alonzo H. Cushing   Sergt. Frederick Fuger

July 1. Marched from Uniontown Md. at 2 P. M. Went into position at 11 P. M. on the Taneytown Road three miles from Gettysburg.

July 2. Moved with the Corps at daylight and went into position on the Corps battle line in the order from right to left as mentioned. The batteries were engaged toward night with some loss.

July 3. Engaged with the Confederate artillery in front at 8 A. M. and along the whole line at 1 P. M. and assisted in repulsing Longstreet's assault in the afternoon.

Casualties   Killed 3 Officers 24 Men   Wounded 5 Officers 114 Men
Captured or Missing 3 Men   Total 149

No. 128U   Tablet on Granite Pedestal located—Hancock Avenue, the Angle

---

ARMY OF THE POTOMAC
SECOND CORPS
ARTILLERY BRIGADE
BATTERY I FIRST U. S. ARTILLERY
Six 12 Pounders
Lieut. George A. Woodruff   Commanding
Lieut. Tully McCrea   Commanding

July 2 & 3. Arrived and took position in Ziegler's Grove on the left of Evergreen Cemetery actively engaged and assisted in repelling Longstreet's assault. Lieut. Woodruff was mortally wounded on the 3D and the command devolved on Lieut. Tully McCrea.

Casualties   Killed 1 Man   Wounded 1 Officer and 23 Men

No. 129U   Tablet on Granite Marker located—North Hancock Avenue, Ziegler's Grove

---

ARMY OF THE POTOMAC
SECOND CORPS
ARTILLERY BRIGADE
BATTERY A FOURTH U. S. ARTILLERY
Six 3 Inch Rifles

Lieut. Alonzo H. Cushing and Sergt. Frederick Fuger Commanding

July 2. Arrived and took position with the brigade of Brig. General A. S. Webb Second Division Second Corps and took part in the artillery engagements during the day.

July 3. Engaged in the repulse of Longstreet's assault and lost all its officers killed or wounded and all the guns but one and all its horses but three were disabled. Lieut. Cushing was killed while firing the last shot from the only effective gun. After the repulse of Longstreet's assault the Battery was withdrawn.

Casualties   Killed 1 Officer and 5 Men   Wounded 1 Officer and 31 Men

No. 130U   Tablet on Granite Marker located—Hancock Avenue, the Angle

---

ARMY OF THE POTOMAC
SIXTH CORPS
ARTILLERY BRIGADE
Col. Charles H. Tompkins
Mass. 1st Battery A   Six 12 Pounders
Capt. William H. McCartney
New York 1st Battery   Six 3 Inch Rifles
Capt. Andrew Cowan
New York 3D Battery   Six 10 Pounders
Capt. William A. Harn
1st Rhode Island Battery C   Six 3 Inch Rifles
Capt. Richard Waterman
1st Rhode Island Battery G   Six 10 Pounder Parrotts
Capt. George W. Adams
2D U. S. Battery D   Six 12 Pounders
Lieut. Edward B. Williston
2D U. S. Battery G   Six 12 Pounders
Lieut. John H. Butler
5th U. S. Battery F   Six 10 Pounder Parrotts
Lieut. Leonard Martin

July 2. Arrived in the afternoon and evening from Manchester Md. and the artillery was placed under the orders of Brig. Gen. H. J. Hunt Chief of Artillery of the Army.

July 3. The batteries were placed in reserve on different portions of the field so as to be available but with exception of 1st New York Battery were not actively engaged.

Casualties   Killed 4 Men   Wounded 2 Officers 6 Men   Total 12

No. 131U   Tablet on Granite Pedestal located—Sedgwick Avenue

———

ARMY OF THE POTOMAC
SIXTH CORPS
ARTILLERY BRIGADE
BATTERY D SECOND U. S. ARTILLERY
Four Light 12 Pounders
Lieut. Edward B. Williston   Commanding

July 2. Arrived with the Corps and took position and remained on Taneytown Road.

Not Engaged

No. 132U   Tablet on Granite Marker located—Taneytown Road, north of Wheatfield Road

---

ARMY OF THE POTOMAC
SIXTH CORPS
ARTILLERY BRIGADE
BATTERY G SECOND U. S. ARTILLERY
Six 12 Pounders
Lieut. John H. Butler   Commanding

July 2. Arrived in the afternoon with the Corps and held in Reserve.

July 3. Brought up to Ziegler's Grove in rear of Third Division Second Corps on repulse of Longstreet's assault.

No. 133U   Tablet on Granite Marker located—Ziegler's Grove, at Cyclorama Center

---

ARMY OF THE POTOMAC
SIXTH CORPS
ARTILLERY BRIGADE
BATTERY F FIFTH U. S. ARTILLERY
Six 10 Pounder Parrotts
Lieut. Leonard Martin   Commanding

July 2. Arrived in the afternoon with the Corps and held in reserve.

July 3. Brought up to Ziegler's Grove in rear of Third Division Second Corps on the repulse of Longstreet's assault.

No. 134U   Tablet on Granite Marker located—Ziegler's Grove, at Cyclorama Center

---

ARMY OF THE POTOMAC
CAVALRY CORPS   HORSE ARTILLERY
FIRST BRIGADE
Capt. James M. Robertson

9th Michigan Battery
Capt. Jabez J. Daniels

July 3. Engaged on Cemetery Ridge south of Pleasonton Avenue subject to the orders of Major Gen. J. Newton.

6th New York Battery
Capt. Joseph W. Martin
In Reserve
2D U. S. Batteries B and L
Lieut. Edward Heaton
In Reserve
2D U. S. Battery M
Lieut. A. C. M. Pennington Jr.

July 3. With the Cavalry on the right.

4th U. S. Battery E
Lieut. Samuel S. Elder

July 3. With First Brigade Third Division on left.

Casualties   Killed 2 Men   Wounded 1 Officer 5 Men   Total 8

No. 135U   Tablet on Granite Pedestal located—Pleasonton Avenue

━━━━━━━━━━━━━━

ARMY OF THE POTOMAC
CAVALRY CORPS
FIRST BRIGADE   HORSE ARTILLERY
BATTERIES B & L SECOND ARTILLERY
Six 3 Inch Rifles
Lieut. Edward Heaton   Commanding

July 2. Arrived near the battlefield at 5.30 A. M. and reported to Major General Alfred Pleasonton who ordered the Battery to be held in reserve until near dark when it was moved back two miles on the Baltimore Pike for the night.

July 3. Moved to the front and was ordered to the position occupied the day before but being subject to the severe artillery fire the Battery was ordered to retire out of range and there remained until the close of the battle.

No. 136U   Tablet on Granite Marker located—Pleasonton Avenue

Note: No casualty figures were listed. A second tablet for these batteries is located on Granite Schoolhouse Road.

━━━━━━━━━━━━━━

ARMY OF THE POTOMAC
CAVALRY CORPS
FIRST BRIGADE   HORSE ARTILLERY
BATTERIES B & L SECOND U. S. ARTILLERY
Six 3 Inch Rifles
Lieut. Edward Heaton   Commanding

July 2. Arrived at 5.30 A. M. In reserve during the day and at night withdrew two miles on the Baltimore Pike.

July 3. Advanced to former position in the morning and ordered to the Reserve Artillery and for a time exposed to a severe fire. In the evening was withdrawn to the position of the previous night.

No. 137U   Tablet on Granite Marker located—Granite Schoolhouse Road

Note: No casualty figures are given on this tablet.

ARMY OF THE POTOMAC
CAVALRY CORPS
SECOND DIVISION   FIRST BRIGADE
3RD PENNA. HEAVY ARTILLERY
SECTION BATTERY H
Two 3 Inch Rifles
Captain William D. Rank

July 2. Marched with the 2D Cavalry Division and went into position on the Hanover Road 3 miles from Gettysburg.

July 3. In position here in early morning and was engaged in the afternoon assisting in the repulse of Longstreet's assault.

Loss   Missing 1 Man

No. 138U   Cast Iron Tablet located—Hancock Avenue, south of Pennsylvania Monument

---

ARMY OF THE POTOMAC
CAVALRY CORPS
FIRST BRIGADE   HORSE ARTILLERY
BATTERY M SECOND U. S. ARTILLERY
Six 3 Inch Rifles
Lieut. A. C. M. Pennington   Commanding

July 2. Engaged with the Confederates at Hunterstown.

July 3. Engaged in Brig. General Custer's Brigade with Major General J. E. B. Stuart's Confederate Cavalry on the right of the Union Army.

Casualties Wounded 1 Officer

No. 139U   Tablet on Granite Marker located—East Cavalry Avenue, East Cavalry Field

Note: Tablet location is shown on Cavalry Battle Tablet Location Map, page 161.

ARMY OF THE POTOMAC
CAVALRY CORPS
FIRST BRIGADE   HORSE ARTILLERY
BATTERY E FOURTH U. S. ARTILLERY
Four 3 Inch Rifles
Lieut. Samuel S. Elder   Commanding

July 3. Arrived on the field and took position on a hill southwest of Round Top and engaged under Brig. General E. J. Fransworth in the afternoon against the Confederate right.

Casualties Killed 1 Man

No. 140U   Tablet on Granite Marker located—southwest of Round Top, Bushman Woods

---

ARMY OF THE POTOMAC
CAVALRY CORPS   HORSE ARTILLERY
SECOND BRIGADE
Capt. John C. Tidball

1st U. S. Batteries E and G
Capt. Alanson M. Randol

July 2 and 3. With Cavalry on right under Brig. Gen. D. Mcm. Gregg.

1st U. S. Battery K
Capt. William M. Graham

July 3. With the Reserve Cavalry Brigade on extreme left.

2D U. S. Battery A
Lieut. John H. Calef

July 1. With First Brigade First Division on the right and left of Chambersburg Pike.

July 2. In front of Little Round Top.

3D U. S. Battery C
Lieut. William L. Fuller

With Second Brigade Second Division at Manchester. Not engaged.

Casualties   Killed 2 Men Wounded 13 Men   Total 15

No. 141U   Tablet on Granite Pedestal located—East Cavalry Avenue, East Cavalry Field

Note: Tablet location is shown on Cavalry Battle Tablet Location Map, page 161.

━━━━━━━━━━

ARMY OF THE POTOMAC
CAVALRY CORPS
BATTERIES E & G FIRST U. S. ARTILLERY
Four 12 Pounders
Capt. Alanson M. Randol   Commanding

July 1 & 2. With First Brigade Second Cavalry Division. Not engaged.

July 3. One section under Lieut. James Chester was ordered to Second Brigade Third Cavalry Division and took position west of Low Dutch Road and with Brig. General Custer's Second Brigade Third Division Cavalry Corps was hotly engaged in repelling the attack of Major General Stuart's Confederate Cavalry Division. The one section under Lieut. Ernest L. Kinney remained near the Hanover Road.

No. 142U   Tablet on Granite Marker located—East Cavalry Avenue near Low Dutch Road

Note: Tablet location is shown on Cavalry Battle Tablet Location Map, page 161.

━━━━━━━━━━

ARMY OF THE POTOMAC
CAVALRY CORPS
BATTERIES E & G FIRST U. S. ARTILLERY
Four 12 Pounders
Capt. Alanson M. Randol

July 1&2. With First Brigade Second Cavalry Division. Not engaged.

July 3. One section under Lieut. James Chester was ordered to Second Brigade Third Cavalry Division and took position west of the Low Dutch Road and with Brig. General Custer's Second Brigade Third Division Cavalry Corps was hotly engaged in repelling the attack of Major General Stuart's Confederate Cavalry Division. The one section under Lieut. Ernest L. Kinney remained near Hanover Road.

No. 143U Tablet on Granite Marker located—East Cavalry Avenue near Hanover Road

Note: This tablet is a duplicate of the one for this battery located on East Cavalry Avenue near Low Dutch Road.

ARMY OF THE POTOMAC
CAVALRY CORPS
SECOND BRIGADE   HORSE ARTILLERY
BATTERY K FIRST U. S. ARTILLERY
Six 3 Inch Rifles
Captain William M. Graham

July 3. Arrived on the field and took position on the left with Cavalry and engaged during the attack of Brig. General E. J. Farnsworth's and Brig. General W. Merritt's Brigades on the Confederate right.

Casualties   Killed 2 Men   Wounded 1 Man

No. 144U   Tablet on Granite Marker located—Emmitsburg Road, South Cavalry Field

---

ARMY OF THE POTOMAC
CAVALRY CORPS
SECOND BRIGADE   HORSE ARTILLERY
BATTERY A SECOND U. S. ARTILLERY
SIX 3 INCH RIFLES
Lieut. John H. Calef   Commanding

June 30. Arrived in the evening from Emmitsburg and took position on the Chambersburg Pike.

July 1. Advanced with the Cavalry went into position with right section on right of the road left section on the left and centre with Col. Wm. Chamble's Brigade on the right of Fairfield Road. The first Union gun of the battle was fired from right section and the positions held under a severe fire until the First Corps arrived about 10 A. M. The Battery was then relieved by Capt. J. A. Hall's 2D Maine Battery and after being supplied with ammunition returned about 3 P. M. but under a front and enfilading fire it retired to a line in front of Cemetery Ridge and towards night moved to the left about a mile and bivouacked for the night near the Third Corps.

July 2. A. M. marched with the First Brigade of Major General John Buford's Division to Taneytown en route to Westminster.

Casualties   Wounded 12 Men

Lost   13 Horses Killed

No. 145U   Tablet on Granite Marker located—South Reynolds Avenue

------

ARMY OF THE POTOMAC
CAVALRY CORPS
SECOND BRIGADE   HORSE ARTILLERY
BATTERY A SECOND U. S. ARTILLERY
SIX 3 INCH RIFLES
Lieut. John H. Calef   Commanding

June 30. Arrived in the evening from Emmitsburg and took position on the Chambersburg Pike.

July 1. Advanced with the First Division Cavalry Corps the right and left sections on the Chambersburg Pike. The centre section under Sergt. Chas. Percel posted here with the First Brigade First Division Cavalry Corps and assisted in repulsing an attack of the Confederate Infantry. This section having been withdrawn joined the Battery in the rear and again advanced with left section and relieved Battery B First Maine Artillery on Chambersburg Pike in the afternoon but was soon compelled by a front and enfilading fire to retire. Rejoined the Battery in position with the Cavalry on the left in front of Cemetery Ridge and remained during the night.

Casualties   Wounded 12 Men

13 Horses Killed

No. 146U   Tablet on Granite Marker located—Chambersburg Pike at Stone Avenue

Note: This tablet describes the activity of the center section of this battery.

ARMY OF THE POTOMAC
CAVALRY CORPS
SECOND BRIGADE   HORSE ARTILLERY
BATTERY C THIRD U. S. ARTILLERY
Six 3 Inch Rifles
Lieut. William D. Fuller   Commanding

July 1. Proceeded under orders to Manchester Md. and picketed and held all roads until afternoon of July 3 when ordered to Emmitsburg and marched to Westminster.

Not engaged

No. 147U Tablet on Granite Marker located—Taneytown Road at Granite School-house Road

———————

ARMY OF THE POTOMAC
ARTILLERY RESERVE
Brigadier General Robert O. Tyler
Captain James M. Robertson

Headquarters Guard
Thirty Second Massachusetts Infantry Co. C   Captain Josiah G. Fuller

First Regular Brigade   Captain Dunbar R. Ransom
Four Batteries

First Volunteer Brigade   Lieutenant Colonel Freeman McGilvery
Four Batteries

Second Volunteer Brigade   Captain Elijah D. Taft
Four Batteries

Third Volunteer Brigade   Captain James F. Huntington
Four Batteries

Fourth Volunteer Brigade   Captain Robert H. Fitzhugh
Five Batteries

Train Guard
Fourth New Jersey (Seven Companies)   Major Charles Ewing

Casualties   Killed 2 Officers 41 Men   Wounded 15 Officers 172 Men
Captured or Missing 12 Men   Total 242

No. 148U   Tablet on Granite Marker located—Taneytown Road at Pleasonton Avenue

---

ARMY OF THE POTOMAC
ARTILLERY RESERVE
FIRST REGULAR BRIGADE
Capt. Dunbar R. Ransom

1st U. S. Battery H
Lieut. Chandler P. Eakin   Lieut. Philip D. Mason

July 2. And 3. Engaged on Cemetery Hill.

3D U. S. Batteries F and K
Lieut. John G. Turnbull

July 2. Engaged on Emmitsburg Road on right of the Smith House.

July 3. On and near Cemetery Ridge.

4th U. S. Battery C
Lieut. Evan Thomas

July 2 and 3. Engaged on Cemetery Ridge on left of Second Corps.

5th U. S. Battery C
Lieut. Culian V. Weir

July 2 and 3. Engaged on Cemetery Ridge and in front on left of Second Corps.

Casualties   Killed 1 Officer 12 Men   Wounded 4 Officers 49 Men   Captured or Missing 2 Men   Total 68

No. 149U   Tablet on Granite Pedestal located—Hancock Avenue at Pennsylvania Monument

---

ARMY OF THE POTOMAC
ARTILLERY RESERVE
FIRST REGULAR BRIGADE
BATTERY H FIRST U. S. ARTILLERY
Six 12 Pounders
Lieut. Chandler P. Eakin   Commanding

July 2. In position on Cemetery Hill facing the Emmitsburg Road. Engaged July 2nd and 3rd. Lieut. Eakin severely wounded after his guns went into battery and the command devolved on Lieut. Philip D. Mason.

Casualties Killed 1 Man Wounded 1 Officer and 7 Men Missing 1 Man

No. 150U   Tablet on Granite Marker located—National Cemetery

---

ARMY OF THE POTOMAC
ARTILLERY RESERVE
FIRST REGULAR BRIGADE
BATTERIES F & K THIRD U. S. ARTILLERY
Six 12 Pounders
Lieut. John C. Turnbull

July 1. Took position on crest of hill near General Meade's Headquarters.

July 2. Moved to a position on the right of a log house on the Emmitsburg Road on the line held by Brig. General A. A. Humphreys's Second Division Third Corps and became immediately engaged but was compelled to retire with the loss of 45 horses and 4 guns which were soon afterwards recaptured.

July 3. Went into position on the crest of the hill at the left of the Evergreen Cemetery and near Army Headquarters and there remained until the close of the battle.

Casualties Killed 1 Officer and 8 Men Wounded 14 Men Missing 1 Man

No. 151U   Tablet on Granite Marker located—Emmitsburg Road and Sickles Avenue

---

ARMY OF THE POTOMAC
ARTILLERY RESERVE
FIRST REGULAR BRIGADE
BATTERIES F & K THIRD U. S. ARTILLERY
Six 12 Pounders
Lieut. John C. Turnbull   Commanding

July 1. Took position on crest of hill near General Meade's Headquarters.

July 2. Moved to a position at the right of a log house on the Emmitsburg Road with Brig. General A. A. Humphreys's Division Third Corps. Engaged here but was compelled to retire with the loss of 45 horses killed and 4 guns which were afterwards recaptured.

July 3. Went into position near the Taneytown Road on the left of Cemetery Hill.

Casualties Killed 1 Officer and 8 Men Wounded 14 Men Missing 1 Man

No. 152U Tablet on Granite Marker located—east of Hancock Avenue, Old Meade Avenue

Note: This tablet is essentially a duplicate of the one for this battery located on Emmitsburg Road.

ARMY OF THE POTOMAC
ARTILLERY RESERVE
FIRST REGULAR BRIGADE
BATTERY C FOURTH U. S. ARTILLERY
Six 12 Pounders
Lieut. Evan Thomas Commanding

July 2. Arrived and took position on crest of hill near General Meade's Headquarters on the left of the Second Corps and was actively engaged in repelling the attack of the Confederates.

July 3. In position near the left of the Second Corps line.

Casualties Killed 1 Man Wounded 1 Officer and 16 Men

No. 153U Tablet on Granite Marker located—Hancock Avenue

ARMY OF THE POTOMAC
ARTILLERY RESERVE
FIRST REGULAR BRIGADE
BATTERY C FIFTH U. S. ARTILLERY
Six 12 Pounders
Lieut. Culian V. Weir Commanding

July 2. Arrived at Gettysburg from near Taneytown and in the afternoon was ordered to the front and by direction of Major General W. S. Hancock took position 500 yards further to the front and by order of Brig. General John Gibbon opened fire on the Confederates on the left front. The Confederates in front advanced to within a few yards no infantry opposing.

Three of the guns were captured by the Confederates and drawn off to the Emmitsburg Road but were recaptured by the 13th Vermont and another regiment.

July 3. In the rear of the line until Longstreet's assault was made when the Battery was moved up to Brig. General A. S. Webb's line and opened with canister at short range on the advancing Confederates. At 6.30 P. M. returned to the Artillery Reserve.

Casualties   Killed 2 men   Wounded 2 Officers and 12 Men

No. 154U   Tablet on Granite Marker located—Hancock Avenue

ARMY OF THE POTOMAC
ARTILLERY RESERVE
FIRST VOLUNTEER BRIGADE
Lieut. Col. Freeman McGilvery

5th Mass. Battery E (10th New York Attached)
Capt. Charles A. Phillips

July 2. Engaged on Third Corps line on the Wheatfield Road.

9th Mass. Battery
Capt. John Bigelow   Lieut. Richard S. Milton

July 2. Engaged on Third Corps line on the Wheatfield Road.
July 3. In Ziegler's Grove.

15th New York Battery
Capt. Patrick Hart

July 2. Engaged on Third Corps line on the Wheatfield Road.
July 3. On Second Corps line south of Pleasonton Avenue.

Penna. Batteries C and F
Capt. James Thompson

July 2. Engaged in Peach Orchard.
July 3. On line with Battery K 4th U. S. on right and Hart's Battery on left.

Casualties   Killed 1 Officer 16 Men   Wounded 10 Officers 61 Men
Captured or Missing 5 Men   Total 93

No. 155U   Tablet on Granite Pedestal located—Hancock Avenue, south of Pennsylvania Monument

Note: A tablet describing this brigade's activity on July 2 is located on Wheatfield Road.

━━━━━━━━━━

ARMY OF THE POTOMAC
ARTILLERY RESERVE
FIRST VOLUNTEER BRIGADE
Lieut. Col. Freeman McGilvery
5th Mass. Battery E
(10th New York Battery Attached)
Capt. Charles Phillips
9th Mass. Battery
Capt. John Bigelow   Lieut. Richard S. Milton
15th New York Battery
Capt. Patrick Hart
Batteries C and F Penna.
Capt. James Thompson

July 2. Went into action at 3.30 P. M. on this road Batteries C and F Penna. on the right in the Peach Orchard line facing west. About 5 P. M. opened and repulsed a heavy column of infantry charging the Brigade. About 6 P. M. the Confederates gained position on the left and the infantry fell back leaving the artillery without support. Four batteries fell back 250 yards and renewed their fire. Battery B 1st New Jersey and 15th New York Battery retired from the field. The advanced line of the 3rd Corps having been abandoned the Artillery Brigade took up a new position 400 yards in the rear and opened on the enemy with canister and at 8 P. M. retired to the battle line of the army.

No. 156U   Tablet on Granite Pedestal located—Wheatfield Road

━━━━━━━━━━

ARMY OF THE POTOMAC
FIRST BRIGADE   ARTILLERY RESERVE
NEW YORK LIGHT ARTILLERY
15TH BATTERY
Four 12 Pounders
Captain Patrick Hart   Commanding

July 2. Engaged in the Peach Orchard retired about dark and reported to Brig. General R. O. Tyler Artillery Reserve.

July 3. Ordered early to the front and took position in the Battalion on the left of Battery E. 5th Massachusetts. Directed by Maj. General Hancock to open on the Confederate batteries with solid shot and shell. Upon the advance of the Confederate infantry fired shell and shrapnel and canister when the line was within 500 yards. A second line advancing was met with double canister which dispersed it. The fire of the Battery was then directed against the artillery on the Confederate right and several caissons and limbers were exploded by the shells.

July 4. Remained in this position until noon.

Casualties   Killed 3 Men   Wounded 2 Officers and 11 Men   Total 16

No. 157U   Cast Iron Tablet located—Hancock Avenue, south of Pennsylvania Monument

---

ARMY OF THE POTOMAC
FIRST BRIGADE   ARTILLERY RESERVE
MASSACHUSETTS LIGHT ARTILLERY
5TH BATTERY E
Six 3 Inch Rifles
Captain Charles A. Phillips   Commanding

July 2. Withdrew at 5 P. M. from the field near the Peach Orchard and went into battery here.

July 3. About 1.30 P. M. by order of Brig. General H. J. Hunt fired on the Confederate batteries but did little damage. Opened an enfilading fire soon after on Longstreet's advancing line of infantry and assisted in repulsing the assault. A charge was made within the range of the Battery immediately afterwards by the Florida Brigade and at about the same time a Confederate battery opened on the left front which at once received the concentrated fire of the batteries of the Brigade driving the cannoneers from the guns which they abandoned.

July 4. Remained in this position until afternoon.

Casualties   Killed 2 Men   Wounded 1 Officer and 13 Men   Total 16

No. 158U   Cast Iron Tablet located—Hancock Avenue south of Pennsylvania Monument

---

ARMY OF THE POTOMAC
ARTILLERY RESERVE
SECOND VOLUNTEER BRIGADE
Capt. Elijah D. Taft

1st Conn. Heavy Battery B
Capt. Albert F. Brooker
Not engaged

1st Conn. Heavy Battery M
Capt. Franklin A. Pratt
Not Engaged

2D Conn. Battery
Capt. John W. Sterling

July 2. Reinforced Third Corps line and late in the day retired and formed line under Lieut. Col. F. McGilvery on left of Second Corps.

5th New York Battery
Capt. Elijah D. Taft

July 2 and 3. Engaged on Cemetery Hill.

Casualties   Killed 1 Man   Wounded 5 Men   Captured or Missing 2 Men
Total 8

No. 159U   Tablet on Granite Pedestal located—Baltimore Pike at Evergreen Cemetery

---

ARMY OF THE POTOMAC
ARTILLERY RESERVE
SECOND VOLUNTEER BRIGADE
FIFTH NEW YORK LIGHT ARTILLERY
Six 20 Pounder Parrots
Captain Elijah D. Taft

July 2. Arrived and halted in park about 10.30 A. M. Moved to the cemetery at 3.30 P. M. and engaged from 4 P. M. until dark. Four guns south of and facing Baltimore Pike firing on a Confederate battery on Benner's Hill. Two guns firing westwardly.

July 3. Engaged at intervals in same position until 4 P. M. One gun on Baltimore Pike having burst the other three received the section firing westwardly. Remained in this position until the close of the battle.

Casualties   Killed 1 Man   Wounded 2 Men

Ammunition Expended   1114 Rounds

No. 160U   Cast Iron Tablet located—Baltimore Pike at Evergreen Cemetery

ARMY OF THE POTOMAC
ARTILLERY RESERVE
THIRD VOLUNTEER BRIGADE
Capt. James F. Huntington

1st New Hampshire Battery
Capt. Frederick M. Edgell

July 2 and 3. Engaged on Cemetery Hill.

1st Ohio Battery H
Lieut. George W. Norton

July 2 and 3. Engaged on Cemetery Hill.

1st Penna. Batteries F and G
Capt. R. Bruce Ricketts

July 2 and 3. Engaged on East Cemetery Hill.

West Virginia Battery C
Capt. Wallace Hill

July 2 and 3. Engaged on Cemetery Hill.

Casualties   Killed 10 Men   Wounded 1 Officer 23 Men   Captured or Missing 3 Men   Total 37

No. 161U   Tablet on Granite Pedestal located—National Cemetery

---

ARMY OF THE POTOMAC
ARTILLERY RESERVE
FOURTH VOLUNTEER BRIGADE
Capt. Robert H. Fitzhugh

6th Maine Battery F
Lieut. Edwin B. Dow

July 2 and 3. With First Volunteer Artillery Brigade near left of Second Corps line.

Maryland Battery A
Capt. James H. Rigby

July 2 and 3. Engaged on Powers Hill.

1st New Jersey Battery
Lieut. Augustin N. Parsons

July 3. Engaged on line of Second Division Second Corps.

1st New York Battery G
Capt. Nelson Ames

July 2. Engaged in Peach Orchard.
July 3. Engaged on left of Second Corps line.

1st New York Battery K (11th New York Attached)
Capt. Robert H. Fitzhugh

July 3. Engaged on Second Corps line.

Casualties   Killed 2 Men   Wounded 34 Men   Total 36

No. 162U   Tablet on Granite Pedestal located—Hancock Avenue near the Angle

OTHER SUPPORTING UNITS TABLET INSCRIPTIONS
ARMY OF THE POTOMAC

ARMY OF THE POTOMAC
ENGINEER BRIGADE
Brig. Gen. Henry W. Benham

15th New York (3 Companies)
Major Walter L Cassin

50th New York
Col. William H. Pettes

United States Battalion
Capt. George H. Mendell

Engaged in arduous duties from June 13 to July 18 1863 bridging rivers and transporting pontoons to enable the Army to cross the Potomac River and its tributaries into Pennsylvania and to re-cross into Virginia.

No. 163U   Tablet on Granite Pedestal located—Pleasonton Avenue

---

ARMY OF THE POTOMAC
UNITED STATES BATTALION OF ENGINEERS
Capt. George H. Mendell   Commanding

With the Army of the Potomac in the Gettysburg Campaign from the Rappahannock to the Potomac and engaged in arduous duties from June 13th to July 18th bridging rivers and transporting pontoons.

No casualties reported.

No. 164U   Tablet on Granite Marker located—Pleasonton Avenue

---

ARMY OF THE POTOMAC
HEADQUARTERS
PROVOST GUARD
EIGHTH U. S. INFANTRY
Eight Companies
Captain Edwin W. H. Read   Commanding

July 2. Arrived in the morning and engaged in Provost duty until the close of the battle.

No. 165U   Tablet on Granite Marker located—Leister Farm, Meade's Headquarters

———

ARMY OF THE POTOMAC
CAVALRY CORPS SECOND DIVISION
SECOND BRIGADE
Col. Pennock Huey
2D   4th New York   6th Ohio (10 Cos.)
8th Pennsylvania Cavalry

Participated in the Gettysburg Campaign with the Division until it arrived at Hanover Junction Pa.

June 30. The Commander of the Division ordered the Brigade to Manchester and all roads were held by pickets until the afternoon of the 3D.

July 3. Orders were received to go via Westminster to Emmitsburg to take possession of that place.

July 4. Moved to Westminster and received supplies and marched to Emmitsburg arriving at noon.

Pursuant to orders the Brigade joined Third Division Cavalry Corps.

No. 166U   Tablet on Granite Pedestal located—Pleasonton Avenue

Note: This tablet describes the activities of the Second Brigade, Second Cavalry Division in the campaign. The brigade did not reach the battlefield proper.

ARTILLERY UNITS TABLET INSCRIPTIONS
ARMY OF NORTHERN VIRGINIA

C. S. A.
ARMY OF NORTHERN VIRGINIA
HILL'S CORPS   ARTILLERY RESERVE
McINTOSH'S BATTALION
Johnson's   Rice's   Hurt's and Wallace's Batteries
Six Napoleons   Two Whitworths   Eight 3 Inch Rifles

July 1–4. The Battalion was actively engaged on each of the three days of the battle and withdrew from the field under orders in the evening of the fourth day.

Losses   7 men killed   25 wounded of whom 16 were captured.   38 horses killed or disabled.

No. 73C   Tablet on Granite Pedestal located—West Confederate Avenue

---

ARMY OF NORTHERN VIRGINIA
HILL'S CORPS   ARTILLERY RESERVE
McINTOSH'S BATTALION   RICE'S BATTERY
DANVILLE VIRGINIA ARTILLERY
Four Napoleons

July 1. In position near Chambersburg Pike west of Herr's Tavern and firing when Union forces were visible. Enfiladed their line at one time in and near railroad.

July 2. Two guns took position here and were actively engaged under heavy fire of sharpshooters and artillery. The other two guns in reserve.

July 3. All the guns were actively engaged in this position.

July 4. Withdrew at evening to Marsh Creek on Fairfield Road.

Losses not reported in detail.

238

No. 74C   Cast Iron Tablet located—West Confederate Avenue

━━━━━━━━━━━━━━━

ARMY OF NORTHERN VIRGINIA
HILL'S CORPS   ARTILLERY RESERVE
McINTOSH'S BATTALION   RICE'S BATTERY
DANVILLE VIRGINIA ARTILLERY
Four Napoleons

July 2. Two Guns took position here and were actively engaged under the heavy fire of Union sharpshooters and artillery. Two guns of the Battery were in reserve.

July 3. All guns were actively engaged in this position.

July 4. Withdrew in the night to Marsh Creek on the Fairfield Road.

Losses not reported in detail.

No. 75C   Cast Iron Tablet located—East Side West Confederate Avenue

Note: This tablet essentially duplicates the one for this battery located on the other side of the avenue.

━━━━━━━━━━━━━━━

ARMY OF NORTHERN VIRGINIA
HILL'S CORPS   ARTILLERY RESERVE
McINTOSH'S BATTALION   HURT'S BATTERY
HARDAWAY ALABAMA ARTILLERY
Two Whitworths   Two 3 Inch Rifles

July 1. The Whitworths were in position near Chambersburg Pike west of Herr's Tavern and actively engaged.

July 2. All the guns were in position here and actively engaged under heavy fire of sharpshooters and artillery.

July 3. The 3 Inch Rifles remained here. The Whitworths were moved to position on Oak Hill. All were actively engaged. The Whitworths were beyond the range of Union guns whilst their own fire reached all parts of the field.

July 4. Withdrew at evening to Marsh Creek on Fairfield Road.

Losses not reported in detail.

No. 76C   Cast Iron Tablet located—West Confederate Avenue

Note: Another tablet for this battery is located on Oak Hill.

━━━━━━━━━━━━━━━

ARMY OF NORTHERN VIRGINIA
HILL'S CORPS   ARTILLERY RESERVE
McINTOSH'S BATTALION   HURT'S BATTERY
HARDAWAY ALABAMA ARTILLERY
Two Whitworths   Two 3 Inch Rifles

July 1. The Whitworths were in position to the right of the Chambersburg Pike near the position of Pegram's Battalion. Opened fire slowly and effectively shelling the woods occupied by the Union troops to the right of the town.

July 2. The Battery in position on Seminary Ridge south of the Hagerstown Road exposed to a heavy fire from the Union sharpshooters and artillery.

July 3. The Whitworth guns were moved to this position and fired with great effect. The 3 Inch Rifles remaining on Seminary Ridge south of the Hagerstown Road.

July 4. Withdrew at evening to Marsh Creek on the Fairfield Road.

No. 77C   Cast Iron Tablet located—Oak Hill

━━━━━━━━━━━━━━━━

ARMY OF NORTHERN VIRGINIA
HILL'S CORPS   ARTILLERY RESERVE
McINTOSH'S BATTALION   JOHNSON'S VIRGINIA BATTERY
Two Napoleons   Two 3 Inch Rifles

July 1. In position on hill near Fairfield Road west of Willoughby Run. Not engaged though under fire and losing one man killed.

July 2. In position here and actively engaged under a heavy fire of sharpshooters and artillery.

July 3. Remained in this position and was actively engaged.

July 4. Withdrew at evening to Marsh Creek on Fairfield Road.

Losses not reported in detail.

No. 78C   Cast Iron Tablet located—West Confederate Avenue

━━━━━━━━━━━━━━━━

ARMY OF NORTHERN VIRGINIA
HILL'S CORPS   ARTILLERY RESERVE
McINTOSH'S BATTALION   JOHNSON'S VIRGINIA BATTERY
Two Napoleons   Two 3 Inch Rifles

July 2. In position here and actively engaged under the heavy fire of Union sharpshooters and artillery.

July 3. Remained in this position all day and actively engaged.

July 4. Withdrew in the night to Marsh Creek on the Fairfield Road.

Losses not reported in detail.

No. 79C   Cast Iron Tablet located—east side West Confederate Avenue

Note: This tablet essentially duplicates the one for this battery located on the other side of the avenue.

ARMY OF NORTHERN VIRGINIA
HILL'S CORPS   ARTILLERY RESERVE
MCINTOSH'S BATTALION   WALLACE'S BATTERY
SECOND ROCKBRIDGE ARTILLERY
Four 3 Inch Rifles

July 1. In position near Chambersburg Pike west of Herr's Tavern and actively engaged in the evening.

July 2. Occupied this position and was actively engaged. Had one gun disabled.

July 3. Remained here and was actively engaged.

July 4. Withdrew at evening to Marsh Creek on Fairfield Road.

Losses not reported in detail.

No. 80C   Cast Iron Tablet located—West Confederate Avenue

C. S. A.
ARMY OF NORTHERN VIRGINIA
HILL'S CORPS   ARTILLERY RESERVE
PEGRAM'S BATTALION
Marye's   Crenshaw's   Zimmerman's   McGraw's and Brander's Batteries
Ten Napoleons   Four 10 Pounder Parrotts
Four 3 Inch Rifles   Two 12 Pounder Howitzers

July 1–3. The Battalion was actively engaged on each of the three days of the battle. The first cannon-shot of the battle was fired by one of the batteries from a point near the south side of Chambersburg Pike on the ridge west of Herr's Tavern.

July 4. About sunset withdrew and began the march to Hagerstown.

 Losses Killed 10 Wounded 37 Total 47

 Ammunition expended 3800 rounds. Horses killed or disabled 38

No. 81C Tablet on Granite Pedestal located—West Confederate Avenue

———

ARMY OF NORTHERN VIRGINIA
HILL'S CORPS ARTILLERY RESERVE
PEGRAM'S BATTALION MARYE'S BATTERY
THE FREDERICKSBURG ARTILLERY
Two Napoleons Two 10 Pounder Parrotts

July 1. This Battery fired the first cannon-shot of the battle from a point near the south side of the Chambersburg Pike on the ridge west of Herr's Tavern and was actively engaged until the close of the day's conflict.

July 2. Early in the morning took position here. Opened at intervals upon the Union lines and enfiladed their batteries when they sought to concentrate their fire upon the Confederate right.

July 3. Participated actively in all operations of the artillery including the cannonade which preceded Longstreet's assault.

July 4. About sunset withdrew and began the march to Hagerstown.

 Losses not reported in detail.

No. 82C Cast Iron Tablet located—West Confederate Avenue

———

ARMY OF NORTHERN VIRGINIA
HILL'S CORPS ARTILLERY RESERVE
PEGRAM'S BATTALION CRENSHAW'S BATTERY
Two Napoleons Two 12 Pounder Howitzers

July 1. The Napoleons occupied the ridge west of Herr's Tavern and took an active part in the battle. The howitzers were not engaged.

July 2. Early in the morning all the guns took position here and were actively engaged throughout the day. Sometimes annoyed by sharpshooters which the howitzers aided in silencing.

July 3. Remained here and participated in all the operations of the artillery.

July 4. About sunset withdrew and began the march to Hagerstown.

Losses not reported in detail.

No. 83C   Cast Iron Tablet located—West Confederate Avenue

———————

ARMY OF NORTHERN VIRGINIA
HILL'S CORPS   ARTILLERY RESERVE
PEGRAM'S BATTALION   ZIMMERMAN'S BATTERY
THE PEE DEE ARTILLERY
Four 3 Inch Rifles

July 1. Three guns were in position on the ridge west of Herr's Tavern actively engaged and did effective service. The other was disabled for the day by accident while hastening into action.

July 2. Early in the morning took position here and at intervals was engaged with the Union batteries endeavoring especially to enfilade them when they sought to concentrate their fire upon the Confederate right.

July 3. Took an active part in all the operations of the artillery including the cannonade preceding Longstreet's assault.

July 4. Withdrew about sunset and began the march to Hagerstown.

Losses not reported in detail.

No. 84C   Cast Iron Tablet located—West Confederate Avenue

———————

ARMY OF NORTHERN VIRGINIA
HILL'S CORPS   RESERVE ARTILLERY
PEGRAM'S BATTALION   McGRAW'S BATTERY
THE PURCELL ARTILLERY
Four Napoleons

July 1. In position south of the Chambersburg Pike on the ridge west of Herr's Tavern and actively engaged.

July 2. Early in the morning occupied this position and took part in the day's conflict with the Union batteries and now and then dropped a shell among the busy sharpshooters.

July 3. Remained here and actively participated in all the operations of the artillery.

July 4. Withdrew about sunset and began the march to Hagerstown.

Losses not reported in detail.

No. 85C   Cast Iron Tablet located—West Confederate Avenue

━━━━━━━━━━━━━

ARMY OF NORTHERN VIRGINIA
HILL'S CORPS   ARTILLERY RESERVE
PEGRAM'S BATTALION   BRANDER'S BATTERY
THE LETCHER ARTILLERY
Two Napoleons   Two 10 Pounder Parrotts

July 1. In position at first on the ridge west of Herr's Tavern but moved later to a hill east of Willoughby Run about 500 yards from the Union batteries and from that point fired upon the Union infantry with much effect although itself exposed to a heavy fire of canister.

July 2. Occupied this position early in the morning and was engaged at intervals in firing upon the Union lines and batteries.

July 3. Actively participated in all the operations of the artillery including the cannonade preceding Longstreet's assault.

July 4. Withdrew about sunset and began the march to Hagerstown.

Losses not reported in detail.

No. 86C   Cast Iron Tablet located—West Confederate Avenue

━━━━━━━━━━━━━

C. S. A.
HILL'S CORPS   HETH'S DIVISION
GARNETT'S BATTALION
Granby's   Moore's   Lewis's and Maurin's Batteries
Four Napoleons   Two 10 Pounder Parrotts
Seven 3 Inch Rifles   Two 12 Pounder Howitzers

July 1 2 3 4. The Parrotts and Rifles took part in the battle in a different position on each of the three days their most active service being on the second day in this position. The Napoleons and Howitzers were in reserve and not actively engaged at any time. All withdrew from the field on the fourth day but not at the same hour nor by the same route.

Losses   Wounded 5   Missing 17   Total 22
Ammunition expended   1000 rounds.   Horses killed or disabled 13.

No. 87C   Tablet on Granite Pedestal located—West Confederate Avenue

━━━━━━━━━━━━━

ARMY OF NORTHERN VIRGINIA
HILL'S CORPS HETH'S DIVISION
GARNETT'S BATTALION GRANDY'S BATTERY
THE NORFOLK LIGHT ARTILLERY BLUES
Two 3 Inch Rifles Two 12 Pounder Howitzers

July 1. Arrived on the field in the afternoon but was not engaged.

July 2. The Rifles took position here in the morning and participated during the afternoon and evening in the artillery duel with the Union batteries on Cemetery Hill.

July 3. Ordered to the south side of McMillan's Woods and held all day in reserve without firing a shot though sometimes under fire.

July 4. The Howitzers were never actively engaged in the battle but on this day were placed in a position here. At night they rejoined the Rifles and with them began the march to Hagerstown.

Losses not reported in detail.

No. 88C Cast Iron Tablet located—West Confederate Avenue

ARMY OF NORTHERN VIRGINIA
HILL'S CORPS HETH'S DIVISION
GARNETT'S BATTALION MOORE'S BATTERY
THE HUGER ARTILLERY
One 10 Pounder Parrott One 3 Inch Rifle Two Napoleons

July 1. The Parrott and Rifle about 3.30 P. M. relieved some of Pegram's guns on the ridge west of Herr's Tavern their ammunition being exhausted and from that time took part in the conflict.

July 2. Opened fire here at 3 P. M. on East Cemetery Hill and kept it up for some hours. Renewed it at dusk in support of Early's assault.

July 3. Moved under orders to position south of McMillan's Woods and remained inactive all day though sometimes under fire.

July 4. At 8 A. M. marched to Cashtown to reinforce the cavalry escorting the wagon train. The Napoleons took no part in the battle but were in position here on this day and at evening began the march to Hagerstown.

Losses not reported in detail.

No. 89C Cast Iron Tablet located—West Confederate Avenue

ARMY OF NORTHERN VIRGINIA
HILL'S CORPS   HETH'S DIVISION
GARNETT'S BATTALION   LEWIS'S BATTERY
THE LEWIS ARTILLERY
Two 3 Inch Rifles   Two Napoleons

July 1. One of the Rifles at 3.30 P. M. relieved one of Pegram's guns on the ridge west of Herr's Tavern and was engaged until the fight ended.

July 2. Both Rifles were in position here and took an active part in the artillery duel in the afternoon and evening with Union batteries on Cemetery Hill.

July 3. Moved under orders to a point south of McMillan's Woods but not engaged at any time although from time to time under fire.

July 4. The Napoleons were never actively engaged in the battle but on this day were placed in position here. At night they rejoined the Rifles and with them began the march to Hagerstown.

Losses not reported in detail.

No. 90C   Cast Iron Tablet located—West Confederate Avenue

ARMY OF NORTHERN VIRGINIA
HILL'S CORPS   HETH'S DIVISION
GARNETT'S BATTALION   MAURIN'S BATTERY
THE DONALDSONVILLE ARTILLERY
One 10 Pounder   Two 3 Inch Rifles

July 1. About 3.30 P. M. relieved some of Pegram's guns whose ammunition was exhausted on the ridge west of Herr's Tavern and from that time took an active part in the conflict.

July 2. In position here all day but not actively engaged until 3 P. M. when it opened and maintained a steady fire on Cemetery Hill until near sunset and vigorously renewed it at dusk for the purpose of diverting the fire of the Union artillery from the Confederate infantry then assaulting East Cemetery Hill.

July 3. Ordered to a position south of McMillan's Woods and held in reserve sometimes fired upon but not returning the fire.

July 4. Withdrew about 8 A. M and marched to Cashtown to reinforce the cavalry escorting the wagon train.

Losses not reported in detail.

No. 91C   Cast Iron Tablet located—West Confederate Avenue

C. S. A.
ARMY OF NORTHERN VIRGINIA
HILL'S CORPS   PENDER'S DIVISION
POAGUE'S BATTALION
Ward's   Brooke's   Wyatt's and Graham's Batteries
Seven Napoleons   Six 12 Pounder Howitzers
One 10 Pounder Parrott   Two 3 Inch Rifles

July 2. Late in the evening ten of the guns were placed in position at different points ready for service next day. The Howitzers were kept in the rear as no place was found from which they could be used with advantage.

July 3. The ten guns were actively engaged.

July 4. In the evening about dusk began the march to Hagerstown.

Killed 2   Wounded 24   Missing 6   Total 32

Ammunition expended   657 rounds.   Horses killed or disabled 17

No. 92C   Tablet on Granite Pedestal located—West Confederate

---

ARMY OF NORTHERN VIRGINIA
HILL'S CORPS   PENDER'S DIVISION
POAGUE'S BATTALION   WARD'S BATTERY
THE MADISON (MISS.) LIGHT ARTILLERY
Three Napoleons   One 12 Pounder

July 2. Late in the evening the Napoleons were placed in position about 400 yards eastward from this point.

July 3. The Napoleons participated actively in all the operations of the artillery during the day including the cannonade preceding Longstreet's assault withdrawing afterward to a position near here. The Howitzer was kept in the rear and took no part in the battle but was held in readiness to resist any advance of the Union forces.

July 4. In the evening about dusk began the march to Hagerstown.

Losses not reported in detail.

No. 93C   Cast Iron Tablet located—West Confederate Avenue

ARMY OF NORTHERN VIRGINIA
HILL'S CORPS   PENDER'S DIVISION
POAGUE'S BATTALION   BROOKE'S BATTERY
Two Napoleons   Two 12 Pounder Howitzers

July 2. Late in the evening the Napoleons were placed in position about 400 yards eastward from this point.

July 3. The Napoleons participated actively in all the operations of the artillery during the day including the cannonade preceding Longstreet's assault withdrawing afterward to a position near here. The Howitzers were kept in the rear and took no part in the battle but were held in readiness to resist any advance of the Union forces.

July 4. In the evening about dusk began the march to Hagerstown.

Losses not reported in detail.

No. 94C   Cast Iron Tablet located—West Confederate Avenue

━━━━━━━━━━━━

ARMY OF NORTHERN VIRGINIA
HILL'S CORPS   PENDER'S DIVISION
POAGUE'S BATTALION   WYATT'S BATTERY
THE ALBEMARLE VA. ARTILLERY
One 10 Pounder Parrott   Two 3 Inch Rifles   One 12 Pounder Howitzer

July 2. Late in the evening the Parrott and Rifles took position here.

July 3. At 7 A. M. they opened on the Union position but were soon ordered to cease firing as they drew the concentrated fire of several batteries. They afterward took part in all the operations of the artillery during the day including the cannonade preceding Longstreet's assault. The Howitzer remained in the rear and was not engaged in the battle but held in readiness to resist any advance of the Union forces.

July 4. In the evening about dusk began the march to Hagerstown.

Losses not reported in detail.

No.95C   Cast Iron Tablet located—West Confederate Avenue

━━━━━━━━━━━━

ARMY OF NORTHERN VIRGINIA
HILL'S CORPS   PENDER'S DIVISION
POAGUE'S BATTALION   GRAHAM'S BATTERY
THE CHARLOTTE N. C. ARTILLERY
Two Napoleons   Two 12 Pounder Howitzers

July 2. Late in the evening the Napoleons were placed in position here.

July 3. At 7 A. M. they opened on the Union position but were soon ordered to cease firing as they drew concentrated fire of several batteries. They afterward took part in all the operations of the artillery during the day including the cannonade which preceded Longstreet's assault. The Howitzers remained in the rear and were not engaged in the battle but held in readiness to resist any advance of the Union forces.

July 4. In the evening about dusk began the march to Hagerstown.

Losses not reported in detail.

No. 96C   Cast Iron Tablet located—West Confederate Avenue

C. S. A.
ARMY OF NORTHERN VIRGINIA
HILL'S CORPS   ANDERSON'S DIVISION
LANE'S BATTALION
Patterson's   Wingfield's   Ross's Batteries

Three Napoleons   Two 20 Pounder Parrotts   Three 10 Pounder Parrotts
Four 3 Inch Navy Parrotts   Five 12 Pounder Howitzers

July 2–3. Took part in the battle.

July 4. Remained in position near here and about sunset began the march to Hagerstown.

Losses   Killed 3   Wounded 21   Missing 6   Total 30
Ammunition expended   1082 rounds.   Horses killed or disabled 36.

No. 97C   Tablet on Granite Pedestal located—West Confederate Avenue

---

ARMY OF NORTHERN VIRGINIA
HILL'S CORPS   ANDERSON'S DIVISION
LANE'S BATTALION   PATTERSON'S BATTERY
Two Napoleons   Four 12 Pounder Howitzers

July 2. Was detached from the Battalion in the morning together with the Howitzers of Ross's Battery and ordered into position here. In the afternoon opened fire upon the Union positions north of the Peach Orchard and when the infantry advanced at 6 P. M. moved forward with it beyond the Emmitsburg Road and was engaged there until dark.

July 3. Occupied a position near here in reserve and did not take part in the active operations of the day.

July 4. Withdrew about sunset and began the march to Hagerstown.

Losses   Killed 2   Wounded 5   Missing 2

Ammunition expended   170 rounds.   Horses killed or disabled.

No. 98C   Cast Iron Tablet located—West Confederate Avenue

━━━━━━━━━━

ARMY OF NORTHERN VIRGINIA
HILL'S CORPS   ANDERSON'S DIVISION
LANE'S BATTALION   WINGFIELD'S BATTERY
Two 20 Pounder Parrotts   Three 3 Inch Navy Parrotts

July 2. In position here actively engaged and exposed all the while to a heavy fire from the Union artillery.

July 3. Remained here and took part in all artillery conflicts of the day including that which preceded Longstreet's assault.

July 4. Withdrew about sunset and began the march to Hagerstown.

Losses   Wounded 9   Missing 2

Ammunition expended   406 rounds.   Horses killed or disabled 20.

No. 99C   Cast Iron Tablet located—West Confederate Avenue

━━━━━━━━━━

ARMY OF NORTHERN VIRGINIA
HILL'S CORPS   ANDERSON'S DIVISION
LANE'S BATTALION   ROSS'S BATTERY
One Napoleon   Three 10 Pounder Parrotts
One 3 Inch Navy Parrott   One 12 Pounder Howitzer

July 2. Five of the guns were in position here and actively engaged under a heavy fire of artillery. The Howitzer was detached and served with Patterson's Battery south of Spangler's Woods.

July 3. Remained here and participated in all the operations of the artillery including the cannonade preceding Longstreet's assault.

July 4. Withdrew about sunset and began the march to Hagerstown.

Losses   Killed 1   Wounded 7   Missing 2

Ammunition expended   506 rounds.   Horses killed or disabled 9.

No. 100C   Cast Iron Tablet located—West Confederate Avenue

━━━━━━━━━━

C. S. A.
ARMY OF NORTHERN VIRGINIA
EWELL'S CORPS   ARTILLERY RESERVE
DANCE'S BATTALION
FIRST VIRGINIA ARTILLERY
Cunningham's   Smith's   Watson's   Griffin's and Graham's Batteries
Four 20 Pounder Parrotts   Four 10 Pounder Parrotts
Ten 3 Inch Rifles   Two Napoleons

July 1. The Battalion reached the field in evening too late to take part in the battle.

July 2 & 3. The four first named batteries occupied positions at various points on this ridge. Graham's Battery of 20 Pounder Parrotts served east of Rock Creek. All were actively engaged.

July 4. At nightfall began the march to Hagerstown.

Losses   Killed 3   Wounded 19

Ammunition expended   1888 rounds.

No. 101C   Tablet on Granite Pedestal located—Seminary Avenue, north of Hagerstown Road

———

ARMY OF NORTHERN VIRGINIA
EWELL'S CORPS   ARTILLERY RESERVE
DANCE'S BATTALION   CUNNINGHAM'S BATTERY
THE POWHATAN ARTILLERY
Four 3 Inch Rifles

July 1. Reached the field in evening too late to take part in the battle.

July 2. Early in morning took position here. Opened fire about 4 P. M. upon the batteries on Cemetery Hill and continued firing until dark.

July 3. Remained here all day. Took part in the great cannonade preceding Longstreet's final assault. At night withdrew to camp in rear.

July 4. After nightfall began the march to Hagerstown.

Ammunition expended   308 rounds.   Losses not reported in detail.

No.102C   Cast Iron Tablet located—Seminary Road, north of Hagerstown Road

ARMY OF NORTHERN VIRGINIA
EWELL'S CORPS   RESERVE ARTILLERY
DANCE'S BATTALION   SMITH'S BATTERY
THIRD RICHMOND HOWITZERS
Four 3 Inch Rifles

July 1. Reached the field in evening too late to take part in the battle.

July 2. Early in the morning took position here. About 4 P. M. opened fire upon the batteries on Cemetery Hill and continued firing until dark.

July 3. Moved to position south of Fairfield Road. Took part in the great cannonade preceding Longstreet's final assault and kept firing for some time afterwards. Withdrew at night to camp in rear.

July 4. After nightfall began the march to Hagerstown.

Ammunition expended   314 rounds.

Losses   Killed 1   Wounded not reported.

No. 103C   Cast Iron Tablet located—Seminary Avenue, north of Hagerstown Road

---

ARMY OF NORTHERN VIRGINIA
EWELL'S CORPS   ARTILLERY RESERVE
DANCE'S BATTALION   WATSON'S BATTERY
SECOND RICHMOND HOWITZERS
Four 10 Pounder Parrotts

July 1. Reached the field in evening too late to take part in the battle.

July 2. Early in the morning took position on this ridge just north of Western Maryland R. R. cut. Opened fire about 4 P. M. upon the batteries on Cemetery Hill and continued firing until dark.

July 3. Moved to this position. Took part in the great cannonade preceding Longstreet's final assault and kept firing for some time afterwards. Withdrew at night to camp in rear.

July 4. After nightfall began the march to Hagerstown.

Ammunition expended   661 rounds.   Losses not reported in detail.

No. 104C   Cast Iron Tablet located—West Confederate Avenue, south of Hagerstown Road

ARMY OF NORTHERN VIRGINIA
EWELL'S CORPS   ARTILLERY RESERVE
DANCE'S BATTALION   WATSON'S BATTERY
SECOND RICHMOND HOWITZERS
Four 10 Pounder Parrotts

July 3. Moved to this position. Took part in the cannonade preceding Longstreet's final assault and continued firing for some time afterwards. Moved at night to rear of this line.

July 4. In the night withdrew and began the march to Hagerstown.

Ammunition expended   661 rounds. Losses not reported in detail.

No. 105C   Cast Iron Tablet located—West Confederate Avenue, south of Hagerstown Road

Note: This tablet essentially duplicates the one for this battery located on the opposite side of the avenue.

1st VIRGINIA ARTILLERY   HUPP'S BATTERY
SALEM VIRGINIA ARTILLERY
Two 3 Inch Rifles   Two Napoleons

July 1. The Battery reached the field too late to participate in the engagement of the day.

July 2. Held in reserve near the W. M. Railroad cut.

July 3. The Rifle guns were in position near Fairfield Road. The Napoleons were placed at the railroad cut and remained until night but were not engaged.

July 4. At midnight began the march to Hagerstown.

Casualties not reported.   Ammunition expended 154 rounds.

No. 106C   Cast Iron Tablet located—Seminary Ridge, north side of railroad cut

Note: There is no heading on this tablet other than that shown. This battery is also identified on tablet No. 107C as Griffin's Battery, Dance's Battalion. Hupp's Battery is not listed on the tablets for either reserve artillery battalion of Ewell's Corps.

ARMY OF NORTHERN VIRGINIA
EWELL'S CORPS   RESERVE ARTILLERY
DANCE'S BATTALION   GRIFFIN'S BATTERY
THE SALEM ARTILLERY
Two 3 Inch Rifles   Two Napoleons

July 1. Reached the field too late to take part in the battle.

July 2. Remained in reserve on this ridge north of the railroad.

July 3. The Rifles were moved to this position early in the morning and took part in the cannonade preceding Longstreet's assault and continued firing for some time afterward. Withdrew at night to camp in rear.

July 4. The Napoleons occupied a position on this ridge south of the Railroad cut but did no firing. After nightfall they joined the Rifles and with them began the march to Hagerstown.

No losses reported.   Ammunition expended 154 rounds.

No. 107C   Cast Iron Tablet located—West Confederate Avenue

ARMY OF NORTHERN VIRGINIA
EWELL'S CORPS   ARTILLERY RESERVE
DANCE'S BATTALION   GRAHAM'S BATTERY
ROCKBRIDGE ARTILLERY
Four 20 Pounder Parrotts

July 1. The Battery arrived on the field too late to participate in the engagement of the day. Was ordered to report to Lieut. Colonel H. P. Jones commanding Artillery Early's Division and moved into position on the left to the south and east of town.

July 2. Remained in position on the left firing occasionally.

July 3. Remained in position during the day and rejoined the Battalion during the night.

July 4. Took up line of march to Hagerstown.

Ammunition expended 439 rounds.   Losses not reported in detail.

No. 108C   Cast Iron Tablet located—Benner's Hill, south of Hanover Road

C. S. A.
ARMY OF NORTHERN VIRGINIA
EWELL'S CORPS   ARTILLERY RESERVE
NELSON'S BATTALION
Kirkpatrick's   Massie's and Milledge's Batteries

One 10 Pounder Parrott   Four 3 Inch Rifles   Six Napoleons

July 1 The Battalion arrived on the field too late to participate in the engagement of the day. Was ordered to report to the Chief of Artillery Rodes's Division.

July 2. Took position on Seminary Ridge ¼ mile north of Chambersburg Pike. About 11 A. M. moved to the rear of Pennsylvania College and remained until night when the Battalion returned to the position of the morning.

July 3. Ordered to the extreme left of the Confederate line to find a position to withdraw the fire from the Confederate infantry. Opened about 12 M. firing 20 to 25 rounds. At midnight moved with Johnson's Division to Seminary Ridge.

July 4. Was ordered to take position on the ridge west of town. At night took up the line of march to Hagerstown.

Ammunition expended   48 rounds.   Casualties not reported.

No. 109C   Tablet on Granite Pedestal located—north of Hanover Road

———

ARMY OF NORTHERN VIRGINIA
EWELL'S CORPS   ARTILLERY RESERVE
NELSON'S BATTALION   KIRKPATRICK'S BATTERY
AMHERST VA. ARTILLERY
One 3 Inch Rifle   Three Napoleons

July 1. The Battery arrived too late on the field to participate in the engagement of the day.

July 2. Took position on Seminary Ridge ¼ mile north of Chambersburg Pike. About 11 A. M. moved to the rear of Pennsylvania College and remained until night when the Battery returned to the position of the morning.

July 3. Ordered to the extreme left of the Confederate line. At midnight moved with Johnson's Division to Seminary Ridge.

July 4. Took position on the ridge west of town and at midnight took up the line of march to Hagerstown.

No report of casualties or ammunition expended.

No. 110C   Cast Iron Tablet located—Benner's Hill, north of Hanover Road

───────────

ARMY OF NORTHERN VIRGINIA
EWELL'S CORPS   RESERVE ARTILLERY
NELSON'S BATTALION   MASSIE'S BATTERY
FULVANNA VIRGINIA ARTILLERY
One 3 Inch Rifle   Three Napoleons

July 1. The Battery arrived on the field too late to participate in the engagement of the day.

July 2. Took position on Seminary Ridge ¼ mile north of Chambersburg Pike. About 11 A. M. moved to the rear of Pennsylvania College and remained until night when the Battery returned to the position of the morning.

July 3. Ordered to the extreme left of Confederate line. At midnight moved with Johnson's Division to Seminary Ridge.

July 4. Took position on the ridge west of town and at midnight moved on the march to Hagerstown.

No report of casualties or ammunition expended.

No. 111C   Cast Iron Tablet located—Benner's Hill, north of Hanover Road

───────────

ARMY OF NORTHERN VIRGINIA
EWELL'S CORPS   ARTILLERY RESERVE
NELSON'S BATTALION   MILLEDGE'S BATTERY
GEORGIA ARTILLERY
One 10 Pounder Parrott   Two 3 Inch Rifles

July 1. The Battery arrived on the field too late to participate in the engagement of the day.

July 2. Took position on Seminary Ridge ¼ mile north of Chambersburg Pike. About 11 A. M. moved to the rear of Pennsylvania College and remained until night when the Battery returned to the position of the morning.

July 3. Ordered to the extreme left of the Confederate line to find a position to withdraw the fire from the Confederate infantry. Opened about 12 M. firing from 20 to 25 rounds.

July 4. Took position west of town and at midnight moved on the march to Hagerstown.

Ammunition expended   48 rounds.

No. 112C   Cast Iron Tablet located—Benner's Hill, north of Hanover Road

---

C. S. A.
ARMY OF NORTHERN VIRGINIA
EWELL'S CORPS   RODES'S DIVISION
CARTER'S BATTALION
Carter's   Fry's   Page's and Reese's Batteries
Four 10 Pounder Parrotts   Six 3 Inch Rifles   Six Napoleons

July 1. Arrived on the field soon after noon and rendered very effective service in the day's battle.

July 2. Held in readiness for action but was not engaged.

July 3. The Parrotts and Rifled guns were placed on Seminary Ridge near the railroad cut and took part in the great cannonade preceding Longstreet's assault.

July 4. After nightfall began the march to Hagerstown.

Losses   Killed 6   Wounded 35   Missing 24   Total 65
Ammunition expended   1898 rounds.

No. 113C   Tablet on Granite Pedestal located—Oak Hill

ARMY OF NORTHERN VIRGINIA
EWELL'S CORPS   RODES'S DIVISION
T. H. CARTER'S BATTALION   W. P. CARTER'S BATTERY
THE KING WILLIAM ARTILLERY
Two 10 Pounder Parrotts   Two Napoleons

July 1. Soon after arriving here it opened an enfilading fire on the Union forces near the Chambersburg Pike causing some to seek shelter in the railroad cuts. Their guns replied slowly but not without inflicting some losses on the Battery in its exposed position. Later in the day it moved to the foot of the ridge to aid Doles's Brigade in repelling the Eleventh Corps and rendered effective service. When the fight ended by the withdrawal of the First Corps it pursued the Union forces to the edge of the town.

July 2. In position but was not engaged.

July 3. The Parrott guns on Seminary Ridge near the railroad cut took part in the cannonade preceding Longstreet's assault.

July 4. After nightfall began the march to Hagerstown.

Losses   Killed 4   Wounded 7

Ammunition expended   572 rounds.

No. 114C   Cast Iron Tablet located—Oak Hill

―――――――――

ARMY OF NORTHERN VIRGINIA
EWELL'S CORPS   RODES'S DIVISION
CARTER'S BATTALION   FRY'S BATTERY
THE ORANGE ARTILLERY
Two 10 Pounder Parrotts   Two 3 Inch Rifles

July 1. Opened fire soon after arriving here upon the Union troops near the Chambersburg Pike to which their artillery replied with a heavy fire that caused some loss. Soon afterward the Union forces extended their line northward to the Mummasburg Road and this Battery by its enfilading fire aided our infantry in the severe conflict which ended with the withdrawal of the First Corps from Seminary Ridge.

July 2. In position but was not engaged.

July 3. All its guns were on Seminary Ridge near the Railroad cut and took part in the cannonade preceding Longstreet's assault.

Losses not reported.   Ammunition expended 882 rounds.

No. 115C   Cast Iron Tablet located—Oak Hill

―――――――――

ARMY OF NORTHERN VIRGINIA
EWELL'S CORPS   RODES'S DIVISION
CARTER'S BATTALION   PAGE'S BATTERY
THE MORRIS ARTILLERY
Four Napoleons

July 1. Not engaged until Union forces on Seminary Ridge extended their line to the right when it opened upon them with a rapid enfilading fire in support of the infantry in the conflict which ensued. Meanwhile it suffered from the fire of Union artillery in the valley north of the town. Afterward moved to the foot of the ridge and aided in dislodging both the artillery and infantry of the Eleventh Corps.

July 2. Held in readiness to move into position but was not engaged.

July 3. On Seminary Ridge in reserve.

July 4. After nightfall began the march to Hagerstown.

Losses   Killed and Mortally Wounded 4   Wounded 26
Ammunition expended   215 rounds.   Horses killed or disabled 17.

No.116C   Cast Iron Tablet located—Oak Hill

ARMY OF NORTHERN VIRGINIA
EWELL'S CORPS   RODES'S DIVISION
CARTER'S BATTALION   REESE'S BATTERY
THE JEFF DAVIS ARTILLERY
Four 3 Inch Rifles

July 1. Was placed in position near here in support of Dole's Brigade against two divisions of the Eleventh Corps which were massing on his front and left flank. It rendered effective service not only in protecting Dole's flank but also aided in dislodging the Union infantry and artillery from their position in the fields north of the town.

July 2. Remained in Reserve.

July 3. In position on Seminary Ridge near the railroad cut and took part in the cannonade preceding Longstreet's assault.

July 4. After nightfall began the march to Hagerstown.

Ammunition expended   229 rounds.

No. 117C   Cast Iron Tablet located—Oak Hill

C. S. A.
ARMY OF NORTHERN VIRGINIA
EWELL'S CORPS   EARLY'S DIVISION
JONES ARTILLERY BATTALION
Carrington's   Tanner's   Green's   Garber's Batteries

Two 10 Pounder Parrotts   Six 3 Inch   Eight Napoleons

July 1. Arrived on the field with Early's Division about 2.45 P. M. Moved into battery 400 yards east of this position opened an effective enfilading fire on infantry retiring from Seminary Ridge. Ceased firing as the Confederate infantry advanced.

July 2. The Battalion remained in the same position. Not actively engaged.

July 3. Occupied same position. Not actively engaged.

N0. 118C   Tablet on Granite Pedestal located—Harrisburg Road, .5 mile north of Rock Creek

---

ARMY OF NORTHERN VIRGINIA
EWELL'S CORPS   EARLY'S DIVISION
JONES'S ARTILLERY BATTALION   CARRINGTON'S BATTERY
CHARLOTTESVILLE (VIRGINIA) ARTILLERY
Four Napoleons

July 1. Arrived on the field with Early's Division in the afternoon. Was ordered to cross Rock Creek and move in rear of Gordon's Brigade then advancing. Went into battery on a street in suburbs of the town and remained until near dark when ordered to a position near the railroad.

July 2. Remained near the railroad. Not engaged.

July 3. Occupied the same position. Not engaged.

July 4. Moved in the rear of Early's Division.

Casualties not reported.

No. 119C   Cast Iron Tablet located—Harrisburg Road, .5 mile north of Rock Creek

---

ARMY OF NORTHERN VIRGINIA
EWELL'S CORPS   EARLY'S DIVISION
JONES'S ARTILLERY BATTALION   TANNER'S BATTERY
COURTNEY (VIRGINIA) ARTILLERY
Four 3 Inch Rifles

July 1. Arrived on the field with Early's Division. Moved into battery on north side of Rock Creek. Opened an effective fire on Union infantry on south side of the creek. Ceased firing as the Confederate infantry advanced.

July 2. Took position of the day before remained until 3 P. M. Ordered to report on the York Road and remained until the morning of the 3rd. Not engaged.

July 3. Moved nearer the town and remained until night. Ordered to the wagon park to move with train to the rear.

Casualties not reported. Ammunition expended 595 rounds.

No. 120C   Cast Iron Tablet located—Harrisburg Road, .5 mile north of Rock Creek

---

ARMY OF NORTHERN VIRGINIA
EWELL'S CORPS   EARLY'S DIVISION
JONES'S ARTILLERY BATTALION   GREEN'S BATTERY
LOUISIANA GUARD ARTILLERY
Two 10 Pounder Parrotts   Two 3 Inch Rifles

July 1. Arrived on the field with Early's Division. Placed in position to the right of Tanner's Battery on the north side of Rock Creek and opened fire on Union troops on south side of creek continued firing with effect until the Confederate infantry was in position and advancing.

July 2. Occupied the position of the previous day before sunset was ordered to General Hampton at Hunterstown with a section of Parrott guns. Engaged Battery M 2nd U. S. Fell back a mile and remained for the night.

July 3. Moved forward with the cavalry about 2 P. M. Guns placed in position and opened on a column of advancing cavalry. Received a severe fire and ordered to be withdrawn. Again engaged in the afternoon.

Casualties   Killed 2   Wounded 5
Ammunition expended   161 rounds

No. 121C   Cast Iron Tablet located—Harrisburg Road, .5 mile north of Rock Creek

Note: Another tablet for this battery is located on Confederate Cavalry Avenue, East Cavalry Field.

ARMY OF NORTHERN VIRGINIA
EWELL'S CORPS   EARLY'S DIVISION
JONES'S BATTALION   GREEN'S BATTERY
LOUISIANA GUARD ARTILLERY
Two 10 Pounder Parrotts   Two 3 Inch Rifles

July 3. After taking part in the fighting on the previous two days at Gettysburg and Hunterstown this Battery being detached from its Battalion brought its Parrott guns here and rendered important service in the cavalry battle not withdrawing until after dark.

Losses   Killed 2   Wounded 5   Total 7   Horses disabled 2.

No.122C   Cast Iron Tablet located—Confederate Cavalry Avenue, East Cavalry Field

---

ARMY OF NORTHERN VIRGINIA
EWELL'S CORPS   EARLY'S DIVISION
JONES'S ARTILLERY BATTALION   GARBER'S BATTERY
STAUNTON (VIRGINIA) ARTILLERY
Four Napoleons

July 1. Reached the field with Early's Division and immediately went into battery near this position. Fired with effect on Howard's 11th Corps and on infantry retiring from Seminary Ridge. Ceased firing as the Confederate infantry advanced.

July 2. Occupied the same position. Not engaged.

July 3. Remained in the same position. Not engaged.

Casualties   Wounded 1

Ammunition expended   106 rounds.

No. 123C   Cast Iron Tablet located—Harrisburg Road, .5 mile north of Rock Creek

---

C. S. A.
ARMY OF NORTHERN VIRGINIA
EWELL'S CORPS   JOHNSON'S DIVISION
LATIMER'S BATTALION
Brown's   Carpenter's   Dement's   Raine's Batteries

Two 20 Pounder Parrotts   Five 10 Pounder Parrotts
Three 3 Inch Rifles   Six Napoleons

July 1. After dark crossed Rock Creek and encamped on this ridge.

July 2. At 4 P. M. the Battalion except the 20 pounder Parrotts took position here. and was engaged more than two hours in a heavy cannonade with the Union artillery on Cemetery Hill Steven's Knoll and Culp's Hill. Ammunition exhausted and losses severe the guns were withdrawn except four to cover the advance of Johnson's infantry against Culp's Hill. In the renewed firing Major S. W. Latimer was mortally wounded. In the cannonading the 20 pounder Parrotts in position half a mile north took an active part.

July 3. The 20 pounder Parrotts took part in the great cannonade while the other batteries were in reserve.

July 4. The Battalion withdrew and began the march to Hagerstown.

Losses   Killed 10   Wounded 40   Horses killed 30.

No. 124C   Tablet on Granite Pedestal located—Benner's Hill, south of Hanover Road

---

ARMY OF NORTHERN VIRGINIA
EWELL'S CORPS   JOHNSON'S DIVISION
LATIMER'S BATTALION   BROWN'S BATTERY
THE CHESAPEAKE MD. ARTILLERY
Four 10 Pounder Parrotts

July 2. Took position here about 4 P. M. and was engaged for over two hours in a severe conflict with the Union batteries on East Cemetery Hill and Stevens Knoll. Capt. Brown being severely wounded one of his guns disabled and his ammunition almost exhausted the Battery was withdrawn by order of Gen. Johnson.

July 3. Remained in reserve and not engaged.

July 4. Withdrew from the field with the Battalion.

Losses   Killed 4   Wounded 12   Horses killed 9

No. 125C   Cast Iron Tablet located—Benner's Hill, south of Hanover Road

---

ARMY OF NORTHERN VIRGINIA
EWELL'S CORPS   JOHNSON'S DIVISION
LATIMER'S BATTALION   CARPENTER'S BATTERY
THE ALLEGHANY ARTILLERY
Two Napoleons   Two 3 Inch Rifles

July 2. The Battery took a prominent part in the cannonade against the Union artillery on East Cemetery Hill and other points which began about 4 P. M. and continued over two hours. Some of the Union guns on the left enfiladed the Battalion and caused the Battery to suffer severely and having exhausted its ammunition it was ordered to withdraw.

July 3. Remained in reserve and not engaged.

July 4. Withdrew from the field with the Battalion.

Losses   Killed 5   Wounded 24   Horses killed 9

No. 126C   Cast Iron Tablet located—Benner's Hill, south of Hanover Road

---

ARMY OF NORTHERN VIRGINIA
EWELL'S CORPS   JOHNSON'S DIVISION
LATIMER'S BATTALION   DEMENT'S BATTERY
FIRST MARYLAND BATTERY
Four Napoleons

July 2. In position here about 4 P. M. and took part in the cannonade against the Union batteries on East Cemetery Hill and Culp's Hill which continued over two hours. When the Battalion was withdrawn two guns of the Battery were left here to aid in repelling any attack. Soon afterward they reopened fire in support of the attack of Johnson's infantry on Culp's Hill which drew from the Union guns a heavy responsive fire by which Maj. Latimer was mortally wounded.

July 3. Remained in reserve and was not engaged.

July 4. Withdrew from the field with the Battalion.

Losses   Killed 1   Wounded 4   Horses killed 9.   One caisson exploded and one disabled.

No. 127C   Cast Iron Tablet located—Benner's Hill, south of Hanover Road

---

ARMY OF NORTHERN VIRGINIA
EWELL'S CORPS   JOHNSON'S DIVISION
LATIMER'S BATTALION   RAINE'S BATTERY
THE LEE BATTERY
Two 20 Pounder Parrotts   One 10 Pounder Parrott   One 3 Inch Rifle

July 2. The 10 Pounder Parrott and 3 Inch Rifle took position here about 4 P. M. and were engaged in the severe cannonade that lasted over two hours. They also aided in supporting the attack of Johnson's infantry on Culp's Hill and did not retire to the rear until dark. The 20 Pounder Parrots took an active part in the cannonade from their position some distance in the rear of the other guns.

July 3. The 20 Pounder Parrotts were actively engaged in the great cannonade.

July 4. Withdrew from the field with the Battalion.

Losses   Wounded 8   Horses killed 3

No. 128C   Cast Iron Tablet located—Benner's Hill, south of Hanover Road

———

C. S. A.
ARMY OF NORTHERN VIRGINIA
LONGSTREET'S CORPS   ARTILLERY RESERVE
ALEXANDER'S BATTALION
Woolfolk's   Jordan's   Parker's   Taylor's   Moody's   Rhett's Batteries

Two 20 Pounder Parrotts   One 10 Pounder Parrott   Seven 3 Inch Rifles
Six Napoleons
Four 24 Pounder Howitzers   Four 12 Pounder Howitzers

July 2. Came into position on this line about 4 P. M. Advanced soon after with the infantry and occupied a line on the crest near the Peach Orchard.

July 3. In the line on ridge from Peach Orchard to N. E. corner of Spangler's Woods. Aided in the cannonade and supported Longstreet's assault.

July 4. In position here until 4 P. M. Then withdrew to Marsh Creek on Fairfield Road.

Losses   Killed 19   Wounded 114   Missing 6   Horses killed or disabled 116.

No. 129C   Tablet on Granite Pedestal located—West Confederate Avenue

———

ARMY OF NORTHERN VIRGINIA
LONGSTREET'S CORPS   ARTILLERY RESERVE
ALEXANDER'S BATTALION   WOOLFOLK'S BATTERY
THE ASHLAND VIRGINIA ARTILLERY
Two 20 Pounder Parrotts   Two Napoleons

July 2. Took position here 4.30 P. M. and opened fire. Joined soon in the advance of the infantry. During remainder of the day occupied position on the crest near Peach Orchard and was actively engaged in firing upon the new line of the Union forces.

July 3. In position near N. E. corner of Spangler's Woods on left of the artillery line which occupied the ridge from Peach Orchard to that point. Took part in the cannonade preceding Longstreet's assault followed and supported it. Aided then in repelling sharpshooters and withdrew at midnight.

July 4. In position near here until 4 P. M. Then withdrew to Marsh Creek on Fairfield Road.

Losses heavy but not reported in detail.

No. 130C   Cast Iron Tablet located—West Confederate Avenue

———————

ARMY OF NORTHERN VIRGINIA
LONGSTREET'S CORPS   ARTILLERY RESERVE
ALEXANDER'S BATTALION   JORDAN'S BATTERY
THE BEDFORD VIRGINIA ARTILLERY
Four 3 Inch Rifles

July 2. Took position here 4.30 P. M. Fired a few rounds at the Peach Orchard. Joined in the infantry charge and afterwards occupied position on crest near the Peach Orchard and was actively engaged until night.

July 3. Remained near the same position which was on the main artillery line. Took part in the cannonade preceding Longstreet's final assault and aided in supporting that assault. Retired from the front after night.

July 4. In position near here until 4 P. M. Then withdrew to Marsh Creek on Fairfield Road.

Losses serious but not reported in detail.

No. 131C   Cast Iron Tablet located—West Confederate Avenue

———————

ARMY OF NORTHERN VIRGINIA
LONGSTREET'S CORPS   ARTILLERY RESERVE
ALEXANDER'S BATTALION   PARKER'S BATTERY
One 10 Pounder Parrott   Three 3 Inch Rifles

July 2. Took position here 4 P. M. and opened fire on Peach Orchard. Joined at 5 P. M. in the infantry charge advancing to position east of

Emmitsburg Road and 200 feet north of Peach Orchard continuing actively engaged until night.

July 3. Remained near the same position which was on the main artillery line took part in the cannonade preceding Longstreet's assault and aided in supporting that assault. Retired from the front after night.

July 4. In position near here until 4 P. M. Then withdrew to Marsh Creek on Fairfield Road.

Losses heavy but not reported in detail.

No. 132C   Cast Iron Tablet located—West Confederate Avenue

ARMY OF NORTHERN VIRGINIA
LONGSTREET'S CORPS   ARTILLERY RESERVE
ALEXANDER'S BATTALION   TAYLOR'S BATTERY
Four Napoleons

July 2. Took position here 4 P. M. and opened fire on Peach Orchard. Advanced at 5 P. M. with the infantry to a position about 400 feet north of Peach Orchard and east of Emmitsburg Road continuing actively engaged until night.

July 3. Took position 3 A. M. in main artillery line near Smith House northeast of Sherfy House on Emmitsburg Road and held it all day. Took part in the cannonade preceding Longstreet's final assault supported that assault and aided in repelling sharpshooters afterwards. Retired from the front after night.

July 4. In position near here until 4 P. M. Then withdrew to Marsh Creek on Fairfield Road.

Losses   Killed 2   Wounded 10

No. 133C   Cast Iron Tablet located—West Confederate Avenue

ARMY OF NORTHERN VIRGINIA
LONGSTREET'S CORPS   ARTILLERY RESERVE
ALEXANDER'S BATTALION   MOODY'S BATTERY
THE MADISON LIGHT ARTILLERY
Four 24 Pounder Howitzers

July 2. Arrived here and opened fire at 4 P. M. Following the infantry charge upon the Peach Orchard took position near there and with other batteries supported the infantry in its further advance. Aided in so harassing the retiring Union forces as to compel the temporary abandonment of several guns. Kept up a spirited fire until night fall and prevented pursuit of the Confederate advanced lines when they fell back shortly before dark.

July 3. In position at dawn in the artillery line on the ridge running north from the Peach Orchard and on duty there all day. Took part in the cannonade preceding Longstreet's assault and retired from the front after night.

July 4. Remained near here until 4 P. M. and then withdrew to Marsh Creek on the Fairfield Road.

Losses heavy but not reported in detail.

No. 134C   Cast Iron Tablet located—West Confederate Avenue

━━━━━━━━━━━━━━

ARMY OF NORTHERN VIRGINIA
LONGSTREET'S CORPS   ARTILLERY RESERVE
ALEXANDER'S BATTALION   RHETT'S BATTERY
THE BROOKS ARTILLERY
Four 12 Pounder Howitzers

July 2. Took position here at 4 P. M. and opened fire. When the charge was made on the Peach Orchard moved to a point near there and with other batteries supported the infantry in its further advance. Assisted in harassing the retiring Union forces causing them to abandon temporarily several guns. Continued firing until night and aided in preventing pursuit of the Confederate advanced lines when they fell back shortly before dark.

July 3. In position at dawn in the artillery line on the ridge running north from the Peach Orchard and on duty there all day. Took part in the cannonade preceding Longstreet's assault and retired from the front after night.

July 4. Remained near here until 4 P. M. and then withdrew to Marsh Creek on the Fairfield Road.

Losses heavy but not reported in detail.

No. 135C   Cast Iron Tablet located—West Confederate Avenue

━━━━━━━━━━━━━━

C. S. A.
ARMY OF NORTHERN VIRGINIA
LONGSTREET'S CORPS   ARTILLERY RESERVE
ESHLEMAN BATTALION
THE WASHINGTON LOUISIANA ARTILLERY
Miller's Squires's Richardson's Norcom's Batteries
Eight Napoleons Two 12 Pounder Howitzers

July 3. Arrived on the field before daylight and was engaged all day. Captured one 3 inch rifle.

July 4. At 9 A. M. ordered to Cashtown to reinforce the cavalry escorting the wagon train.

Losses Killed 3 Wounded 26 Missing 16 Total 45

Horses killed and disabled 37 Guns disabled 3

No. 136C   Tablet on Granite Pedestal located—West Confederate Avenue

---

ARMY OF NORTHERN VIRGINIA
LONGSTREET'S CORPS   ARTILLERY RESERVE
ESHLEMAN'S BATTALION   MILLER'S BATTERY
Three Napoleons

July 3. Advanced before daylight into position about 100 yards north of the Peach Orchard. This battery fired the signal guns for the cannonade preceding Longstreet's assault took part therein and supported the charge of the infantry by advancing 450 yards and keeping up a vigorous fire. After the repulse of the assault moved to the left and west of the Emmitsburg Road ready to aid in resisting a countercharge if attempted. From loss of horses but one gun could then be used. The others were sent to the rear and that gun was withdrawn after dark.

July 4. At 9 A. M. marched with the Battalion to Cashtown to reinforce the cavalry escorting the wagon train.

Losses heavy but not reported in detail.

No.137C   Cast Iron Tablet located—West Confederate Avenue

ARMY OF NORTHERN VIRGINIA
LONGSTREET'S CORPS   ARTILLERY RESERVE
ESHLEMAN'S BATTALION   SQUIRES'S BATTERY
One Napoleon

July 3. Having but one gun it co-operated all day with Miller's Battery. Advanced before daylight into position about 100 yards north of the Peach Orchard assisted in repelling skirmishers and took part in the cannonade preceding Longstreet's assault. Moved several hundred yards to the left after the repulse of that assault to aid in resisting a countercharge if attempted. Withdrew soon afterward to the rear.

July 4. At 9 A. M. marched with the Battalion to Cashtown to reinforce the cavalry escorting the wagon train.

Losses not reported in detail.

No.138C   Cast Iron Tablet located—West Confederate Avenue

ARMY OF NORTHERN VIRGINIA
LONGSTREET'S CORPS   ARTILLERY RESERVE
ESHLEMAN'S BATTALION   RICHARDSON'S BATTERY
Two Napoleons   One 12 Pounder Howitzer

July 3. The napoleons took position before daylight north of the Peach Orchard but moved at dawn further northward and West of Emmitsburg Road. A Union 3 inch rifle left the day before between the lines was brought in under a heavy fire of skirmishers and served with this Battery which took part in the cannonade preceding Longstreet's assault. After the repulse of that assault was joined by the Howitzer and made preparations to assist in repelling a countercharge if attempted. Withdrew from the front after dark.

July 4. At 9 A. M. marched with the Battalion to Cashtown to reinforce the Cavalry escorting the wagon train.

Losses not reported in detail.

No. 139C   Cast Iron Tablet located—West Confederate Avenue

ARMY OF NORTHERN VIRGINIA
LONGSTREET'S CORPS   ARTILLERY RESERVE
ESHLEMAN'S BATTALION   NORCOM'S BATTERY
Two Napoleons   One 12 Pounder Howitzer

July 3. The Napoleons advanced before daylight into position 150 yards north of Peach Orchard near the Emmitsburg Road but their fire in the forenoon was desultory. Took active part in the cannonade preceding

Longstreet's assault and one of the guns supported the infantry attack by pushing forward 450 yards and keeping up a vigorous fire. After the assault was repulsed the Napoleons were moved several hundred yards to the left but soon disabled and sent to the rear. The Howitzer was brought forward and did effective service until withdrawn after dark.

July 4. At 9 A. M. marched with the Battalion to Cashtown to reinforce the cavalry guarding the wagon train.

Losses not reported in detail.

No. 140C Cast Iron Tablet located—West Confederate Avenue

C. S. A.
ARMY OF NORTHERN VIRGINIA
LONGSTREET'S CORPS HOOD'S DIVISION
HENRY'S BATTALION
Reilly's Bachman's Garden's Latham's Batteries
Eleven Napoleons Four 10 Pounder Parrotts Two 3 Inch Rifles
One 12 Pounder Howitzer One 6 Pounder Bronze Gun

July 2–3. Occupied this line and took active part in the battle as described on the tablets of the several batteries. The Howitzer the Bronze gun and one 3 inch Rifle were disabled and three captured 10 pounder Parrotts substituted.

July 4. On a line a little west of this until 6 P. M. then withdrew from the field.

Ammunition expended 1500 rounds.

Losses Killed 4 Wounded 23

No. 141C Tablet on Granite Pedestal located—South Confederate Avenue

---

ARMY OF NORTHERN VIRGINIA
LONGSTREET'S CORPS HOOD'S DIVISION
HENRY'S BATTALION REILLY'S BATTERY
THE ROWAN ARTILLERY
Two Napoleons Two 10 Pounder Parrotts Two 3 Inch Rifles

July 2. Took position here 4 P. M. and was actively engaged until night. One rifle burst and a captured 10 pounder Parrott was substituted.

July 3. Two Parrotts moved to right. The other guns engaged in firing upon the Union lines within range. About 5 P. M. aided in repelling cavalry under Brig. Gen. Farnsworth which had charged into the valley between this point and Round Top.

July 4. Occupied position near by and west of this until 6 P. M. Then withdrew from the field.

Losses not reported in detail.

No. 142C   Cast Iron Tablet located—South Confederate Avenue

ARMY OF NORTHERN VIRGINIA
LONGSTREET'S CORPS   HOOD'S DIVISION
HENRY'S BATTALION   REILLY'S BATTERY
THE ROWAN ARTILLERY
A Section   Two 10 Pounder Parrotts

July 3. These guns were detached and first occupied position 300 yards west of this hotly engaged with the artillery of the Union Cavalry Division down the Emmitsburg Road. When the cavalry under Brig. Gen. Farnsworth charged into the valley of Plum Run they were placed here aided in repelling that charge and guarded this flank until night.

July 4. Rejoined the Battery and shared in all its movements.

No.143C   Cast Iron Tablet located—South Confederate Avenue

ARMY OF NORTHERN VIRGINIA
LONGSTREET'S CORPS   HOOD'S DIVISION
HENRY'S BATTALION   BACHMAN'S BATTERY
THE GERMAN ARTILLERY
Four Napoleons

July 2. In reserve near here but not engaged.

July 3. In position here and actively engaged in firing upon the Union lines within range. About 5 P. M. aided in repelling cavalry under Brig. Gen. Farnsworth which had charged into the valley between this point and Round Top.

July 4. Occupied position near by and west of this until 6 P. M. Then withdrew from the field.

Losses not reported in detail.

No. 144C   Cast Iron Tablet located—South Confederate Avenue

━━━━━━━━━━━━━

ARMY OF NORTHERN VIRGINIA
LONGSTREET'S CORPS   HOOD'S DIVISION
HENRY'S BATTALION   GARDEN'S BATTERY
THE PALMETTO ARTILLERY
Two Napoleons   Two 10 Pounder Parrotts

July 2. In reserve near here but not engaged.

July 3. In position here and actively engaged in firing upon the Union lines within range. About 5 P. M. aided in repelling cavalry under Brig. Gen. Farnsworth which had charged into the valley between this point and Round Top.

July 4. Occupied position near by and west of this until 6 P. M. Then withdrew from the field.

Losses not reported in detail.

No. 145C   Cast Iron Tablet located—South Confederate Avenue

━━━━━━━━━━━━━

ARMY OF NORTHERN VIRGINIA
LONGSTREET'S CORPS   HOOD'S DIVISION
HENRY'S BATTALION   LATHAM'S BATTERY
THE BRANCH ARTILLERY
Three Napoleons   One 12 Pounder Howitzer   One 6 Pounder Bronze Gun

July 2. Took position here 4 P. M. and actively engaged until night. The Howitzer and Bronze gun were disabled and two captured 10 pounder Parrotts substituted.

July 3. Engaged in firing upon the Union lines within range. About 5 P. M. aided in repelling cavalry under Brig. Gen. Farnsworth which had charged into the valley between this point and Round Top.

July 4. Occupied position near by and west of this until 6 P. M. Then withdrew from the field.

Losses not reported in detail.

No. 146C   Cast Iron Tablet located—South Confederate Avenue

━━━━━━━━━━━━━

C. S. A.
ARMY OF NORTHERN VIRGINIA
LONGSTREET'S CORPS   McLAWS'S DIVISION
CABELL'S BATTALION
Fraser's   McCarthy's   Carlton's   Manly's Batteries
Four Napoleons   Four 10 Pounder Parrotts   Six 3 Inch Rifles
Two 12 Pounder Howitzers

July 2–3. Took an active part in the battle.

July 4. Remained in position near here and withdrew from the field after night.

Ammunition expended   About 3300 rounds.

Losses   Killed 12   Wounded 30   Missing 4   Horses killed or disabled 80.

No. 147C   Tablet on Granite Pedestal located—intersection West Confederate Avenue and Emmitsburg Road

---

ARMY OF NORTHERN VIRGINIA
LONGSTREET'S CORPS   MCLAWS'S DIVISION
CABELL'S BATTALION   FRASER'S BATTERY
THE PULASKI ARTILLERY
Two 10 Pounder Parrotts   Two 3 Inch Rifles

July 2. Took position here 3.30 P. M. and opened fire on Peach Orchard and the Union batteries east of it. At 4 P. M. the Rifles were silenced by loss of men. The fire of the Parrotts continued until Peach Orchard was taken.

July 3. The Parrotts were moved to crest north of Peach Orchard in main artillery line took part in the great cannonade aided in checking pursuit after Longstreet's assault and retired from front after dark. The Rifles were placed under command of Capt. Manly of the N. C. Artillery and served by his men in position with his own Rifles.

July 4. In position near here. After night withdrew from the field. Their ammunition was nearly exhausted.

Losses   Killed 6   Wounded 13   Horses killed or disabled 18

No. 148C   Cast Iron Tablet located—West Confederate Avenue

ARMY OF NORTHERN VIRGINIA
LONGSTREET'S CORPS   McLAWS'S DIVISION
CABELL'S BATTALION   McCARTHY'S BATTERY
FIRST RICHMOND HOWITZERS
Two Napoleons   Two 3 Inch Rifles

July 2. At 3.30 P. M. placed in reserve near here. The rifled guns advanced to this position at 4 P. M. and engaged in severe artillery fight until dark. The men of the Napoleon section sometimes relieved those of the rifled section.

July 3. Advanced and formed part of the main artillery line the rifle section near Emmitsburg Road the Napoleons further to the left all hotly engaged sometimes changing positions. Retired from the front after dark.

July 4. In position near here. One Napoleon aided in checking a hostile advance. All withdrew from the field at night.

Ammunition expended   about 850 rounds.   One rifle was disabled.

Losses   Killed 2   Wounded 8   Horses killed or disabled 25

No.149C   Cast Iron Tablet located—West Confederate Avenue

ARMY OF NORTHERN VIRGINIA
LONGSTREET'S CORPS   McLAWS'S DIISION
CABELL'S BATTALION   CARLTON'S BATTERY
THE TROUP ARTILLERY
First Section   Two 10 Pounder Parrotts

July 2. This section took position here 3.30 P. M. and was actively engaged until near dark.

July 3. In position on the main artillery line on ridge in front of Spangler's Woods. Took part in the great cannonade and after repulse of Longstreet's assault advanced 300 yards and aided in checking pursuit. Retired from the front after dark.

July 4. Remained near here all day inactive short of ammunition. After night withdrew from the field.

Losses of both sections   Killed 1   Wounded 6   Horses of both sections killed or disabled 17

No. 150C   Cast Iron Tablet located—West Confederate Avenue

ARMY OF NORTHERN VIRGINIA
LONGSTREET'S CORPS McLAWS'S DIVISION
CABELL'S BATTALION CARLTON'S BATTERY
THE TROUP ARTILLERY
Second Section Two 12 Pounder Howitzers

July 2. This section took position here at 4 P. M. and was actively engaged until dark.

July 3. In position near main artillery line but under cover of hill in front of Spangler's Woods. After repulse of Longstreet's assault advanced 300 yards and aided in checking pursuit. Retired from the front after dark.

July 4. In position here all day and withdrew from the field after dark. Their ammunition was nearly exhausted.

Losses of both sections Killed 1 Wounded 6 Horses of both sections killed or disabled 17

No. 151C Cast Iron Tablet located—West Confederate Avenue

ARMY OF NORTHERN VIRGINIA
LONGSTREET'S CORPS McLAWS'S DIVISION
CABELL'S BATTALION MANLY'S BATTERY
FIRST NORTH CAROLINA ARTILLERY
Two Napoleons Two 3 Inch Rifles

July 2. Took position here 3.30 P. M. and became actively engaged. At 5 P. M. advanced to Peach Orchard and continued firing until dark. Returned here after night.

July 3. The Napoleons remained here. The two rifles with the two rifles of Fraser's Battery took position at 5 A. M. under Capt. Manly on crest beyond Emmitsburg Road north of Peach Orchard were engaged in the great cannonade and after Longstreet's assault aided in checking pursuit. Continued firing at intervals until 7.30 P. M. Then resumed this position.

July 4. At 10 A. M. aided in checking an advance of three regiments. After night withdrew from the field.

Ammunition expended 1146 rounds.

Losses Killed 3 Wounded 4 Missing 4 Horses killed or disabled 20

No. 152C Cast Iron Tablet located—West Confederate Avenue

C. S. A.
ARMY OF NORTHERN VIRGINIA
LONGSTREET'S CORPS   PICKETT'S DIVISION
DEARING'S BATTALION
Stribling's   Caskie's   Macon's   Blount's Batteries
Two 20 Pounder Parrotts   Three 10 Pounder Parrotts
One 3 Inch Rifle   Twelve Napoleons

July 3. Advanced to the front about daybreak and took a conspicuous part in the battle. In the cannonade preceding Longstreet's assault it fired by battery and very effectively. Having exhausted its ammunition and being unable to obtain a fresh supply it was withdrawn from the field about 4 P. M.

July 4. In line of battle all day with McLaws's Division. Marched at sunset to Black Horse Tavern.

Losses   Killed 8   Wounded 17   Total 25   Horses killed and disabled 37

No. 153C   Tablet on Granite Pedestal located—West Confederate Avenue

———

ARMY OF NORTHERN VIRGINIA
LONGSTREET'S CORPS   PICKETT'S DIVISION
DEARING'S BATTALION   STRIBLING'S BATTERY
THE FAUQUIER ARTILLERY
Two 20 Pounder Parrotts   Four Napoleons

July 3. Advanced to the front about daybreak. Later in the morning took position on the crest of ridge west of Emmitsburg Road and near the Roger's House. Drove back with a dozen well directed rounds a strong line of skirmishers whose fire wounded a few men and horses. Bore a conspicuous part in the cannonade preceding Longstreet's assault. But its ammunition being exhausted about the time the assault began and repeated efforts to obtain a fresh supply proving fruitless the Battery was withdrawn.

July 4. In line of battle all day with the left wing of McLaws's Division. Marched about sunset to Black Horse Tavern.

Losses not reported in detail.

No. 154C   Cast Iron Tablet located—West Confederate Avenue

ARMY OF NORTHERN VIRGINIA
LONGSTREET'S CORPS   PICKETT'S DIVISION
DEARING'S BATTALION   CASKIE'S BATTERY
THE HAMPDEN ARTILLERY
One 10 Pounder Parrott   One 3 Inch Rifle   Two Napoleons

July 3. Advanced to the front about daylight. Later in the morning took
position on the ridge west of the Emmitsburg Road and near the Rogers
House remaining for hours unengaged. When the signal guns were fired
about 1 P. M. moved forward to the crest of the hill and took an active
part in the cannonade. Ammunition was exhausted while Longstreet's
column was advancing the last round being fired at the Union infantry
which assailed his right flank. Efforts to procure a fresh supply of ammunition proving unsuccessful the Battery was withdrawn.

July 4. In line of battle all day with the left wing of McLaws's Division.
Marched at sunset to Black Horse Tavern.

Losses not reported in detail.

No. 155C   Cast Iron Tablet located—West Confederate Avenue

ARMY OF NORTHERN VIRGINIA
LONGSTREET'S CORPS   PICKETT'S DIVISION
DEARING'S BATTALION   MACON'S BATTERY
THE RICHMOND FAYETTE ARTILLERY
Two Napoleons   Two 10 Pounder Parrotts

July 3. Advanced to the front about daybreak. Later in the morning took
position on the ridge west of Emmitsburg Road and near the Rogers
House but remained inactive until the signal guns were fired some time
after noon. Moved forward then to the crest of the hill and took a prominent part in the cannonade. Ammunition was exhausted while Longstreet's
column was advancing the last rounds being fired at Union infantry assailing his right flank. Efforts to procure a fresh supply of ammunition
proving unsuccessful the Battery was withdrawn.

July 4. In line of battle all day with the left wing of McLaws's Division.
Marched at sunset to Black Horse Tavern.

Losses not reported in detail.

No. 156C   Cast Iron Tablet located—West Confederate Avenue

ARMY OF NORTHERN VIRGINIA
LONGSTREET'S CORPS   PICKETT'S DIVISION
DEARING'S BATTALION   BLOUNT'S BATTERY
Four Napoleons

July 3. Advanced to the front about daybreak. Later in the morning took position on the ridge west of the Emmitsburg Road 200 yards from the Roger's House and remained there for hours unengaged. When the signal guns were fired about 1 P. M. moved forward to the crest of the hill and took an active part in the cannonade. But its ammunition being exhausted as Longstreet's infantry was advancing and all efforts to procure a fresh supply proving fruitless the Battery was withdrawn.

July 4. In line of battle all day with the left wing of McLaws's Division. Marched at sunset to Black Horse Tavern.

Losses not reported in detail.

No. 157C   Cast Iron Tablet located—West Confederate Avenue

———————————

C. S. A.
ARMY OF NORTHERN VIRGINIA
STUART'S CAVALRY DIVISION
HORSE ARTILLERY
Major R. F. Beckham Commanding
Breathed's Virginia Battery
Chew's Virginia Battery
Griffin's Maryland Battery
Hart's South Carolina
McGregor's Virginia Battery
Moorman's Virginia Battery

July 3. These batteries were not permanently attached to the cavalry brigades but were sent to them when needed Breathed's Battery with Brig. General W. H. F. Lee's Brigade Chew's Battery Brig. General W. E. Jones's Brigade Griffin's Battery with the Second Army Corps Hart's Battery attached to the Washington Artillery with the Army Trains McGregor's Battery with Brig. Gen. Wade Hampton's Brigade Moorman's Battery no report.

Casualties not reported.

No. 158C   Tablet on Granite Pedestal located—Confederate Cavalry Avenue, East Cavalry Field

Note: Tablet location is shown on Cavalry Battle Tablet Location Map, page 161.

━━━━━━━━━━

ARMY OF NORTHERN VIRGINIA
STUART'S HORSE ARTILLERY
BECKHAM BATTALION   BREATHED'S BATTERY
Four 3 Inch Rifles

July 3. The Battery arrived here about 2 P. M. and took an active part in the fight until its ample supply of ammunition received in the forenoon was exhausted. It was withdrawn from the field about dark.

Losses   Killed 6   Wounded 8   Total 14   Horses killed or disabled 10.

No. 159C   Cast Iron Tablet located—Confederate Cavalry Avenue, East Cavalry Field

Note: Tablet location is shown on Cavalry Battle Tablet Location Map, page 161.

━━━━━━━━━━

ARMY OF NORTHERN VIRGINIA
STUART'S HORSE ARTILLERY
CAPTAIN THOMAS E. JACKSON'S BATTERY
Two 3 Inch rifles   Two Howitzers

July 3. The Battery was attached to Jenkins' Cavalry Brigade and took part in the fight here on the right wing of the Confederates not far from the Rummel barn but its limited supply of ammunition was soon exhausted and it was withdrawn.

Losses not reported.

No. 160C   Cast Iron Tablet located—Confederate Cavalry Avenue, East Cavalry Avenue

Note: Tablet location is shown on Cavalry Battle Tablet Location Map, page 161.

━━━━━━━━━━

ARMY OF NORTHERN VIRGINIA
STUART'S HORSE ARTILLERY
BECKHAM'S BATTALION   McGREGOR'S BATTERY
Two Napoleons   Two 3 Inch Rifles

July 3. The Battery took an active part in the fight arriving about 2 P M. and keeping up its fire until the ample supply of ammunition furnished on its way here in the forenoon was exhausted. It withdrew from the field under orders about nightfall.

Losses   Killed 5   Wounded 7   Total 12

Horses killed and disabled 11

No. 161C   Cast Iron Tablet located—Confederate Cavalry Avenue, East Cavalry Field

Note: Tablet location is shown on Cavalry Battle Tablet Location Map, page 161.

OTHER SUPPORTING UNITS TABLET INSCRIPTIONS
ARMY OF NORTHERN VIRGINIA

C. S. A.
ARMY OF NORTHERN VIRGINIA
STUART'S CAVALRY DIVISION
JONES'S BRIGADE
6th   7th   11th   12th Virginia Cavalry Regiments and 35th Virginia
Cavalry Battalion

July 1. The 12th Regiment was detached and remained on the south side of the Potomac River. White's 35th Virginia Battalion was also detached. The remaining regiments crossed the Potomac at Williamsport Md.

July 2. Marched from near Greencastle Pa. to Chambersburg Pa.

July 3. The Brigade marched from Chambersburg Pa. via Cashtown to Fairfield Pa. Met the 6th U. S. Cavalry about two miles from Fairfield. The 7th Virginia charged in the advance and was repulsed. The 6th Virginia in support charged and forced the Union Regiment to retire with heavy loss. The Brigade encamped at Fairfield for the night.

July 4. The Brigade held the mountain passes and picketed the left flank of the Army.

Casualties   Killed 11   Wounded 30   Missing 6   Total 47

No. 162C   Tablet on Granite Pedestal located—South Reynolds Avenue

Note: This tablet describes the activities of Jones' Brigade in the campaign. The brigade did not reach the battlefield.

C. S. A.
ARMY OF NORTHERN VIRGINIA
STUART'S CAVALRY DIVISION
ROBERTSON'S BRIGADE
4th and 5th North Carolina Cavalry

July 1. The Brigade crossed the Potomac at Williamsport Md. and marched to Greencastle Pa.

July 2. Marched from Greencastle Pa. to Chambersburg Pa.

July 3. Marched to Cashtown and in the direction of Fairfield guarding the flank of the Army.

July 4. Held Jack's Mountain and picketed the left flank of the Army of Northern Virginia.

No report nor details of losses made.

No. 163C   Tablet on Granite Pedestal located—South Reynolds Avenue

Note: This tablet describes the activities of Robertson's Brigade in the campaign. The brigade did not reach the battlefield.

C. S. A.
ARMY OF NORTHERN VIRGINIA
STUART'S CAVALRY DIVISION
IMBODEN'S BRIGADE
18th Virginia Cavalry   62nd Virginia Infantry   Virginia Partisan Rangers and McClanahan's Virginia Battery

July 3. Command guarding ammunition and supply trains. Reached the field at noon and retired with the supply trains at night.

No report nor details of losses made.

No. 164C   Tablet on Granite Pedestal located—South Reynolds Avenue

Note: This tablet describes the activities of Imboden's Brigade in the campaign. The brigade did not reach the battlefield proper.

PART
VI

After the Battle

MARCH TO THE POTOMAC

Dawn on July 4 found the two exhausted armies about a mile apart on the two ridges that they had fought from the past three days. With the pre-dawn movement of Ewell's Corps from Culp's Hill and the streets of Gettysburg to Seminary Ridge, the perilous process of disengaging the two armies was complete. General Lee's Confederates now held a continuous defensive line along Seminary Ridge from southwest of Round Top to Oak Hill. There was no taste for offensive action by either commander. After suffering heavy losses and its supplies exhausted, though not dispirited, Lee knew that his army must return to Virginia for refitting before fighting again—unless cornered. Meade's Federals, also with heavy losses, were not anxious to leave the fish-hook-shaped defensive line that had served them so well. Furthermore, Meade had observed ten months earlier what Lee's seemingly whipped army did when cornered between Antietam Creek and the Potomac River near Sharpsburg, Maryland. He had no intention of repeating that episode.

Lee developed his plans for moving his army back to Virginia during the long night of July 3. The wagon trains under the charge of Imboden's Mounted Infantry Brigade, with the wounded and prisoners, departed during the afternoon of July 4. The trains crossed South Mountain between Cashtown and Chambersburg, Pennsylvania, then moved down the valley to Hagerstown, Maryland, for a crossing of the Potomac near Williamsport, Maryland. Hill's Corps departed soon after dark for a crossing at the same point, by way of Fairfield and Waynesborough, Pennsylvania on the Hagerstown Road. Longstreet's Corps departed next by the same route, followed by Ewell's Corps. Early's Division, forming the rear guard, was the last to leave the field near noon on July 5. Stuart's Cavalry moved to block the mountain passes and protect the left flank of the army.

The Union cavalry that moved from Gettysburg on July 4 to screen the army's southern flank were soon harassing the departing Confederate columns;

but Meade was reluctant to send his infantry after them. The Sixth Corps moved to Fairfield on July 5 but went no further. Meade decided not to make a direct pursuit but to move south into Maryland before turning west toward Williamsport. On July 6, the First, Sixth, and Eleventh Union Corps marched to Emmitsburg, Maryland, leaving only one brigade of infantry and one of cavalry at Fairfield to pursue the departing Confederates. The remainder of the Union cavalry moved toward Williamsport by different routes. Meade moved his headquarters to Frederick, Maryland on July 7 and started moving his infantry toward Middletown and the South Mountain passes to Boonsboro, Maryland. But the ever-cautious Meade would not be rushed. It would be another seven days before he would attempt to force the Confederate defenses at Williamsport.

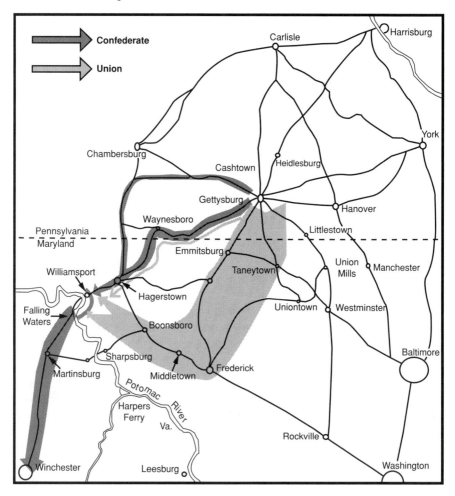

March to the Potomac

Imboden's Brigade reached Williamsport with the Confederate wagon trains in the afternoon of July 5, only to find that Union raiders had destroyed the pontoon bridge there. With the river swollen far above fording level by the recent heavy rains, Imboden could do little but circle the wagons to ward off the harassing Union cavalry and wait for help. Lee, arriving with the head of Longstreet's Corps the next day, assessed the situation as desperate. He quickly ordered construction of a system of defenses, hoping that the river would drop to fording level before his battered army had to use them. Not willing to leave the fate of his army to providence, he also ordered his engineers to construct another pontoon bridge across the river at Falling Waters. A lack of building material made the engineers' task both difficult and time consuming; but Meade's delays gave them just enough time. By the time the Union army moved to attack the Confederate defenses on the morning of July 14, the bridge was finished and Lee's army had crossed safely back into Virginia.

ITINERARY TABLET INSCRIPTIONS
ARMY OF THE POTOMAC

ARMY OF THE POTOMAC

July 4 1863

First and Second Brigades First Cavalry Division marched from Westminster and the Reserve Brigade First Cavalry Division from Gettysburg en route to Frederick. Second Brigade Second Cavalry Division from Westminster via Emmitsburg, to Monterey. The Third Brigade Second Cavalry Division from Gettysburg to Hunterstown and the Third Cavalry Division from Gettysburg via Emmitsburg to Monterey.

Fight at Monterey Gap Pa. and skirmishes at Fairfield Gap Pa. and Emmitsburg, Md.

ARMY OF THE POTOMAC

July 5 1863

Second Corps marched from Gettysburg to Two Taverns   Fifth Corps to Marsh Run   Sixth Corps to Rock Creek   Twelfth Corps to Littlestown First Brigade Second Cavalry Division to Emmitsburg and the Artillery Reserve to Littlestown. First Cavalry Division reached Frederick. The Third Brigade, Second Cavalry Division moved from Hunterstown to Greenwood. Third Cavalry Division and Second Brigade Second Cavalry Division marched from Monterey   via Smithburg to Boonsborough.

Skirmishes at or near Smithsburg Md. and Green Oak   Mercersburg Fairfield   Greencastle   Cunningham's Cross-Roads and Stevens' Furnace (or Caledonia Iron Works) Pa.

290

ARMY OF THE POTOMAC

July 6 1863

First Corps marched from Gettysburg to Emmitsburg   Fifth Corps from Marsh Run to Moritz's Cross-Roads   Sixth Corps from Fairfield to Emmitsburg except the Third Brigade   Second Division which in conjunction with First Brigade   Second Cavalry Division was left at Fairfield to pursue the enemy. Eleventh Corps from Rock Creek to Emmitsburg   First Cavalry Division from Frederick to Williamsport and thence back to Jones' Cross-Roads   Third Cavalry Division and Second Brigade   Second Cavalry Division from Boonsborough   via Hagerstown and Williamsport to Jones' Cross-Roads. The First Brigade Second Cavalry Division from Emmitsburg to Fairfield and the Third Brigade   Second Cavalry Division from Greenwood to Marion.

ARMY OF THE POTOMAC

July 7 1863

Headquarters Army of the Potomac moved from Gettysburg to Frederick. First Corps marched from Emmitsburg to Hamburg   Second Corps from Two Taverns to Taneytown   Third Corps from Gettysburg via Emmitsburg to Mechanicstown   Fifth Corps from Moritz's Cross-Roads via Emmitsburg to Utica. Sixth Corps from Emmitsburg to Mountain Pass near Hamburg   Eleventh Corps from Emmitsburg to Middletown   Twelfth Corps from Littlestown to Walkersville and the Artillery Reserve from Littlestown to Woodborough. First and Third Cavalry Divisions moved from Jones' Cross-Roads to Boonsborough. The Third Brigade   Second Cavalry Division was moving en route from Chambersburg to Middletown. The First Brigade   Second Cavalry Division and the Third Brigade Second Division of the Sixth Corps moved from Fairfield to Waynesborough.

ITINERARY TABLET INSCRIPTIONS
ARMY OF NORTHERN VIRGINIA

ARMY OF NORTHERN VIRGINIA

July 4 1863

Ewell's Corps marched before dawn from the base of Culp's Hill and the streets of Gettysburg to Seminary Ridge and the Army remained in position on that ridge throughout the day. Soon after dark Hill's Corps withdrew and began the march via Fairfield and Waynesborough on the Hagerstown Road.

Pickett's and McLaws' Divisions Longstreet's Corps followed during the night.

ARMY OF NORTHERN VIRGINIA

July 5 1863

The Army on the march to the Potomac Hill's Corps had the advance Longstreet's the centre Ewell's the rear. Hood's Division Longstreet's Corps started after sunrise Early's Division Ewell's Corps started near noon and formed the rear guard. Fitz Lee's and Hampton's Brigades of Cavalry Stuart's Division the latter under Col. Baker marched via Cashtown and Greenwood en route to Williamsport. Chambliss' and Jenkins' Brigades of Cavalry under General Stuart marched via Emmitsburg. Robertson's and Jones' Brigades of Cavalry held Jack Mountain passes. Imboden's Brigade of mounted infantry in charge of the wagon trains reached Greencastle in the morning and Williamsport in the afternoon.

292

PART VII

Organization of the Armies and Tablet Index

INDEX TO THE ARMIES AT GETTYSBURG

Organization of Army of the Potomac and Army of Northern Virginia during the Battle of Gettysburg with the page number(s) where the historical tablet inscription(s) describing the activity of the various commands are located.

BIBLIOGRAPHICAL NOTE

The majority of the content of this book is the history of the Battle of Gettysburg developed by the Gettysburg National Military Park Commission, permanently inscribed on metal tablets and placed on the battlefield to mark where the events occurred. These inscriptions were also the primary source for the narrative summaries of the different phases of the campaign and battle. A secondary source of background for the narrative summaries was selections from *Battles and Leaders of the Civil War*, originally published in 1887 as a four-volume collection of writings primarily by participants in the war. Most useful to this effort were three articles by Henry J. Hunt, brevet major general, U.S.A., chief of artillery, Army of the Potomac, entitled "There was much glory," "I proceed to Cemetery Hill," and "Indescribably grand."

The following selections from the Gettysburg National Military Park Library and Archives were used in the narrative description of the early efforts to preserve the battlefield and activity of the Park Commission:

Harrison, Kathleen Georg. "Patriotic and Enduring Efforts—An Introduction to the Gettysburg Battlefield Commission," March 4, 1995, in Fourth Annual Gettysburg Seminar, G.N.M.P Library.

Harrison, Kathy Georg. "The Location of the Monuments, Markers, and Tablets on Gettysburg Battlefield," G.N.M.P. Library.

Hartwig, D. Scott. "They were Soldiers Once and Young and Brave: The Veterans and Gettysburg National Military Park," March 4, 1995, in Fourth Annual Gettysburg Seminar, G.N.M.P. Library.

Unrau, Harlan D. "Gettysburg Administrative History," Department of Interior, National Park Service, 1991, G.N.M.P. Library.

National Park Service. Gettysburg National Military Park archives, "Reports, Gettysburg National Military Park Commission 1893–1911, Vol. I."

National Park Service. Gettysburg National Military Park archives, "Reports, Gettysburg National Military Park Commission 1912–1921, Vol. II."

I must acknowledge Gettysburg National Military Park historians Kathy Harrison, John Heizer, and Wyona Peterson for their courtesy and assistance. Special thanks is due Supervisory Historian D. Scott Hartwig for encouraging me to proceed with this effort and for his most valuable review and critique of the completed product. Appreciation is also extended to Robert Wilson for the many hours on the battlefield helping me locate and photograph the historical tablets and for his review of the manuscript. Finally, I wish to express my appreciation to my wife Glenda, for her tolerance during the many months that this work has taken.

G. R. L.

INDEX

First names were listed where known.
Specific sites in the battlefield area appear under Gettysburg.

319